1: The Arduous Business of Getting Rescued

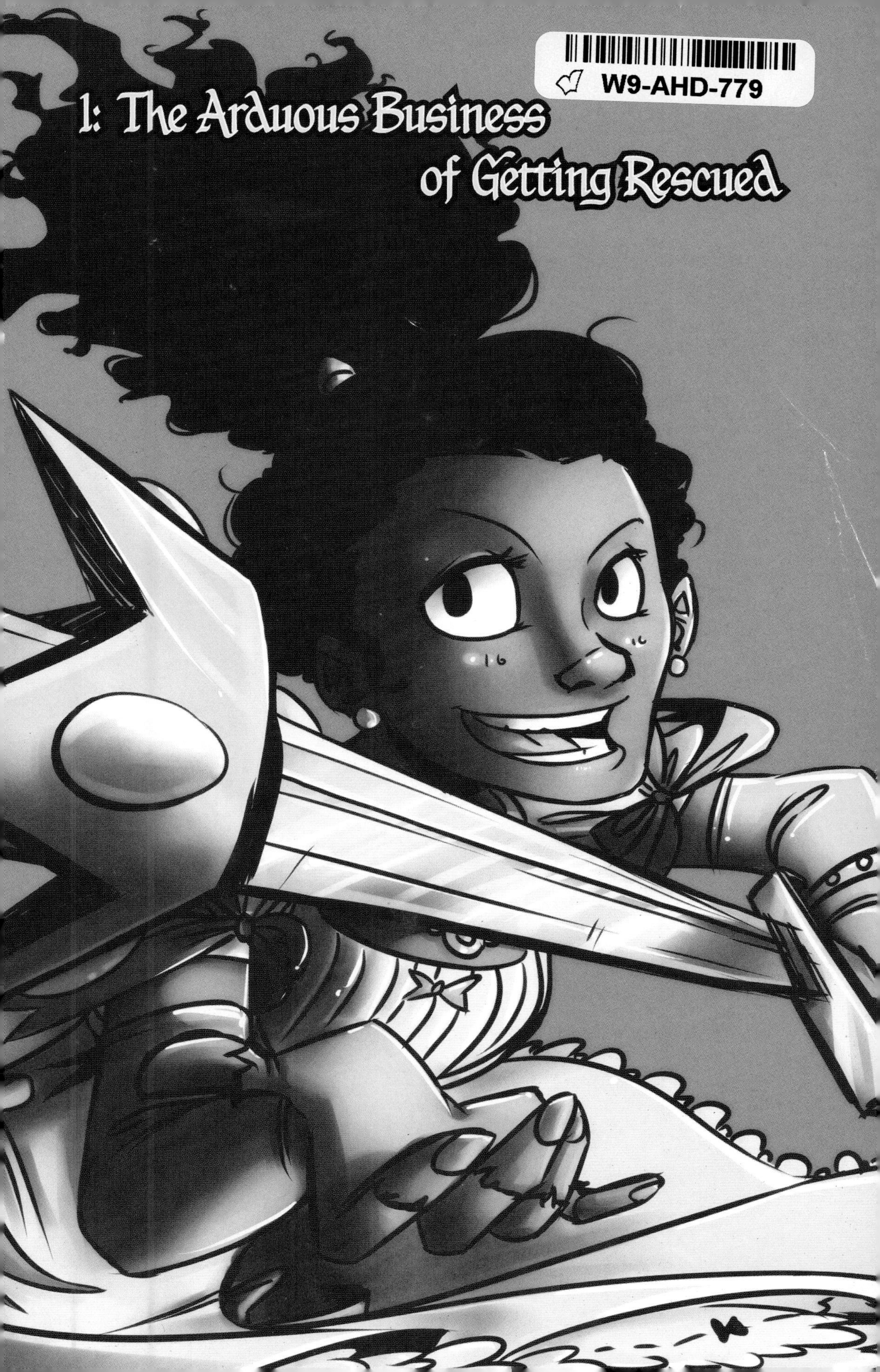

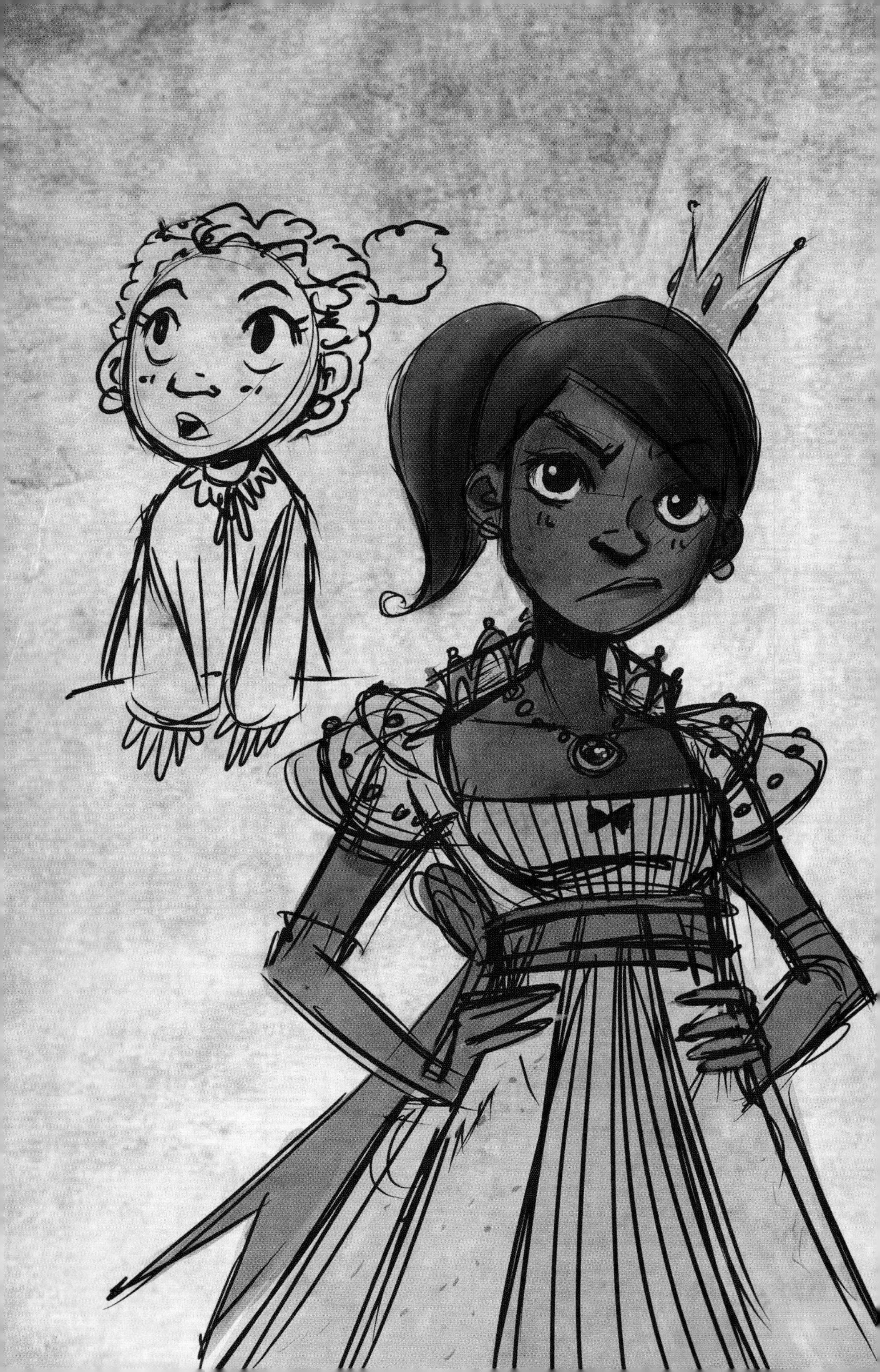

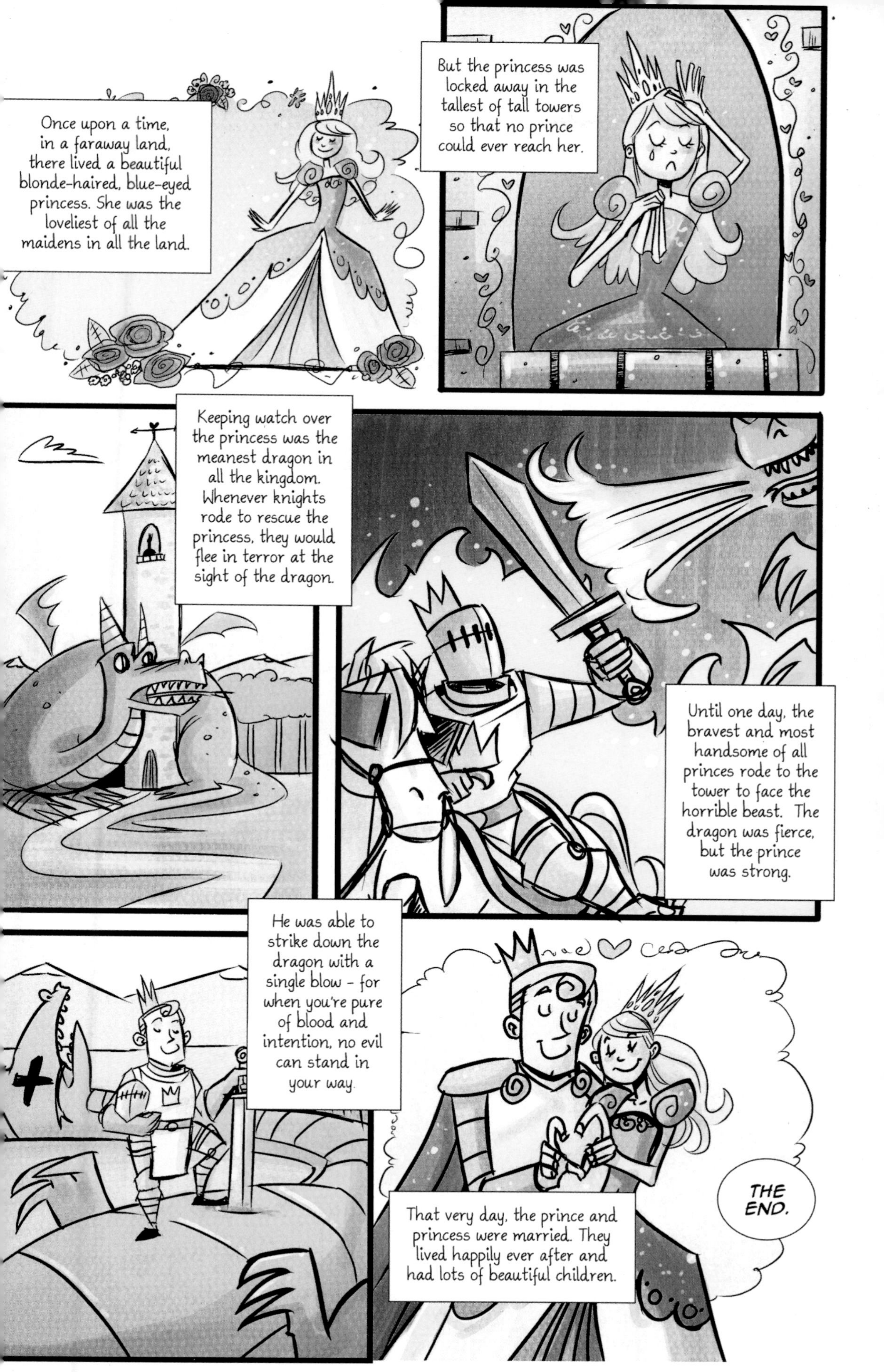
Once upon a time, in a faraway land, there lived a beautiful blonde-haired, blue-eyed princess. She was the loveliest of all the maidens in all the land.
But the princess was locked away in the tallest of tall towers so that no prince could ever reach her.
Keeping watch over the princess was the meanest dragon in all the kingdom. Whenever knights rode to rescue the princess, they would flee in terror at the sight of the dragon.
Until one day, the bravest and most handsome of all princes rode to the tower to face the horrible beast. The dragon was fierce, but the prince was strong.
He was able to strike down the dragon with a single blow - for when you're pure of blood and intention, no evil can stand in your way.
That very day, the prince and princess were married. They lived happily ever after and had lots of beautiful children.
THE END.

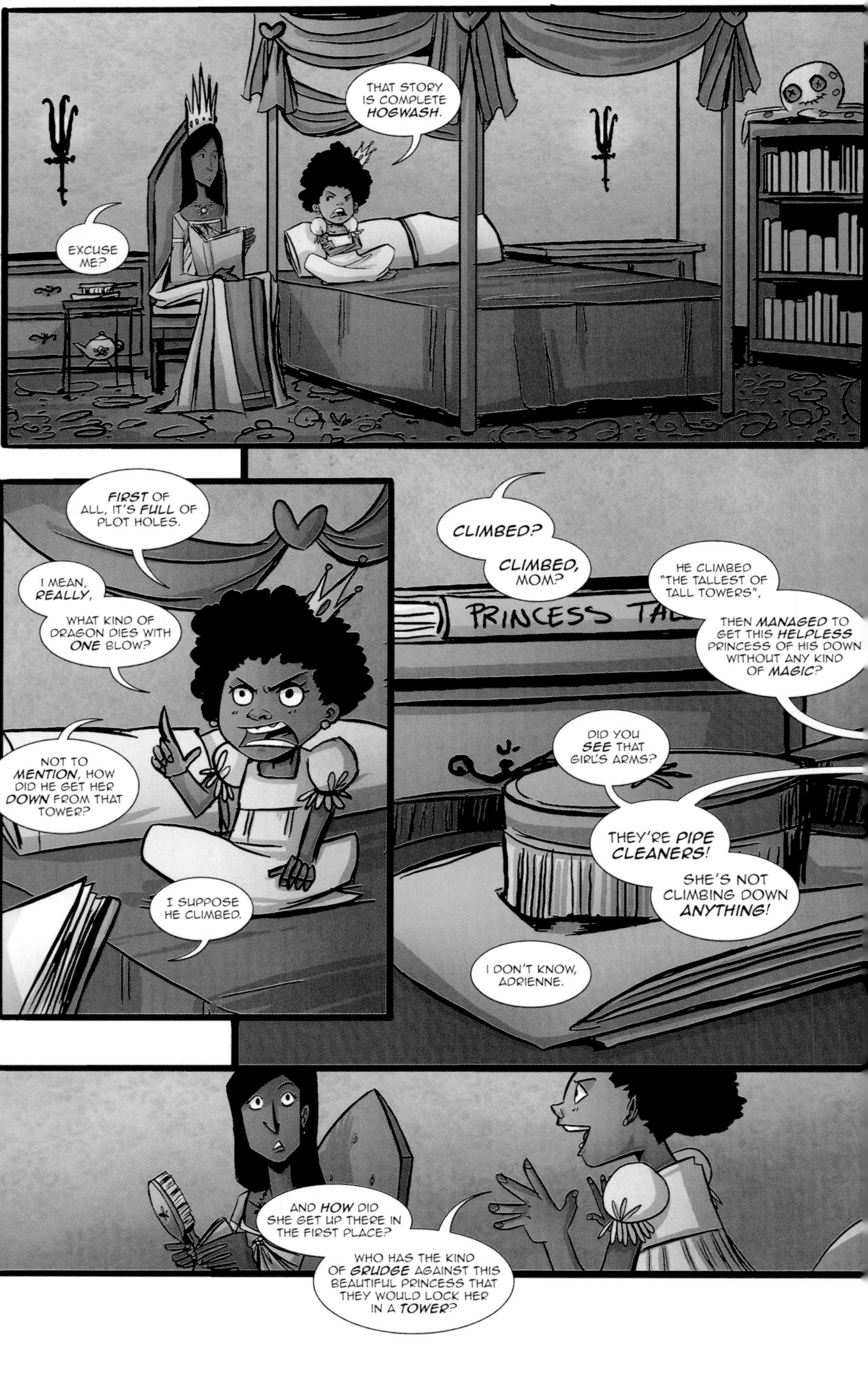

THAT STORY IS COMPLETE HOGWASH.
EXCUSE ME?
FIRST OF ALL, IT'S FULL OF PLOT HOLES.
I MEAN, REALLY,
WHAT KIND OF DRAGON DIES WITH ONE BLOW?
NOT TO MENTION, HOW DID HE GET HER DOWN FROM THAT TOWER?
I SUPPOSE HE CLIMBED.
CLIMBED?
CLIMBED, MOM?
PRINCESS TAL
HE CLIMBED "THE TALLEST OF TALL TOWERS",
THEN MANAGED TO GET THIS HELPLESS PRINCESS OF HIS DOWN WITHOUT ANY KIND OF MAGIC?
DID YOU SEE THAT GIRL'S ARMS?
THEY'RE PIPE CLEANERS!
SHE'S NOT CLIMBING DOWN ANYTHING!
I DON'T KNOW, ADRIENNE.
AND HOW DID SHE GET UP THERE IN THE FIRST PLACE?
WHO HAS THE KIND OF GRUDGE AGAINST THIS BEAUTIFUL PRINCESS THAT THEY WOULD LOCK HER IN A TOWER?

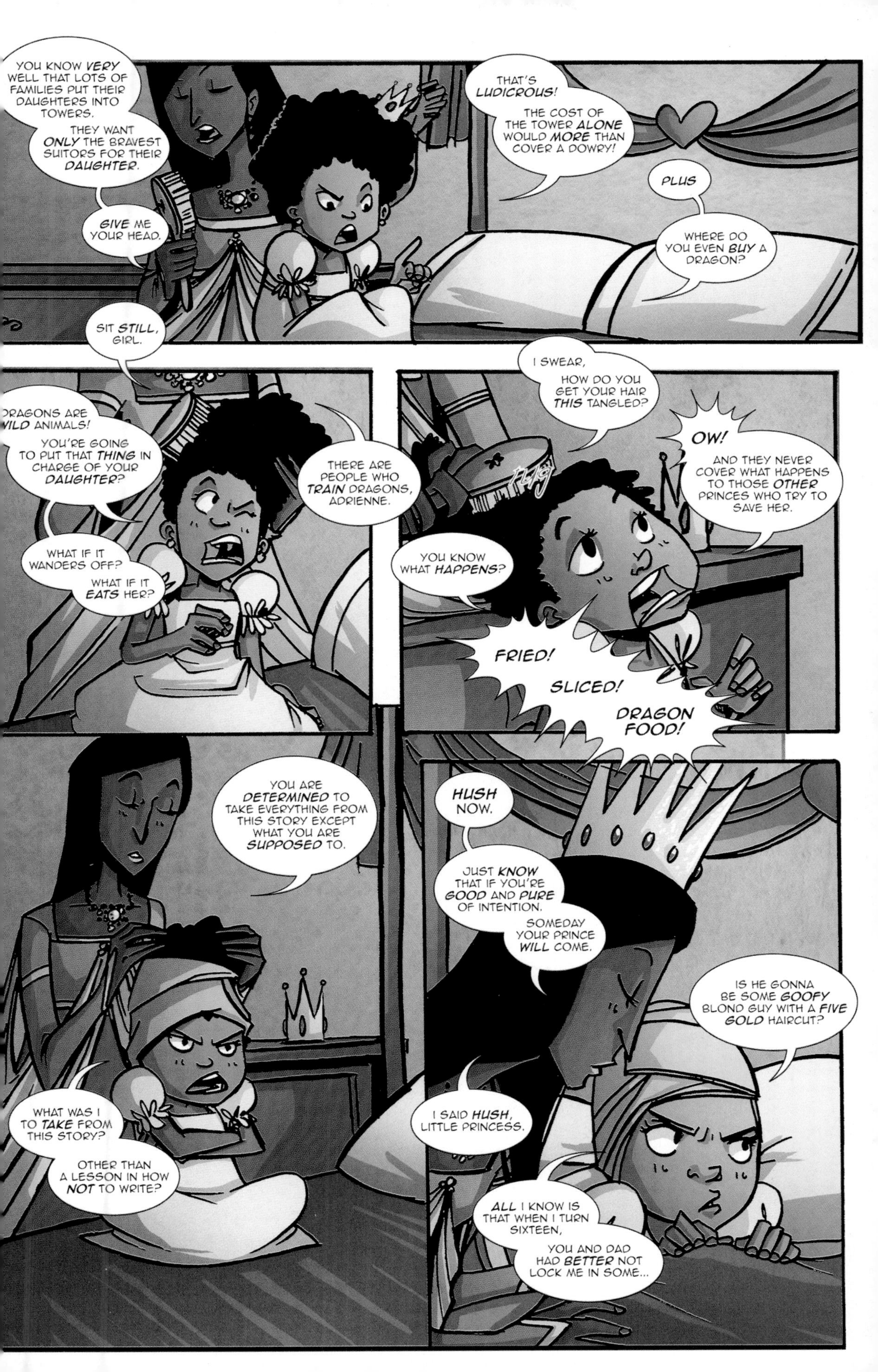
YOU KNOW VERY WELL THAT LOTS OF FAMILIES PUT THEIR DAUGHTERS INTO TOWERS.
THEY WANT ONLY THE BRAVEST SUITORS FOR THEIR DAUGHTER.
GIVE ME YOUR HEAD.
SIT STILL, GIRL.
THAT'S LUDICROUS!
THE COST OF THE TOWER ALONE WOULD MORE THAN COVER A DOWRY!
PLUS
WHERE DO YOU EVEN BUY A DRAGON?
DRAGONS ARE WILD ANIMALS!
YOU'RE GOING TO PUT THAT THING IN CHARGE OF YOUR DAUGHTER?
THERE ARE PEOPLE WHO TRAIN DRAGONS, ADRIENNE.
WHAT IF IT WANDERS OFF?
WHAT IF IT EATS HER?
I SWEAR,
HOW DO YOU GET YOUR HAIR THIS TANGLED?
OW!
AND THEY NEVER COVER WHAT HAPPENS TO THOSE OTHER PRINCES WHO TRY TO SAVE HER.
YOU KNOW WHAT HAPPENS?
FRIED!
SLICED!
DRAGON FOOD!
YOU ARE DETERMINED TO TAKE EVERYTHING FROM THIS STORY EXCEPT WHAT YOU ARE SUPPOSED TO.
WHAT WAS I TO TAKE FROM THIS STORY?
OTHER THAN A LESSON IN HOW NOT TO WRITE?
HUSH NOW.
JUST KNOW THAT IF YOU'RE GOOD AND PURE OF INTENTION.
SOMEDAY YOUR PRINCE WILL COME.
IS HE GONNA BE SOME GOOFY BLOND GUY WITH A FIVE GOLD HAIRCUT?
I SAID HUSH, LITTLE PRINCESS.
ALL I KNOW IS THAT WHEN I TURN SIXTEEN,
YOU AND DAD HAD BETTER NOT LOCK ME IN SOME...

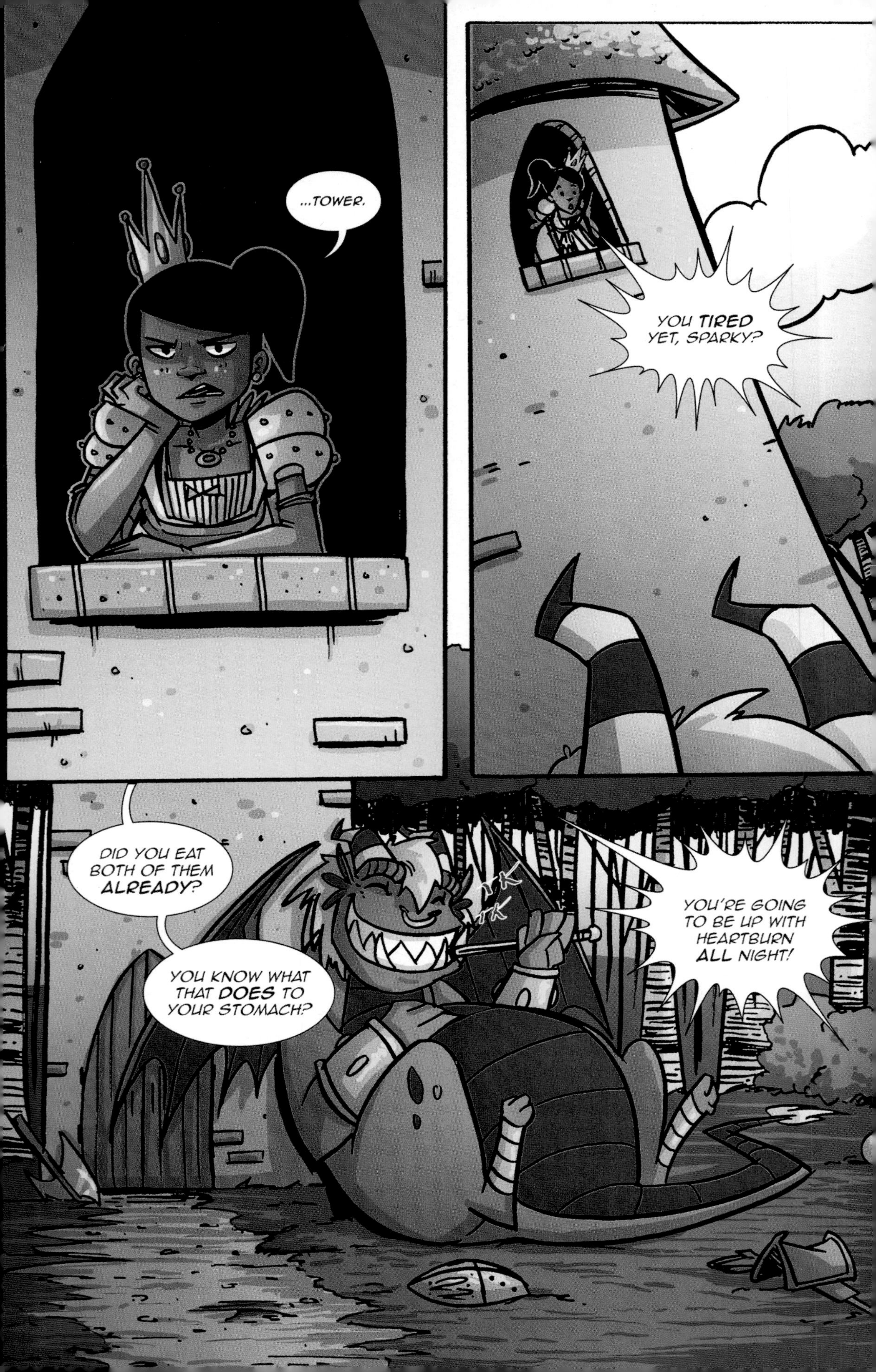
...TOWER.
YOU TIRED YET, SPARKY?
DID YOU EAT BOTH OF THEM ALREADY?
YOU KNOW WHAT THAT DOES TO YOUR STOMACH?
YOU'RE GOING TO BE UP WITH HEARTBURN ALL NIGHT!
TK TK

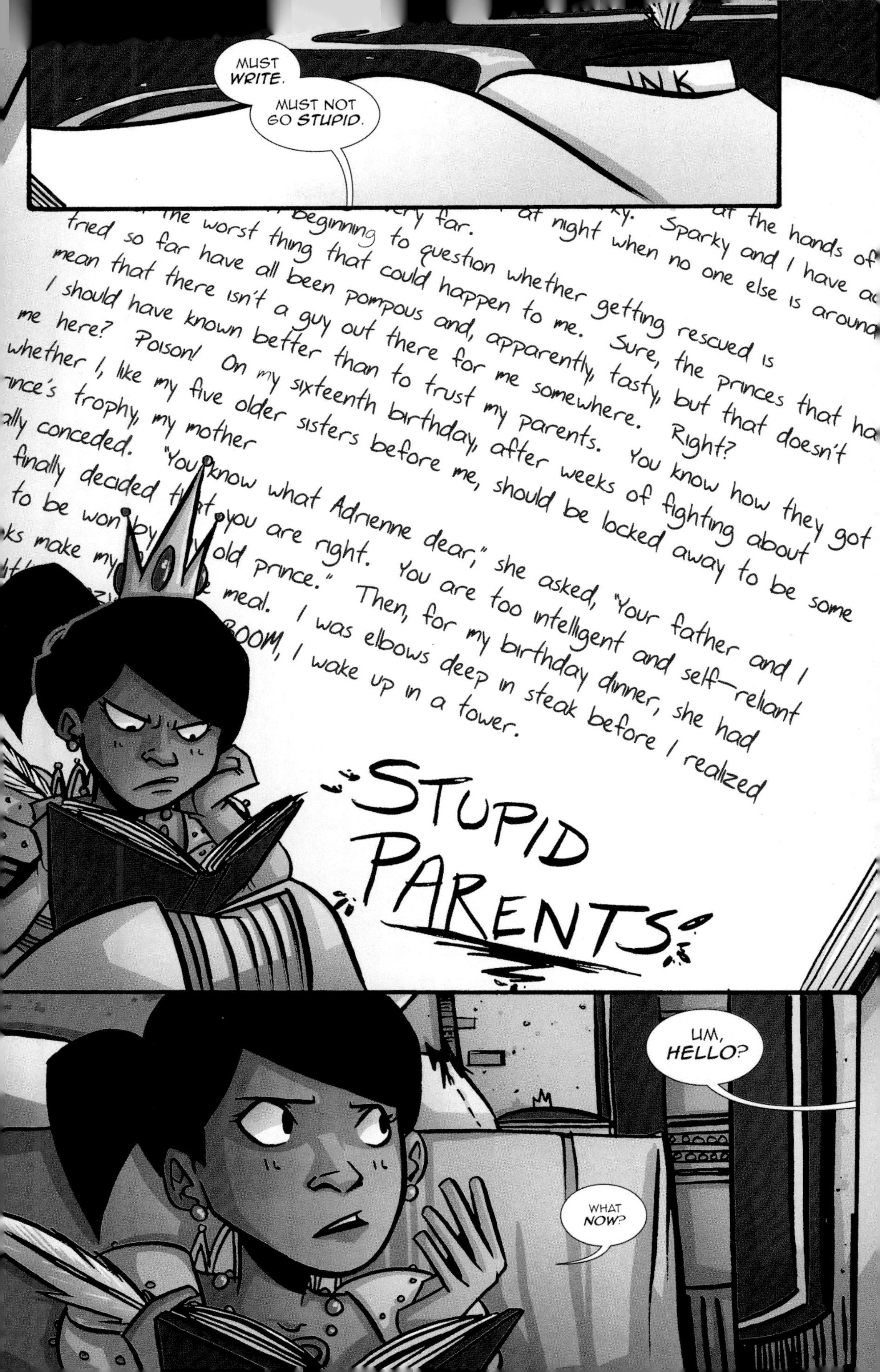
MUST WRITE.
MUST NOT GO STUPID.
INK
at night when no one else is around
Sparky and I have a
at the hands of
beginning to question whether getting rescued is
the worst thing that could happen to me. Sure, the princes that ha
tried so far have all been pompous and, apparently, tasty, but that doesn't
mean that there isn't a guy out there for me somewhere. Right?
I should have known better than to trust my parents. You know how they got
me here? Poison! On my sixteenth birthday, after weeks of fighting about
whether I, like my five older sisters before me, should be locked away to be some
ince's trophy, my mother
ally conceded. "You know what Adrienne dear," she asked, "Your father and I
finally decided that you are right. You are too intelligent and self-reliant
to be won by old prince." Then, for my birthday dinner, she had
meal. I was elbows deep in steak before I realized
BOOM, I wake up in a tower.
STUPID PARENTS!
UM, HELLO?
WHAT NOW?

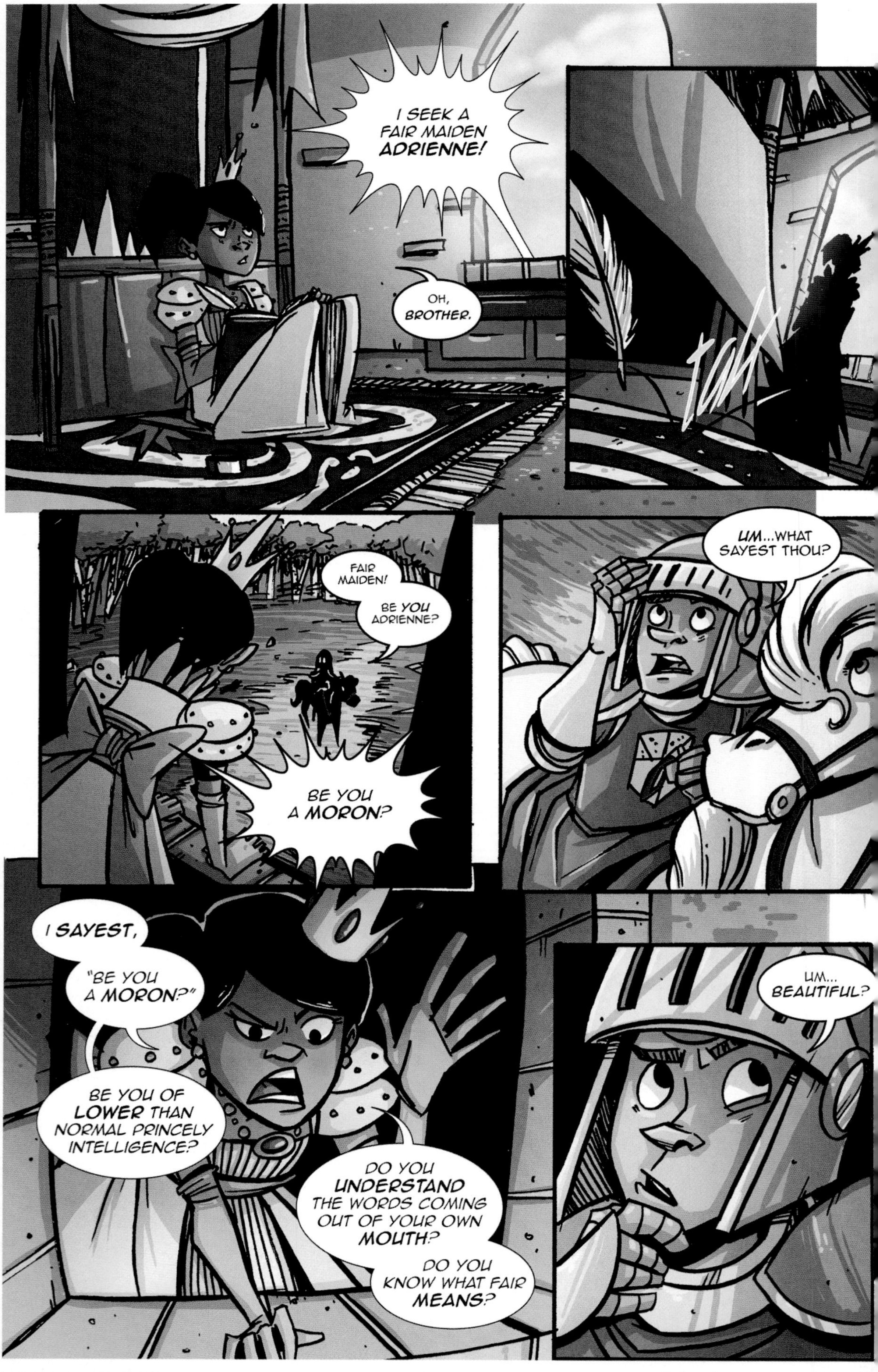
I SEEK A FAIR MAIDEN ADRIENNE!
OH, BROTHER.
FAIR MAIDEN!
BE YOU ADRIENNE?
BE YOU A MORON?
UM...WHAT SAYEST THOU?
I SAYEST,
"BE YOU A MORON?"
BE YOU OF LOWER THAN NORMAL PRINCELY INTELLIGENCE?
DO YOU UNDERSTAND THE WORDS COMING OUT OF YOUR OWN MOUTH?
DO YOU KNOW WHAT FAIR MEANS?
UM... BEAUTIFUL?

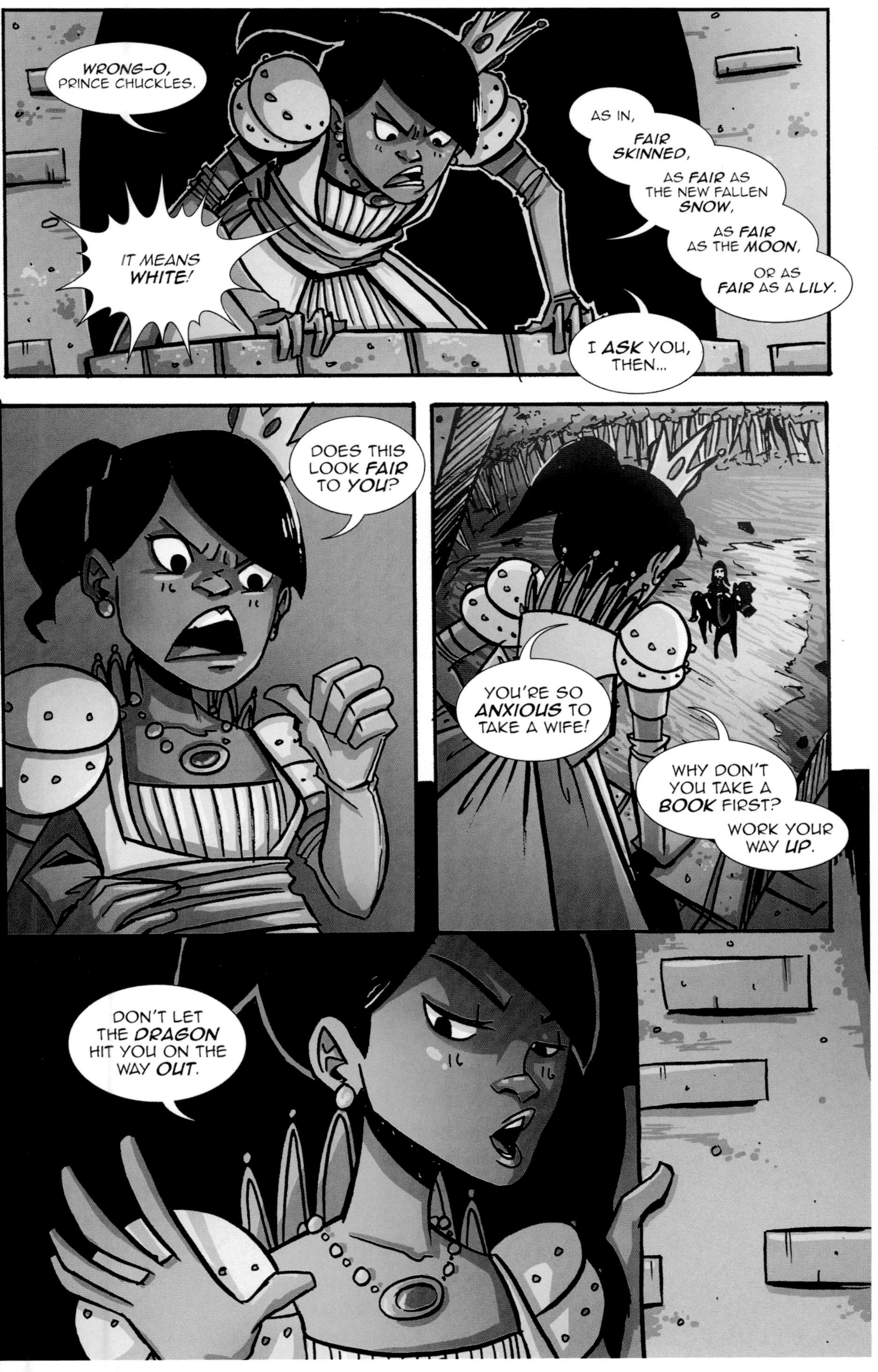
WRONG-O, PRINCE CHUCKLES.
IT MEANS WHITE!
AS IN, FAIR SKINNED,
AS FAIR AS THE NEW FALLEN SNOW,
AS FAIR AS THE MOON,
OR AS FAIR AS A LILY.
I ASK YOU, THEN...
DOES THIS LOOK FAIR TO YOU?
YOU'RE SO ANXIOUS TO TAKE A WIFE!
WHY DON'T YOU TAKE A BOOK FIRST?
WORK YOUR WAY UP.
DON'T LET THE DRAGON HIT YOU ON THE WAY OUT.

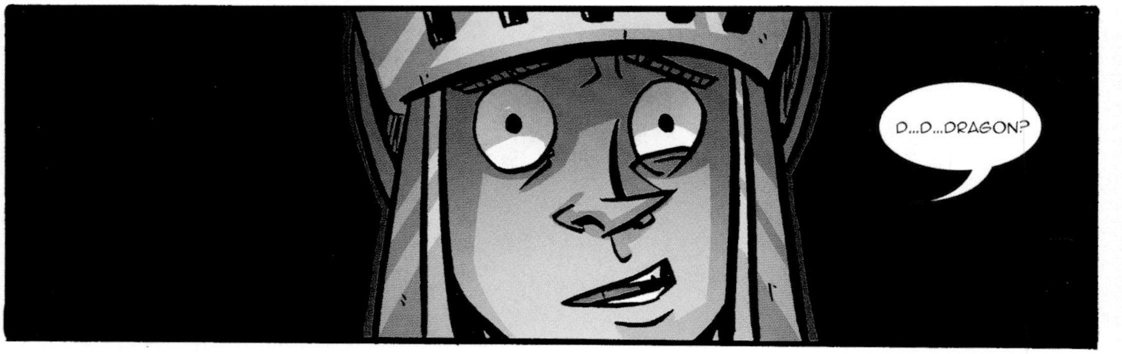
D...D...DRAGON?

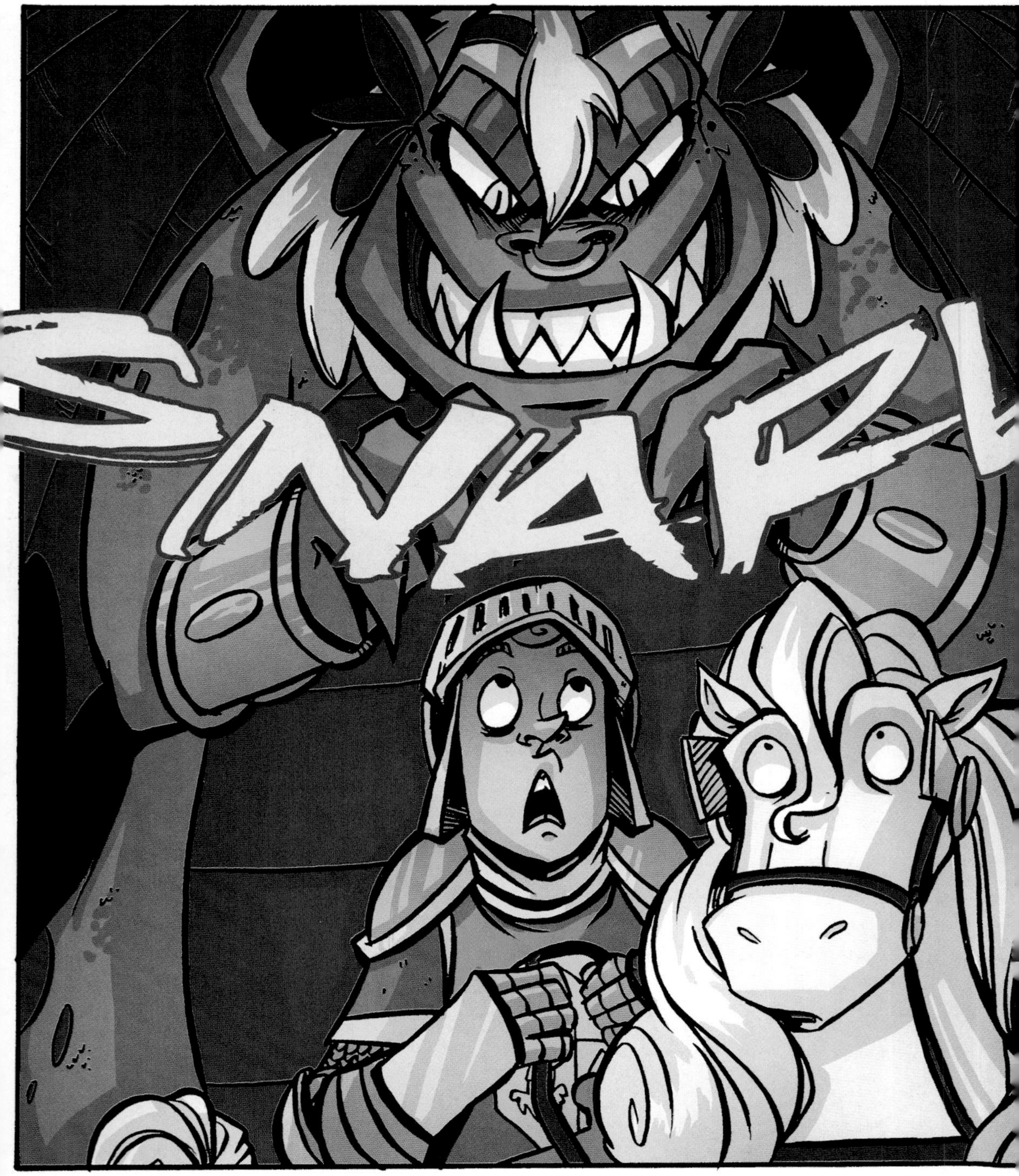
SNAP

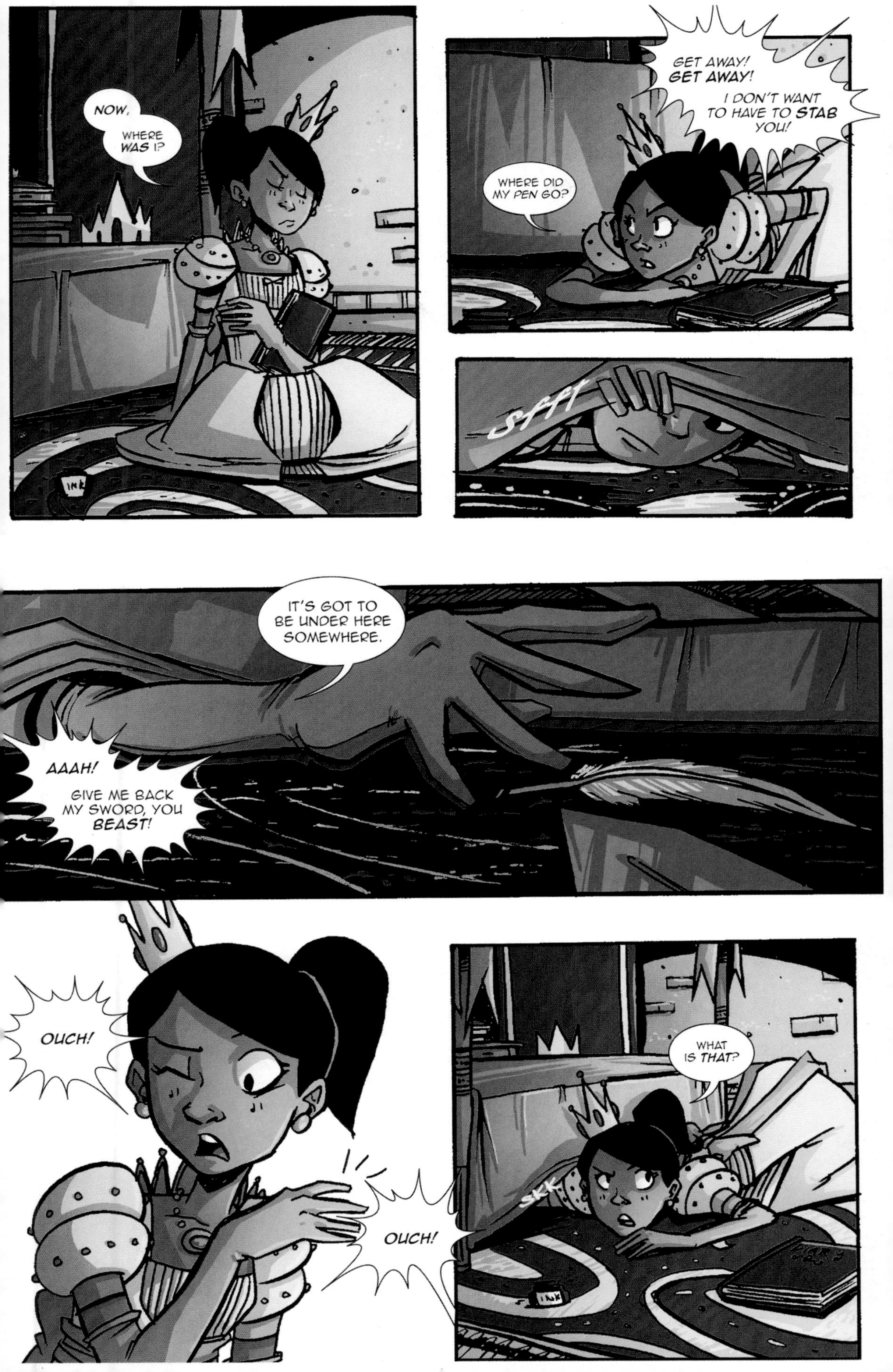
NOW, WHERE WAS I?
GET AWAY! GET AWAY! I DON'T WANT TO HAVE TO STAB YOU!
WHERE DID MY PEN GO?
SFFT
INK
IT'S GOT TO BE UNDER HERE SOMEWHERE.
AAAH! GIVE ME BACK MY SWORD, YOU BEAST!
OUCH!
OUCH!
WHAT IS THAT?
SKK
INK
DIARY

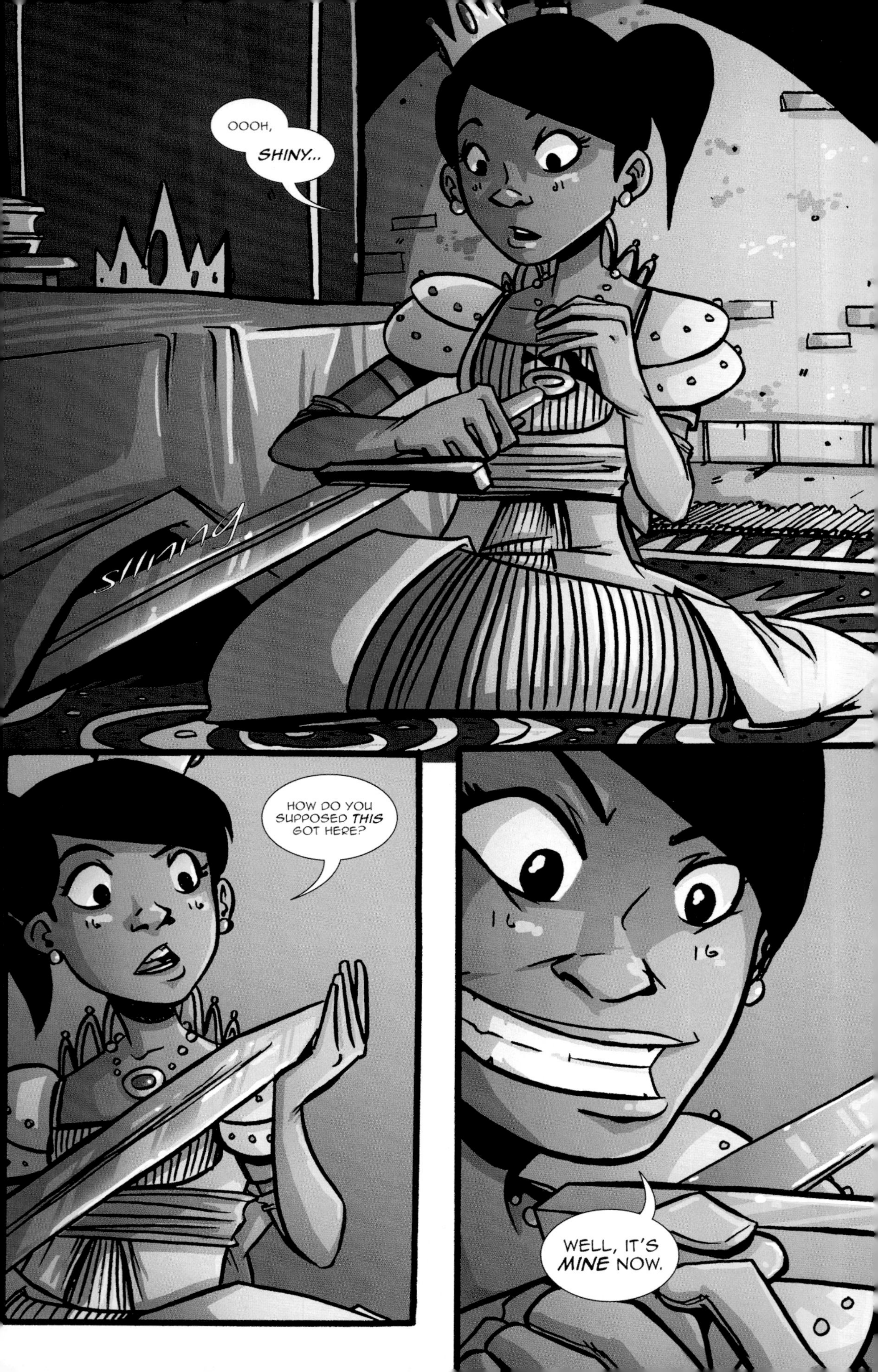
OOOH, SHINY...
shing
HOW DO YOU SUPPOSED THIS GOT HERE?
WELL, IT'S MINE NOW.

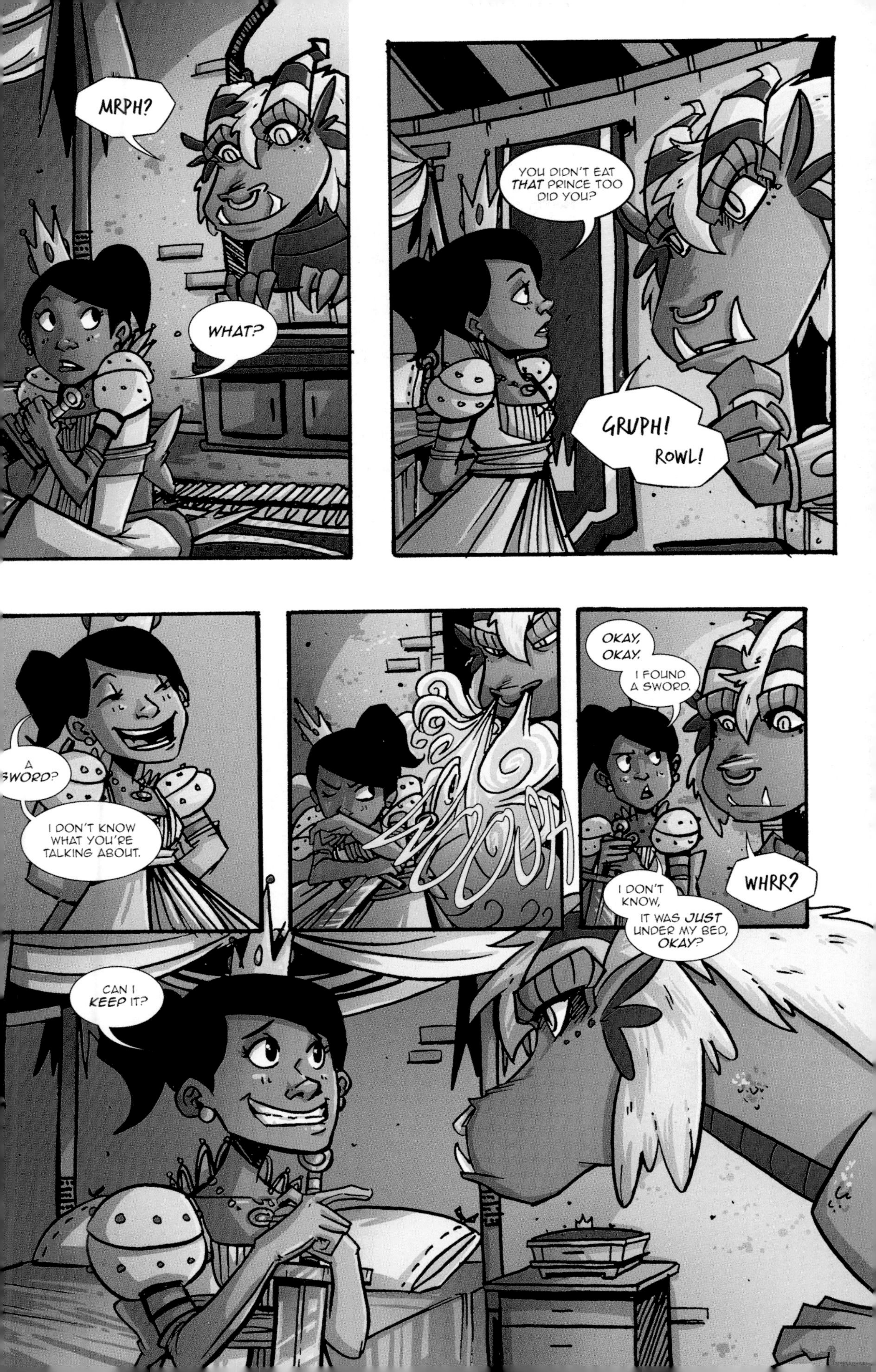
MRPH?
WHAT?
YOU DIDN'T EAT *THAT* PRINCE TOO DID YOU?
GRUPH!
ROWL!
A SWORD?
I DON'T KNOW WHAT YOU'RE TALKING ABOUT.
WOOOSH
OKAY, OKAY.
I FOUND A SWORD.
WHRR?
I DON'T KNOW,
IT WAS *JUST* UNDER MY BED, *OKAY*?
CAN I *KEEP* IT?

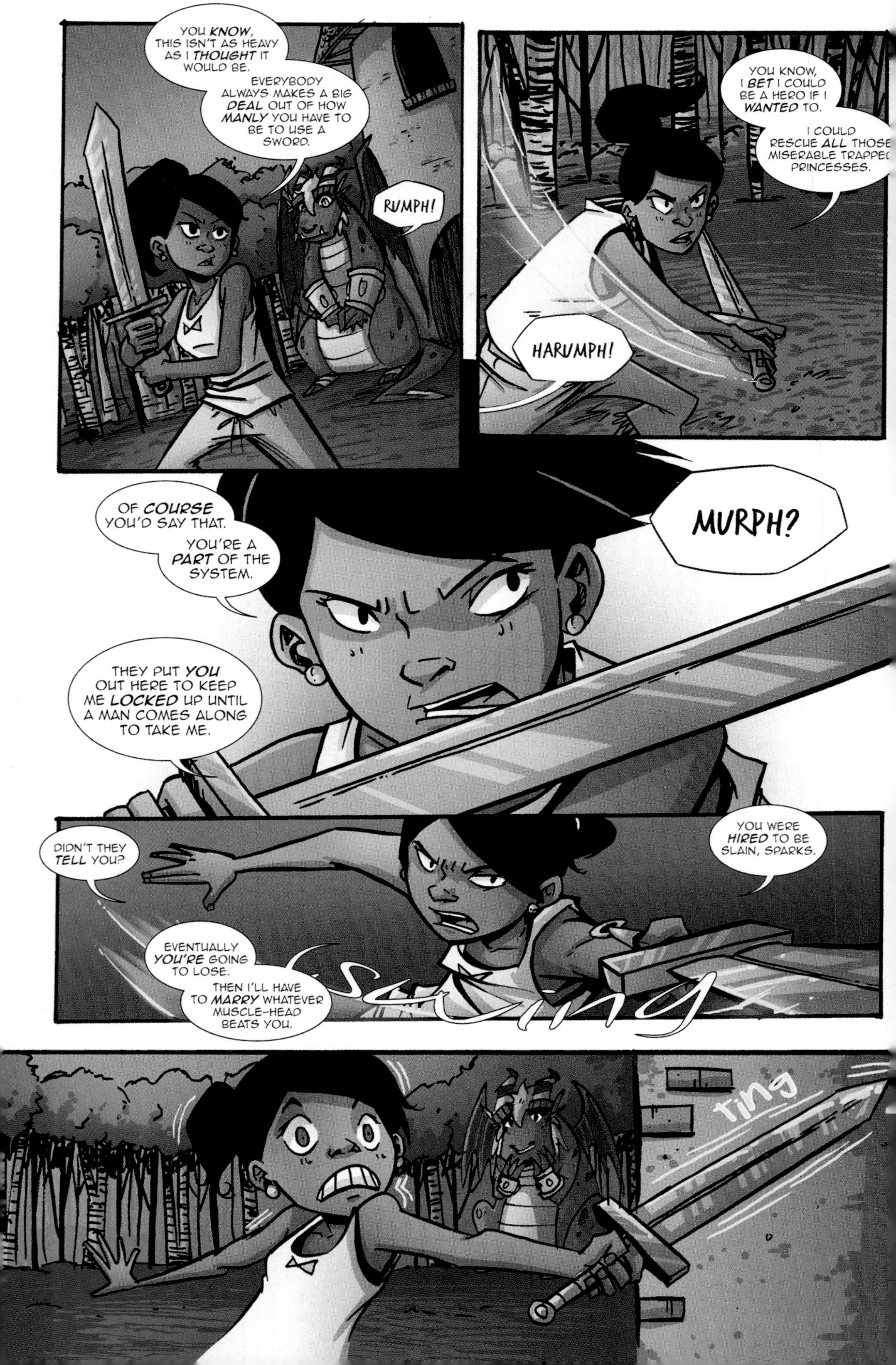

YOU KNOW, THIS ISN'T AS HEAVY AS I THOUGHT IT WOULD BE.
EVERYBODY ALWAYS MAKES A BIG DEAL OUT OF HOW MANLY YOU HAVE TO BE TO USE A SWORD.
RUMPH!
YOU KNOW, I BET I COULD BE A HERO IF I WANTED TO.
I COULD RESCUE ALL THOSE MISERABLE TRAPPED PRINCESSES.
HARUMPH!
OF COURSE YOU'D SAY THAT.
YOU'RE A PART OF THE SYSTEM.
MURPH?
THEY PUT YOU OUT HERE TO KEEP ME LOCKED UP UNTIL A MAN COMES ALONG TO TAKE ME.
DIDN'T THEY TELL YOU?
YOU WERE HIRED TO BE SLAIN, SPARKS.
EVENTUALLY YOU'RE GOING TO LOSE.
THEN I'LL HAVE TO MARRY WHATEVER MUSCLE-HEAD BEATS YOU.
swing
ting

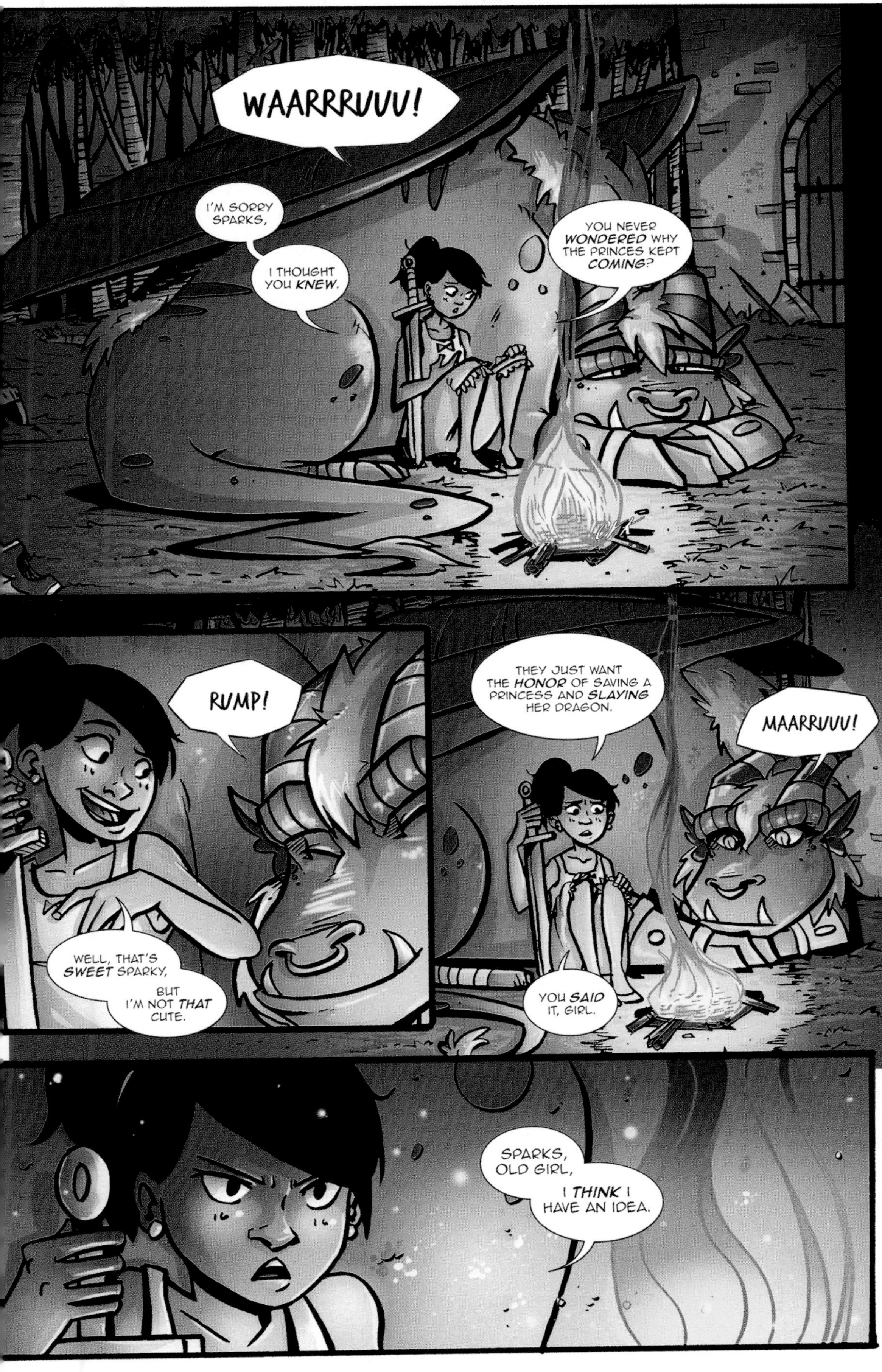
WAARRRUUU!
I'M SORRY SPARKS,
I THOUGHT YOU KNEW.
YOU NEVER WONDERED WHY THE PRINCES KEPT COMING?
RUMP!
WELL, THAT'S SWEET SPARKY,
BUT I'M NOT THAT CUTE.
THEY JUST WANT THE HONOR OF SAVING A PRINCESS AND SLAYING HER DRAGON.
MAARRUUU!
YOU SAID IT, GIRL.
SPARKS, OLD GIRL,
I THINK I HAVE AN IDEA.

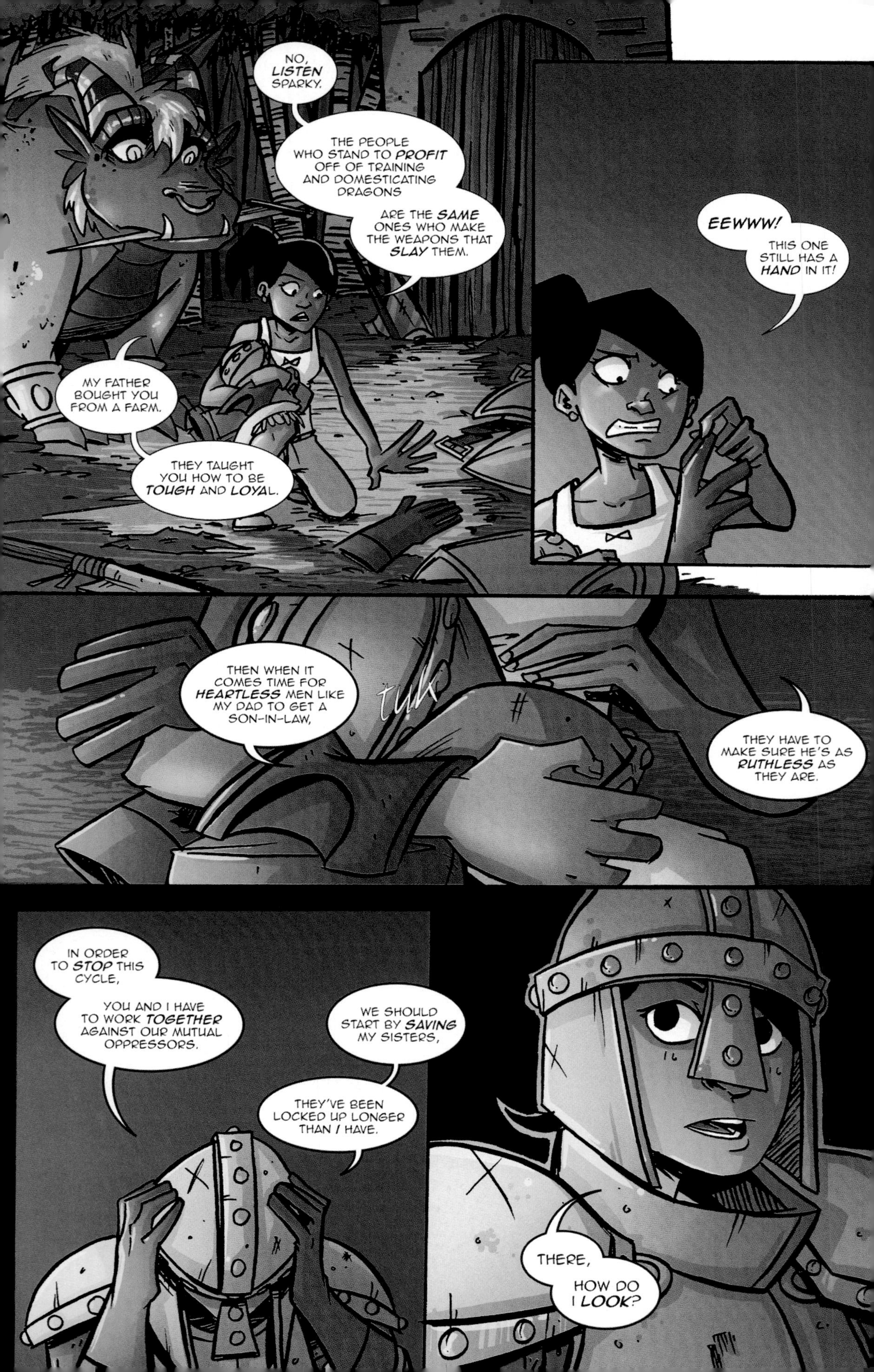
NO, LISTEN SPARKY.
THE PEOPLE WHO STAND TO PROFIT OFF OF TRAINING AND DOMESTICATING DRAGONS
ARE THE SAME ONES WHO MAKE THE WEAPONS THAT SLAY THEM.
MY FATHER BOUGHT YOU FROM A FARM.
THEY TAUGHT YOU HOW TO BE TOUGH AND LOYAL.
EEWWW!
THIS ONE STILL HAS A HAND IN IT!
THEN WHEN IT COMES TIME FOR HEARTLESS MEN LIKE MY DAD TO GET A SON-IN-LAW,
tuk
THEY HAVE TO MAKE SURE HE'S AS RUTHLESS AS THEY ARE.
IN ORDER TO STOP THIS CYCLE,
YOU AND I HAVE TO WORK TOGETHER AGAINST OUR MUTUAL OPPRESSORS.
WE SHOULD START BY SAVING MY SISTERS,
THEY'VE BEEN LOCKED UP LONGER THAN I HAVE.
THERE,
HOW DO I LOOK?

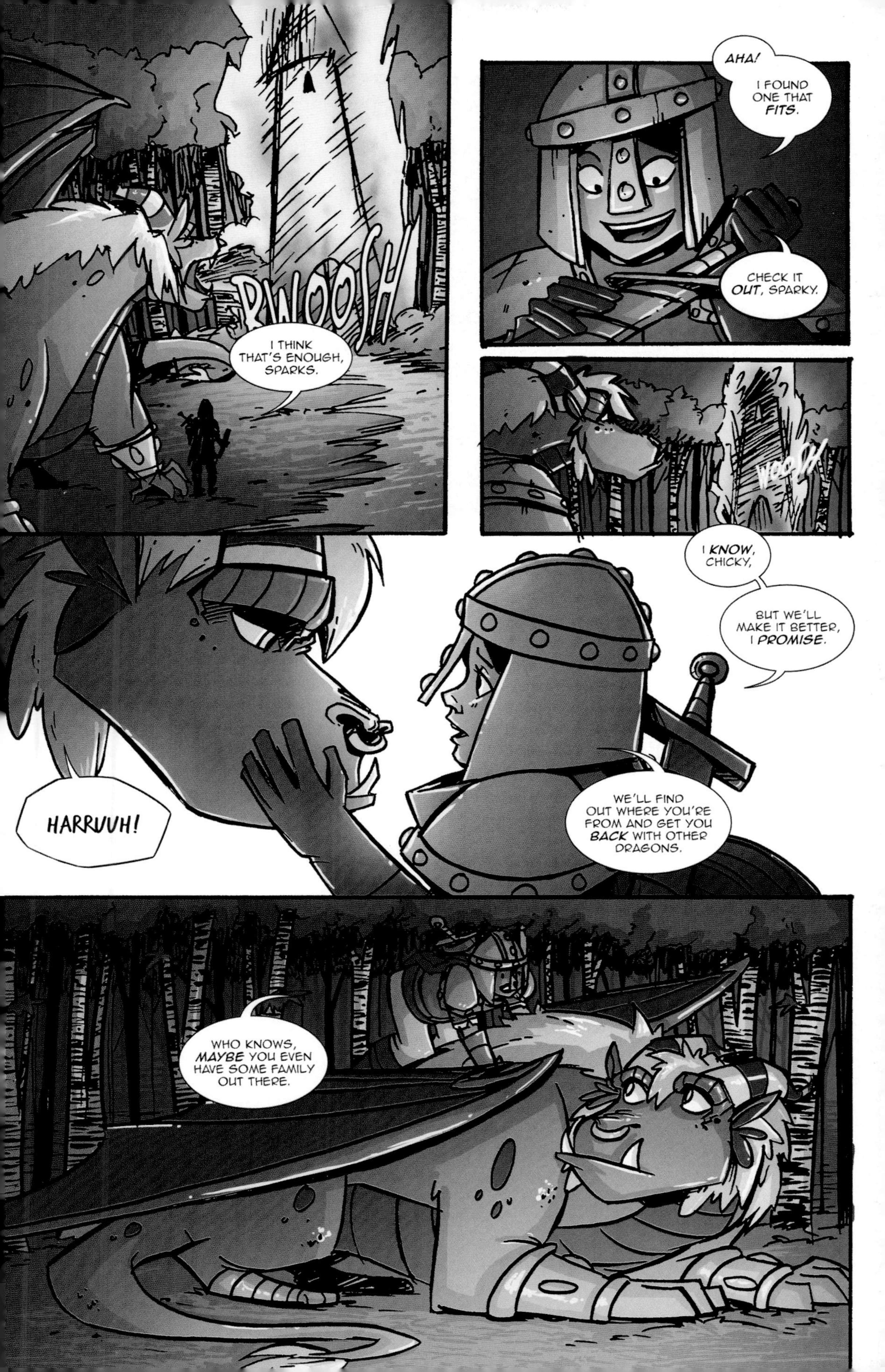
BWOOSH
I THINK THAT'S ENOUGH, SPARKS.
AHA!
I FOUND ONE THAT *FITS*.
CHECK IT *OUT*, SPARKY.
WOOSH
I *KNOW*, CHICKY,
BUT WE'LL MAKE IT BETTER, I *PROMISE*.
HARRUUH!
WE'LL FIND OUT WHERE YOU'RE FROM AND GET YOU *BACK* WITH OTHER DRAGONS.
WHO KNOWS, *MAYBE* YOU EVEN HAVE SOME FAMILY OUT THERE.

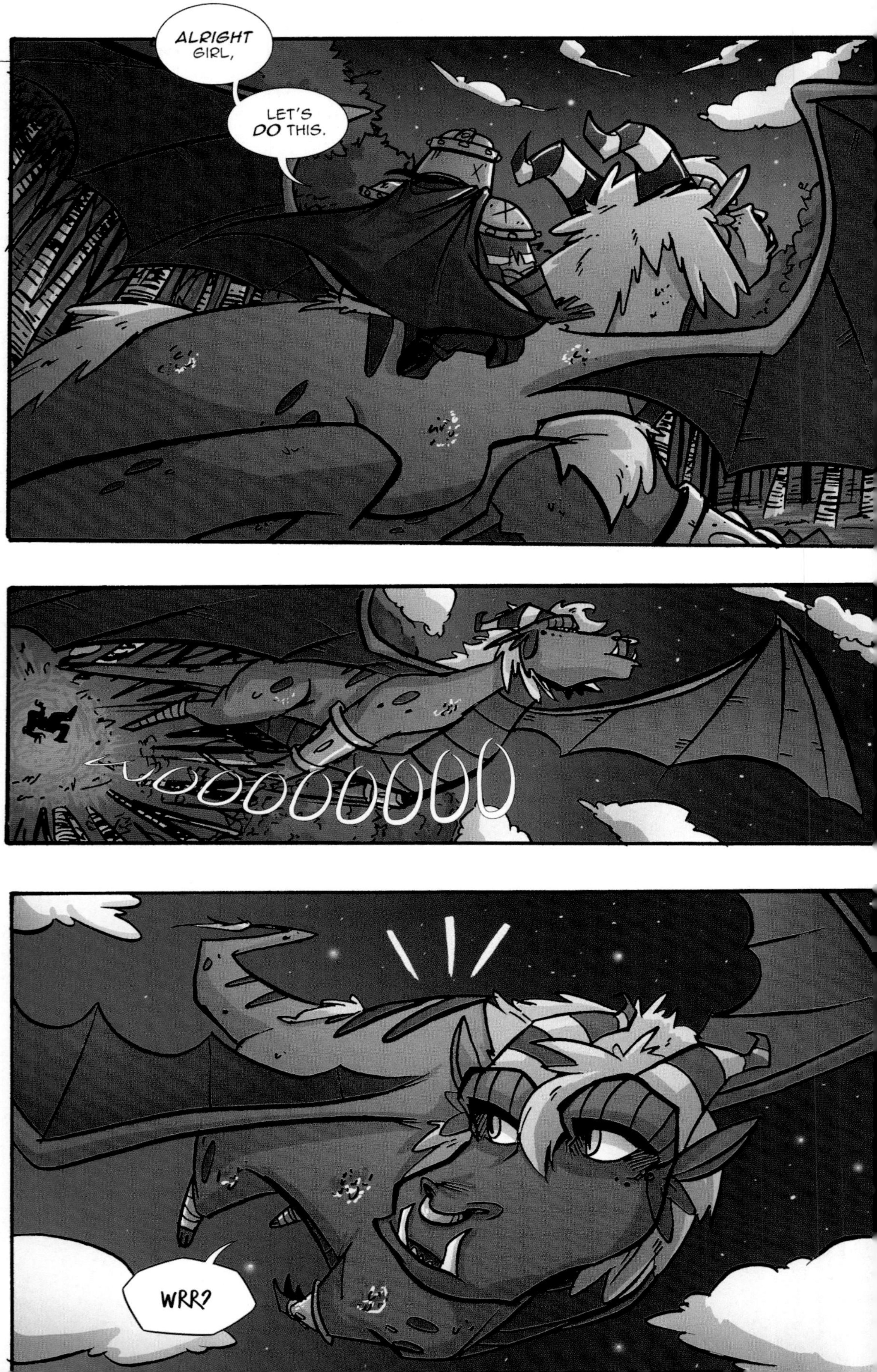
ALRIGHT GIRL,
LET'S DO THIS.
WOOOOOOOOOO
WRR?

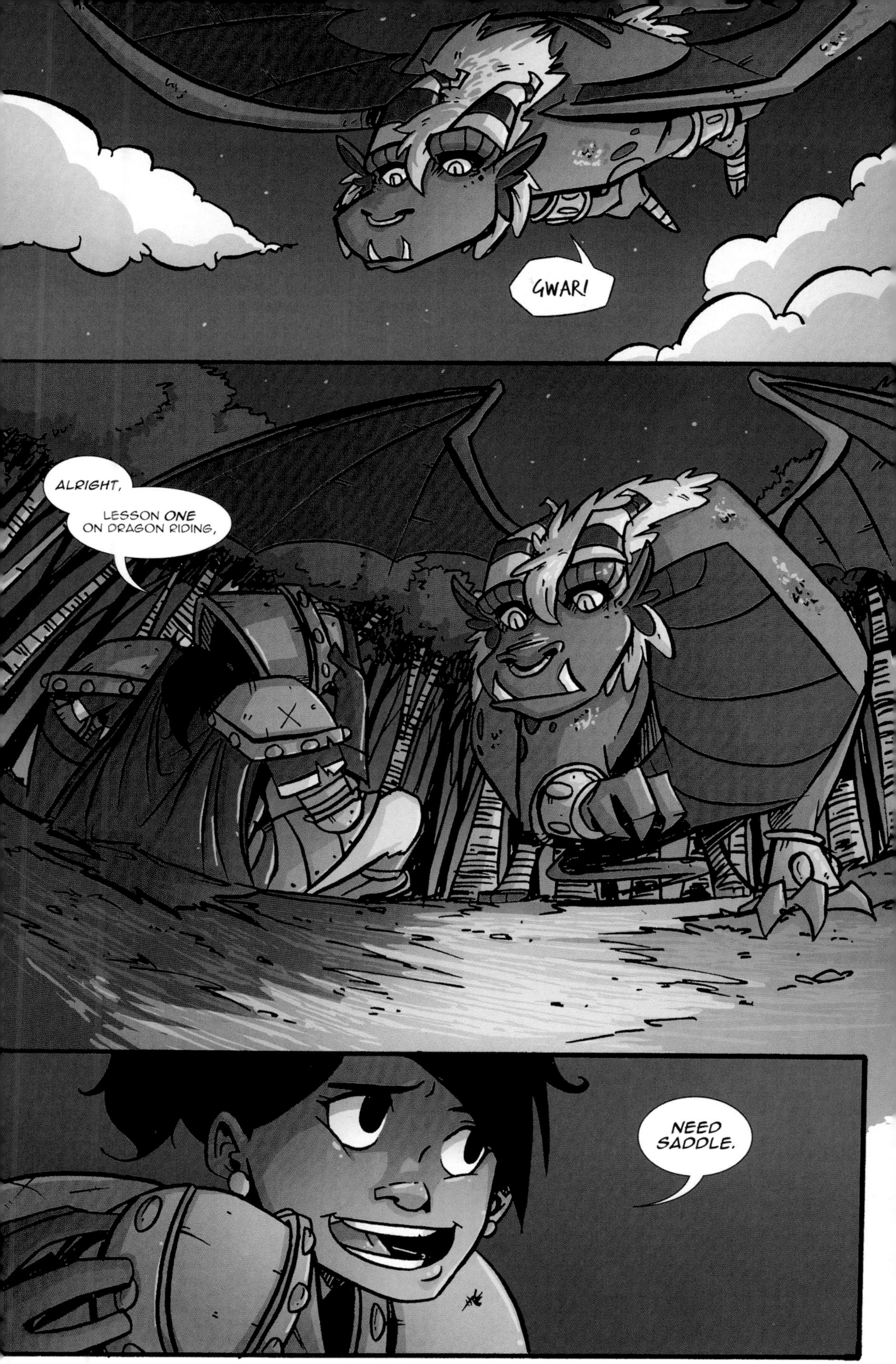
GWAR!
ALRIGHT,
LESSON ONE ON DRAGON RIDING,
NEED SADDLE.

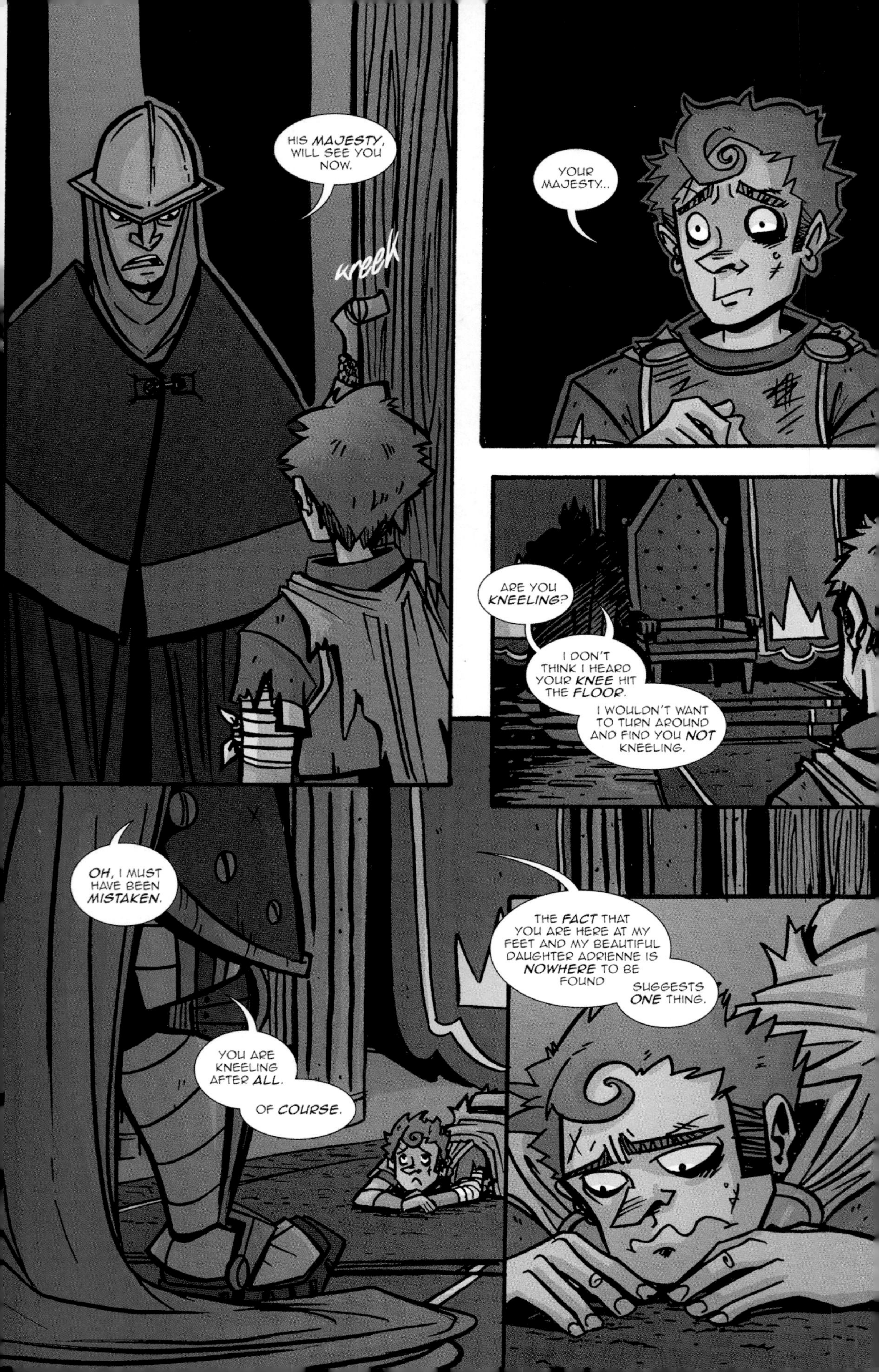

HIS MAJESTY, WILL SEE YOU NOW.
kreek
YOUR MAJESTY...
ARE YOU KNEELING?
I DON'T THINK I HEARD YOUR KNEE HIT THE FLOOR.
I WOULDN'T WANT TO TURN AROUND AND FIND YOU NOT KNEELING.
OH, I MUST HAVE BEEN MISTAKEN.
YOU ARE KNEELING AFTER ALL.
OF COURSE.
THE FACT THAT YOU ARE HERE AT MY FEET AND MY BEAUTIFUL DAUGHTER ADRIENNE IS NOWHERE TO BE FOUND
SUGGESTS ONE THING.

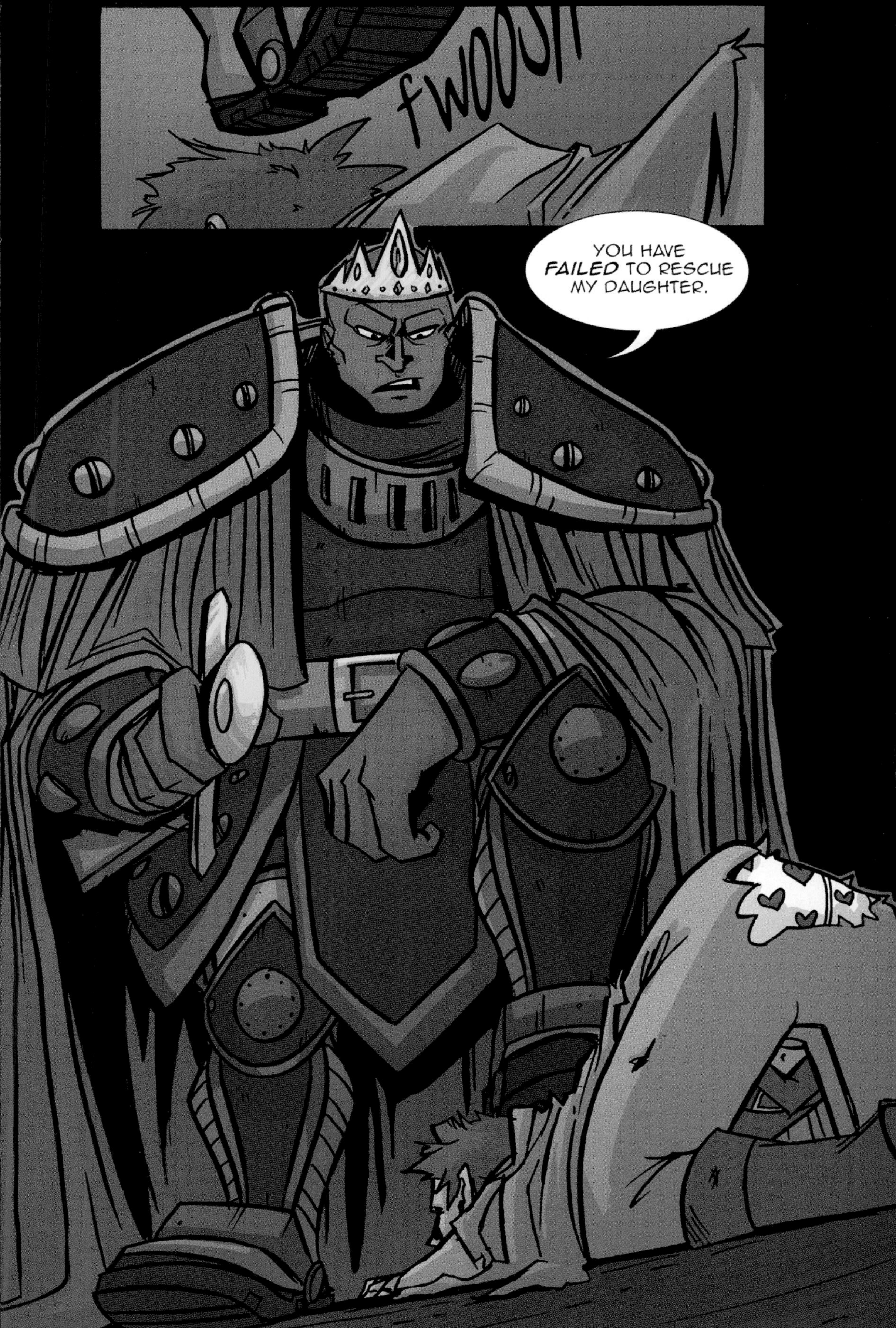
FWOOSH
YOU HAVE *FAILED* TO RESCUE MY DAUGHTER.

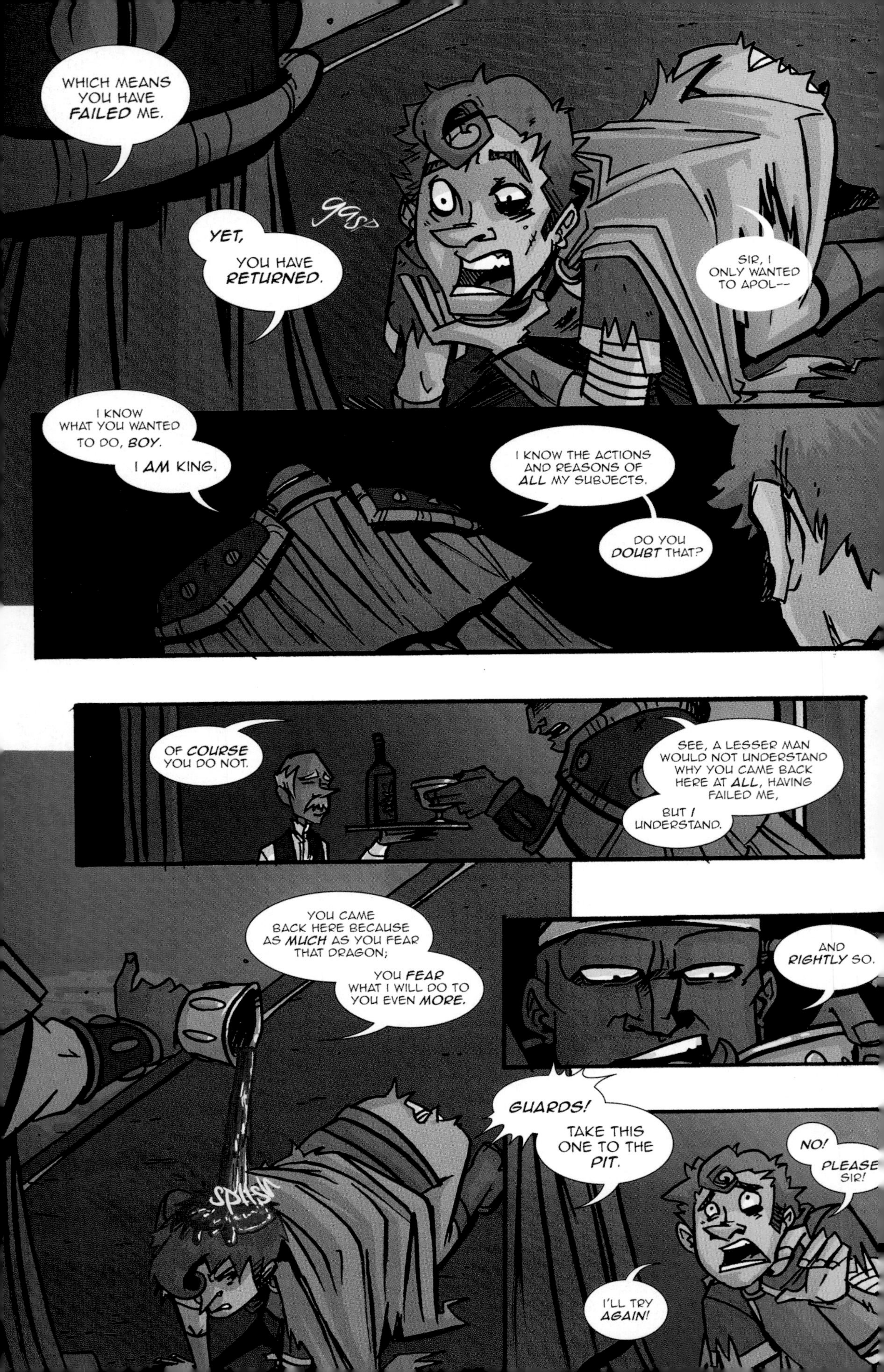
WHICH MEANS YOU HAVE FAILED ME.
gasp
YET, YOU HAVE RETURNED.
SIR, I ONLY WANTED TO APOL--
I KNOW WHAT YOU WANTED TO DO, BOY.
I AM KING.
I KNOW THE ACTIONS AND REASONS OF ALL MY SUBJECTS.
DO YOU DOUBT THAT?
OF COURSE YOU DO NOT.
SEE, A LESSER MAN WOULD NOT UNDERSTAND WHY YOU CAME BACK HERE AT ALL, HAVING FAILED ME,
BUT I UNDERSTAND.
YOU CAME BACK HERE BECAUSE AS MUCH AS YOU FEAR THAT DRAGON;
YOU FEAR WHAT I WILL DO TO YOU EVEN MORE.
AND RIGHTLY SO.
GUARDS!
TAKE THIS ONE TO THE PIT.
splish
NO!
PLEASE SIR!
I'LL TRY AGAIN!

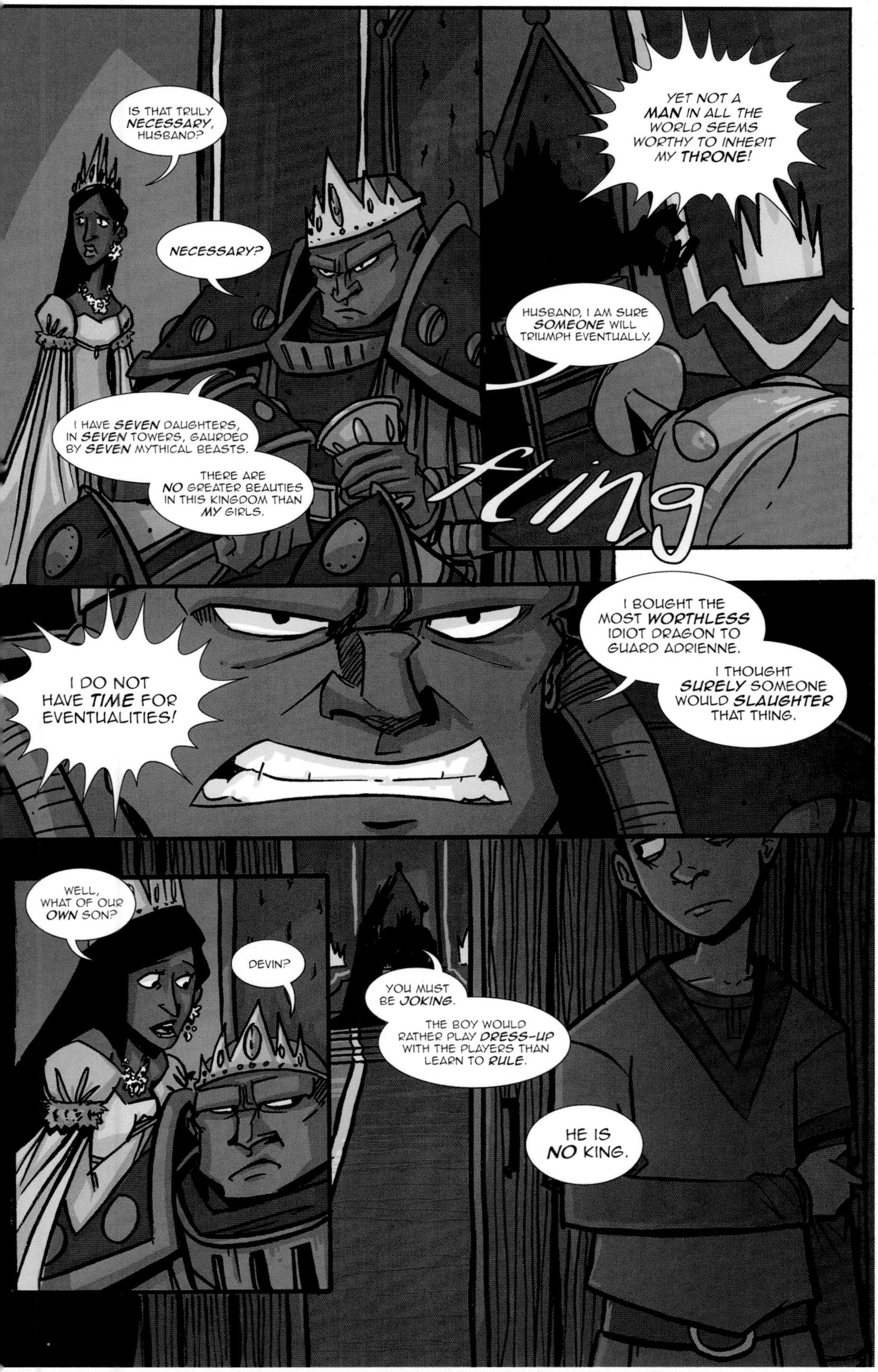

IS THAT TRULY NECESSARY, HUSBAND?
NECESSARY?
I HAVE SEVEN DAUGHTERS, IN SEVEN TOWERS, GAURDED BY SEVEN MYTHICAL BEASTS.
THERE ARE NO GREATER BEAUTIES IN THIS KINGDOM THAN MY GIRLS.
YET NOT A MAN IN ALL THE WORLD SEEMS WORTHY TO INHERIT MY THRONE!
HUSBAND, I AM SURE SOMEONE WILL TRIUMPH EVENTUALLY.
fling
I DO NOT HAVE TIME FOR EVENTUALITIES!
I BOUGHT THE MOST WORTHLESS IDIOT DRAGON TO GUARD ADRIENNE.
I THOUGHT SURELY SOMEONE WOULD SLAUGHTER THAT THING.
WELL, WHAT OF OUR OWN SON?
DEVIN?
YOU MUST BE JOKING.
THE BOY WOULD RATHER PLAY DRESS-UP WITH THE PLAYERS THAN LEARN TO RULE.
HE IS NO KING.

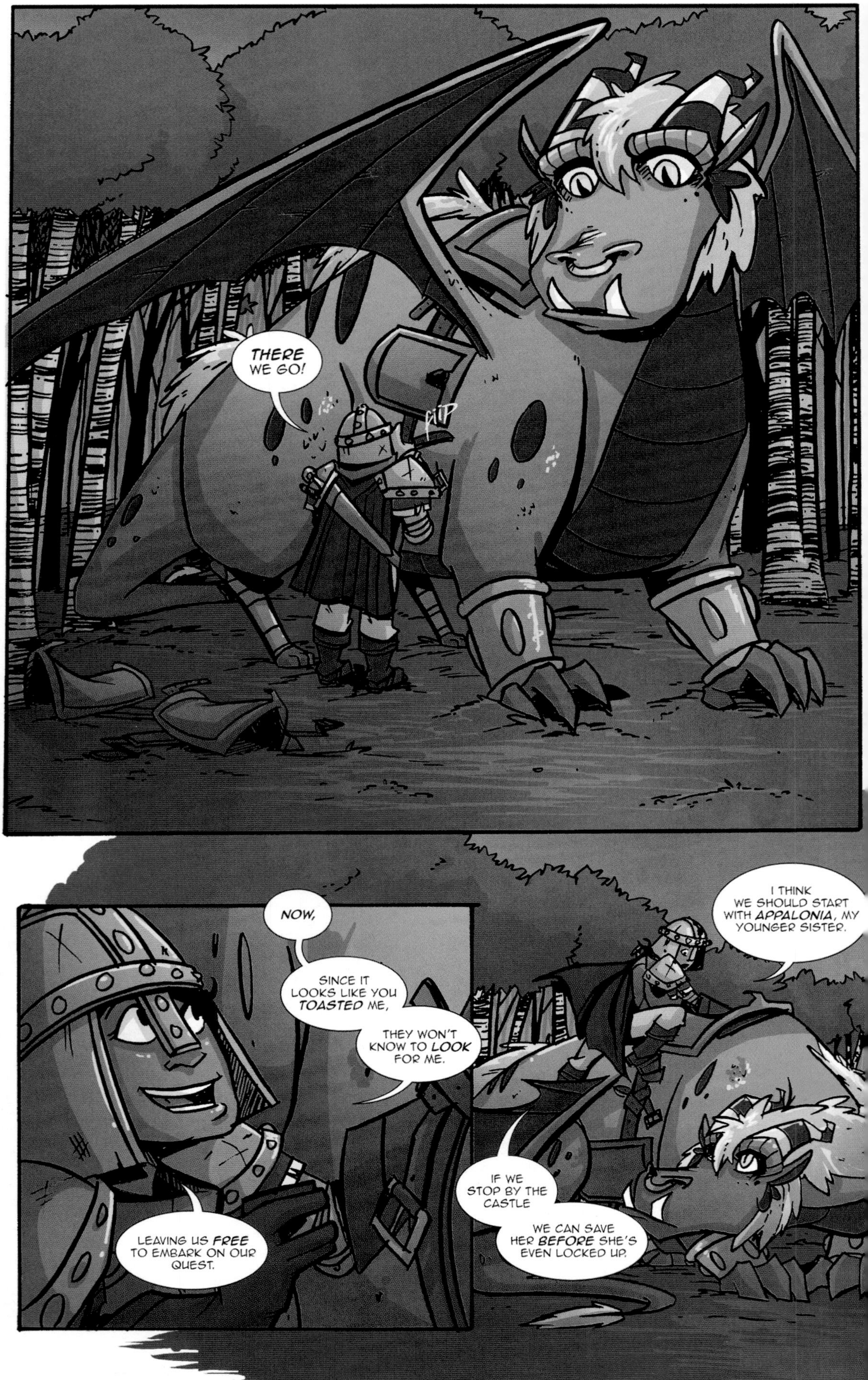
THERE WE GO!
flip
NOW,
SINCE IT LOOKS LIKE YOU TOASTED ME,
THEY WON'T KNOW TO LOOK FOR ME.
LEAVING US FREE TO EMBARK ON OUR QUEST.
I THINK WE SHOULD START WITH APPALONIA, MY YOUNGER SISTER.
IF WE STOP BY THE CASTLE
WE CAN SAVE HER BEFORE SHE'S EVEN LOCKED UP.

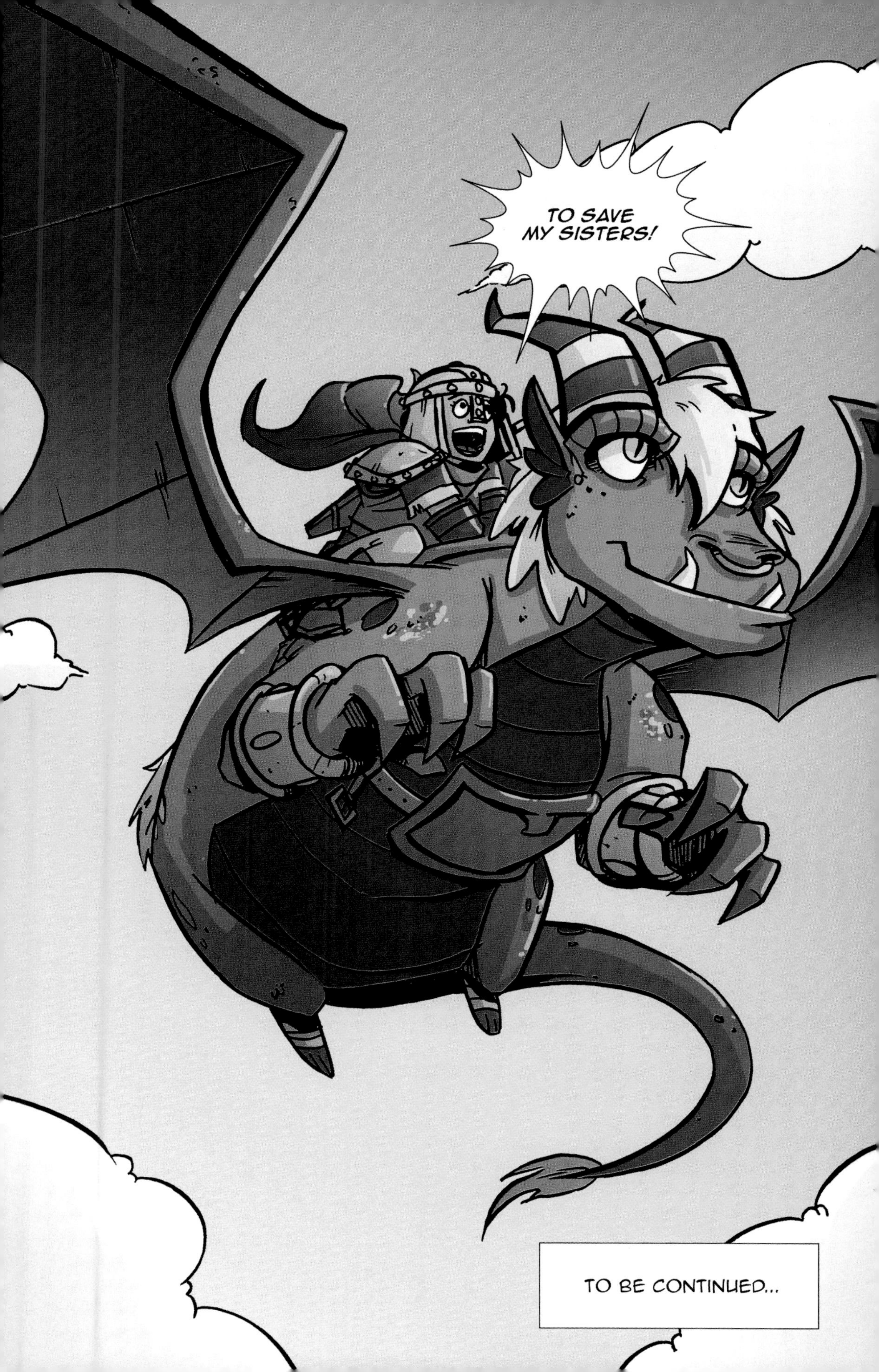
TO SAVE MY SISTERS!
TO BE CONTINUED...

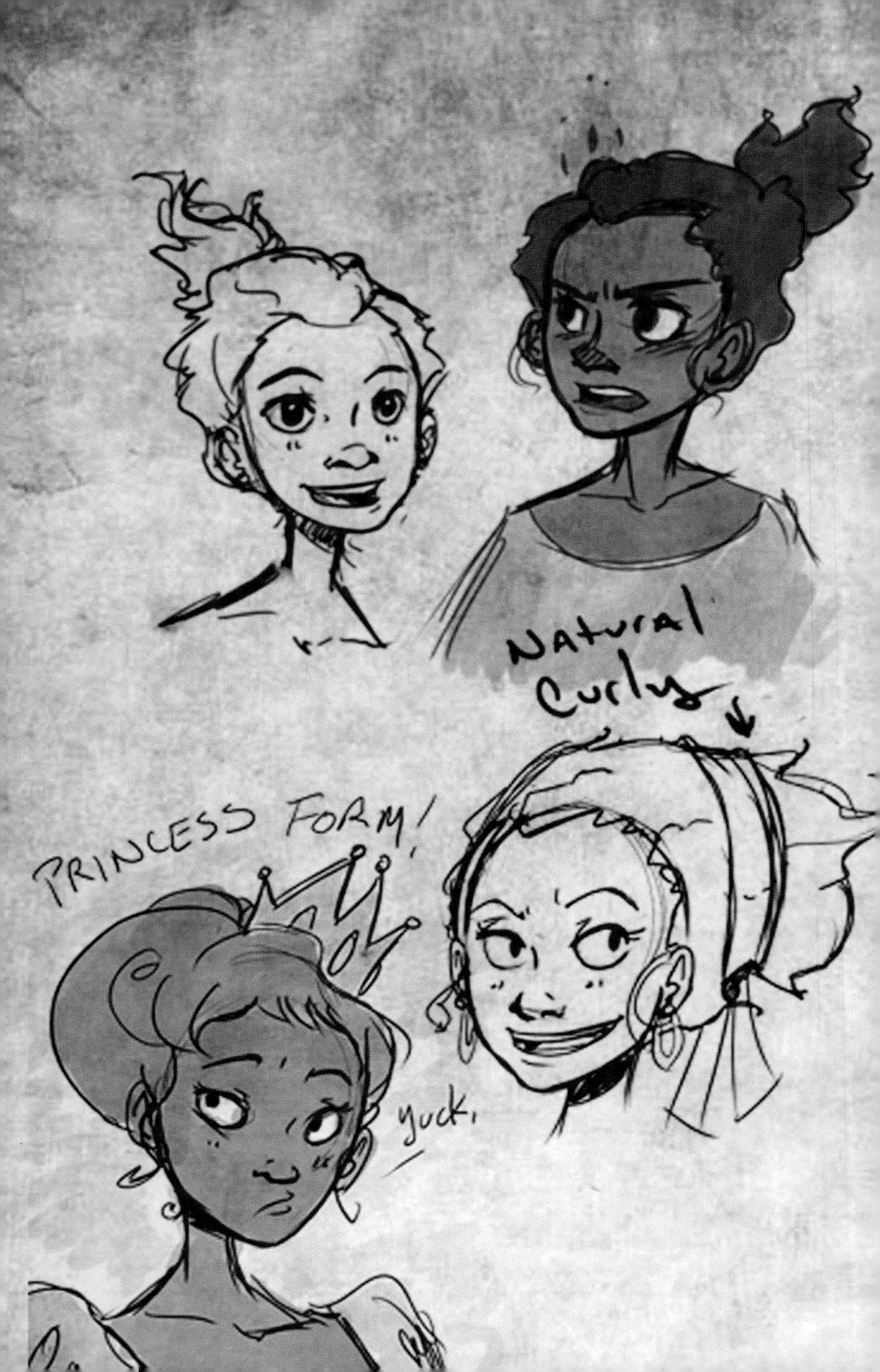
Natural Curls
PRINCESS FORM!
yuck.

2: All for the Want of a Proper Belt

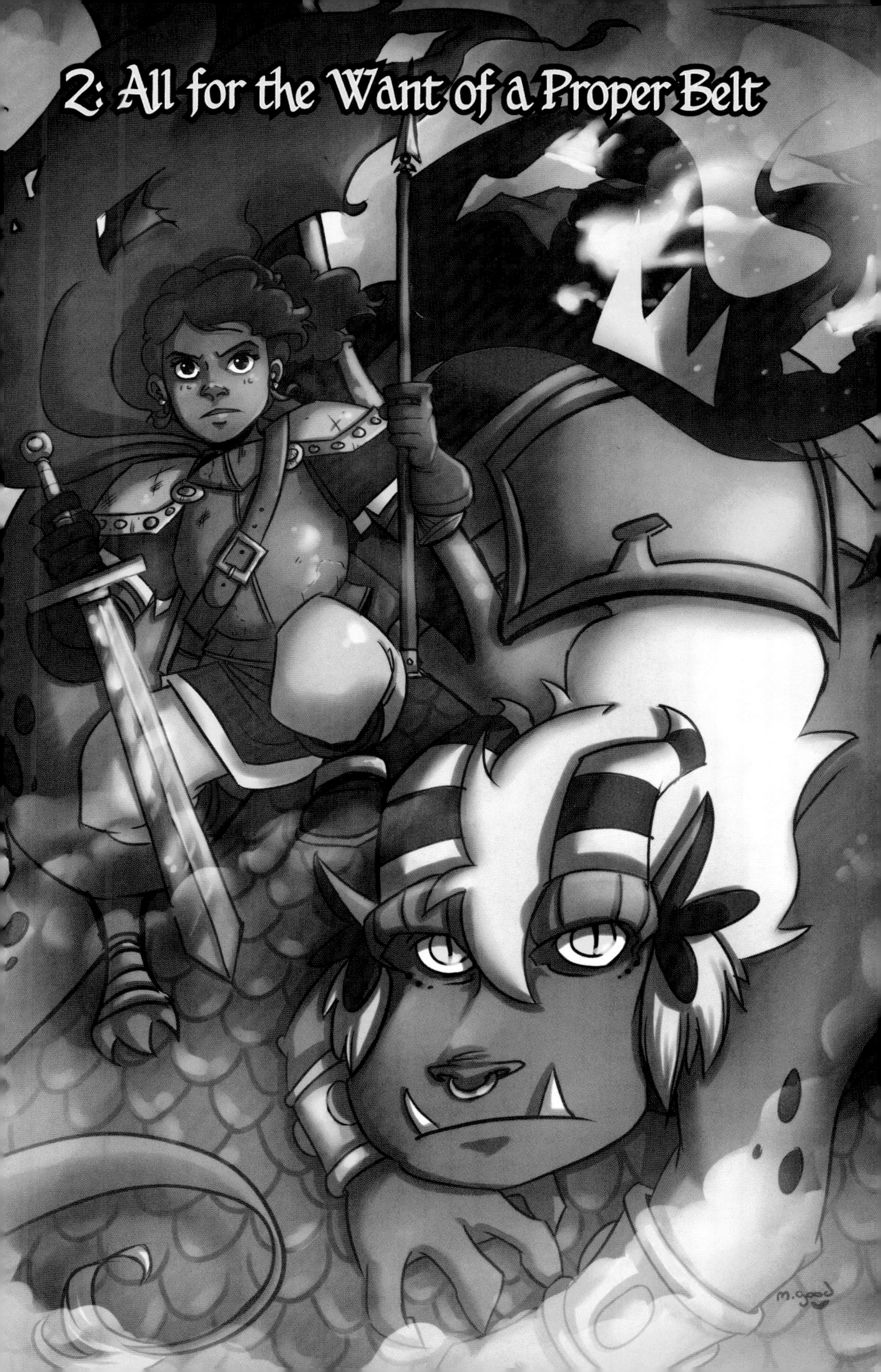

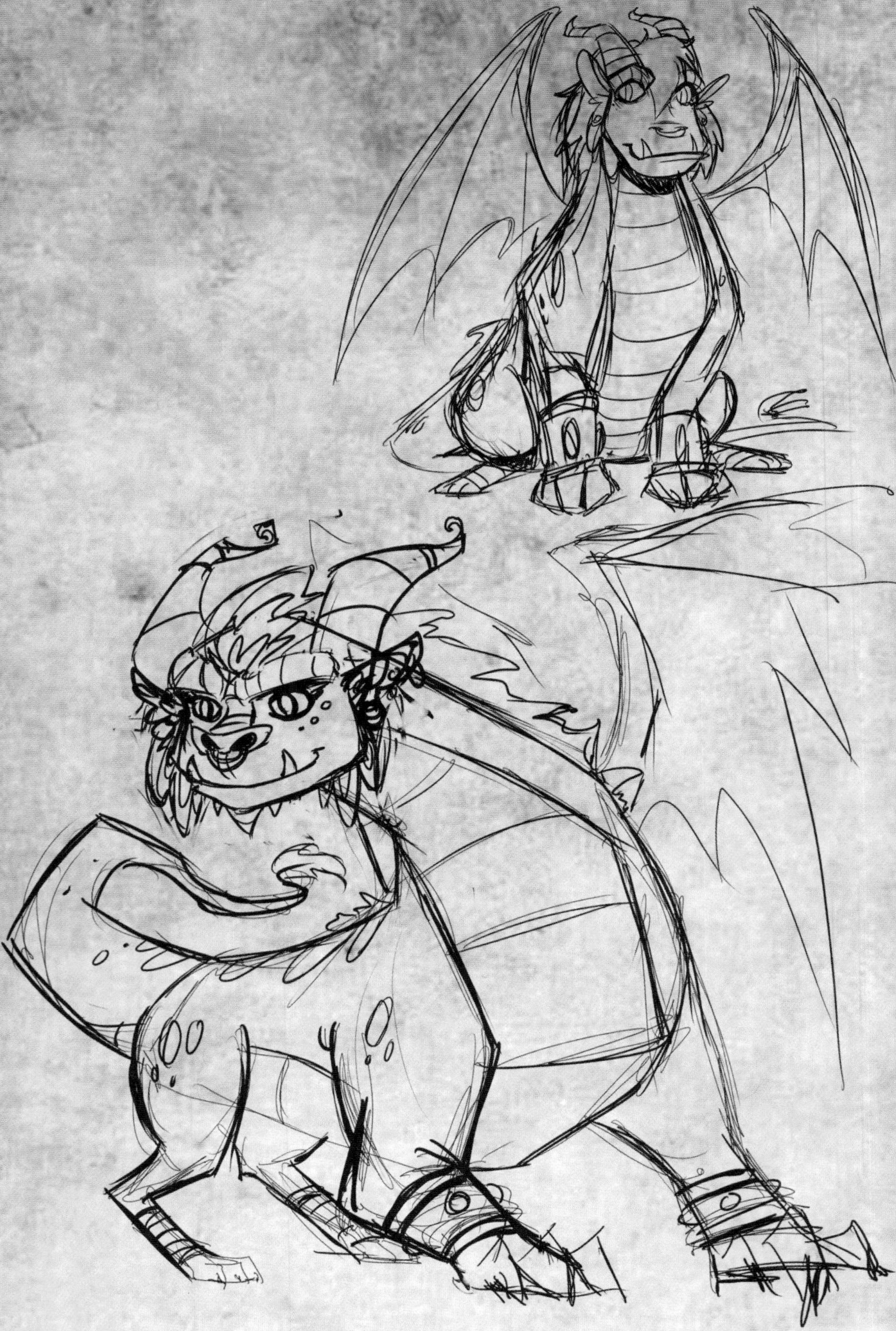

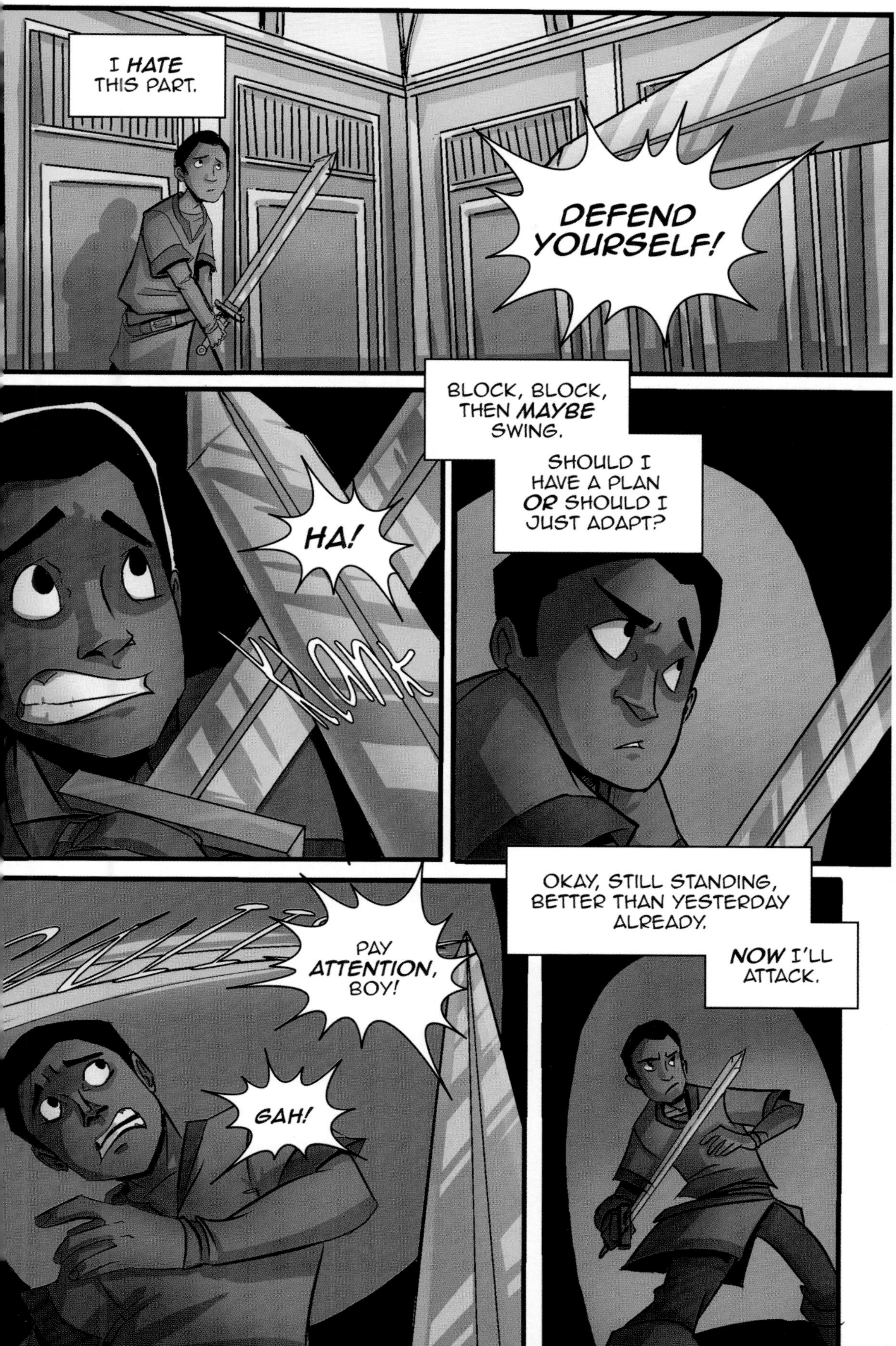
I HATE THIS PART.
DEFEND YOURSELF!
BLOCK, BLOCK, THEN MAYBE SWING.
HA!
SHOULD I HAVE A PLAN OR SHOULD I JUST ADAPT?
PAY ATTENTION, BOY!
GAH!
OKAY, STILL STANDING, BETTER THAN YESTERDAY ALREADY.
NOW I'LL ATTACK.

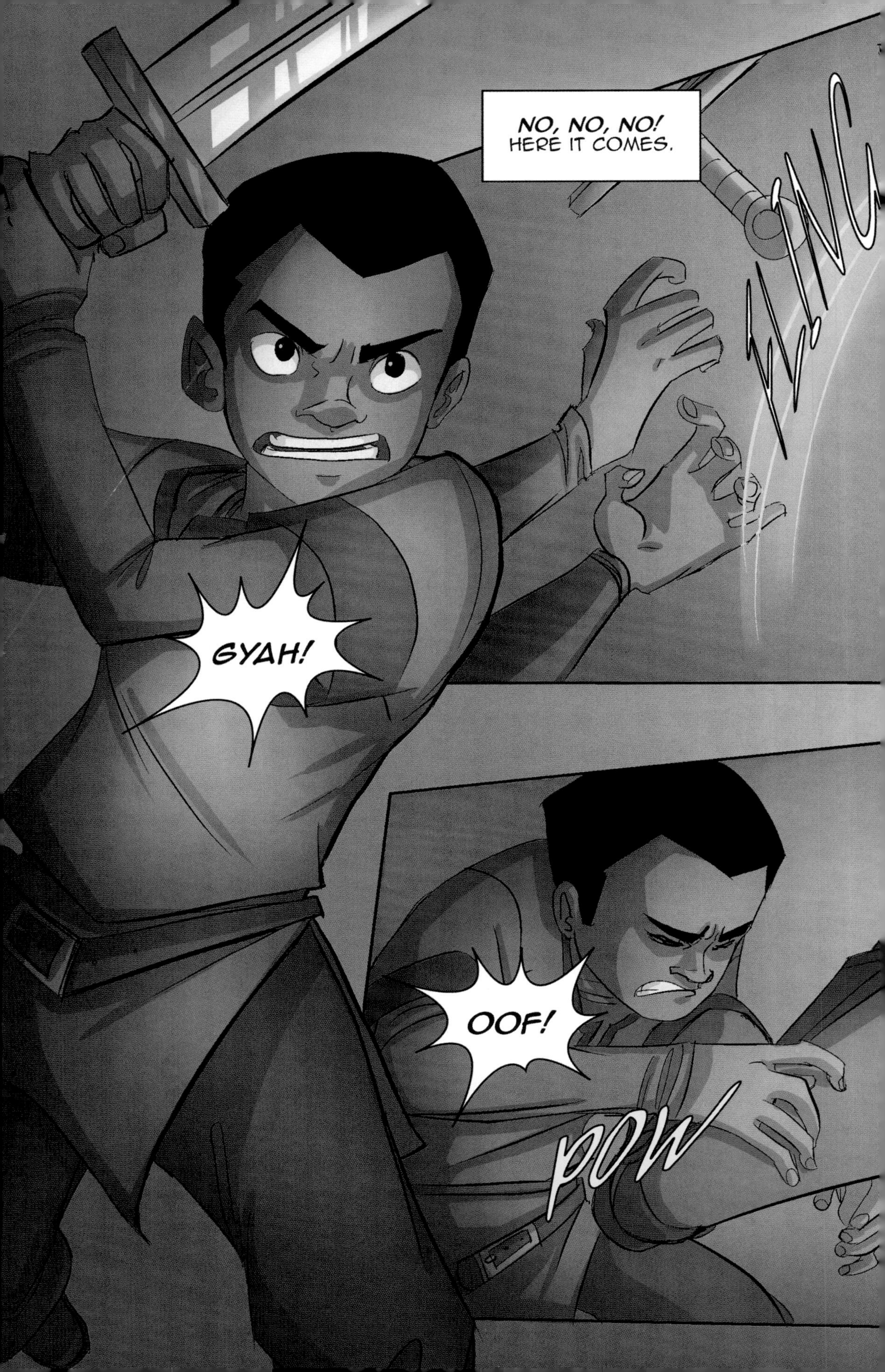
NO, NO, NO!
HERE IT COMES.
ZING
GYAH!
OOF!
POW

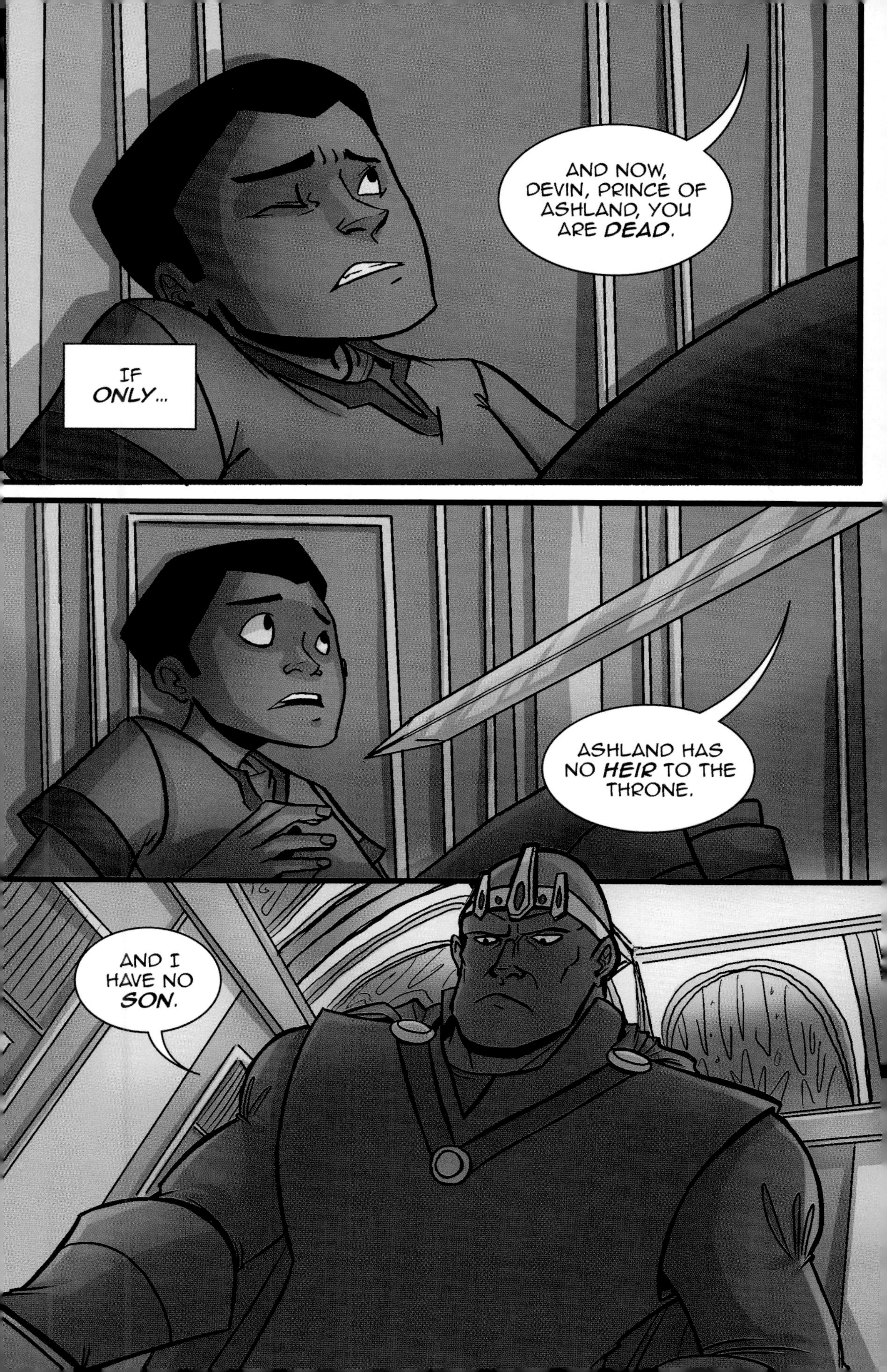
AND NOW, DEVIN, PRINCE OF ASHLAND, YOU ARE DEAD.
IF ONLY...
ASHLAND HAS NO HEIR TO THE THRONE.
AND I HAVE NO SON.

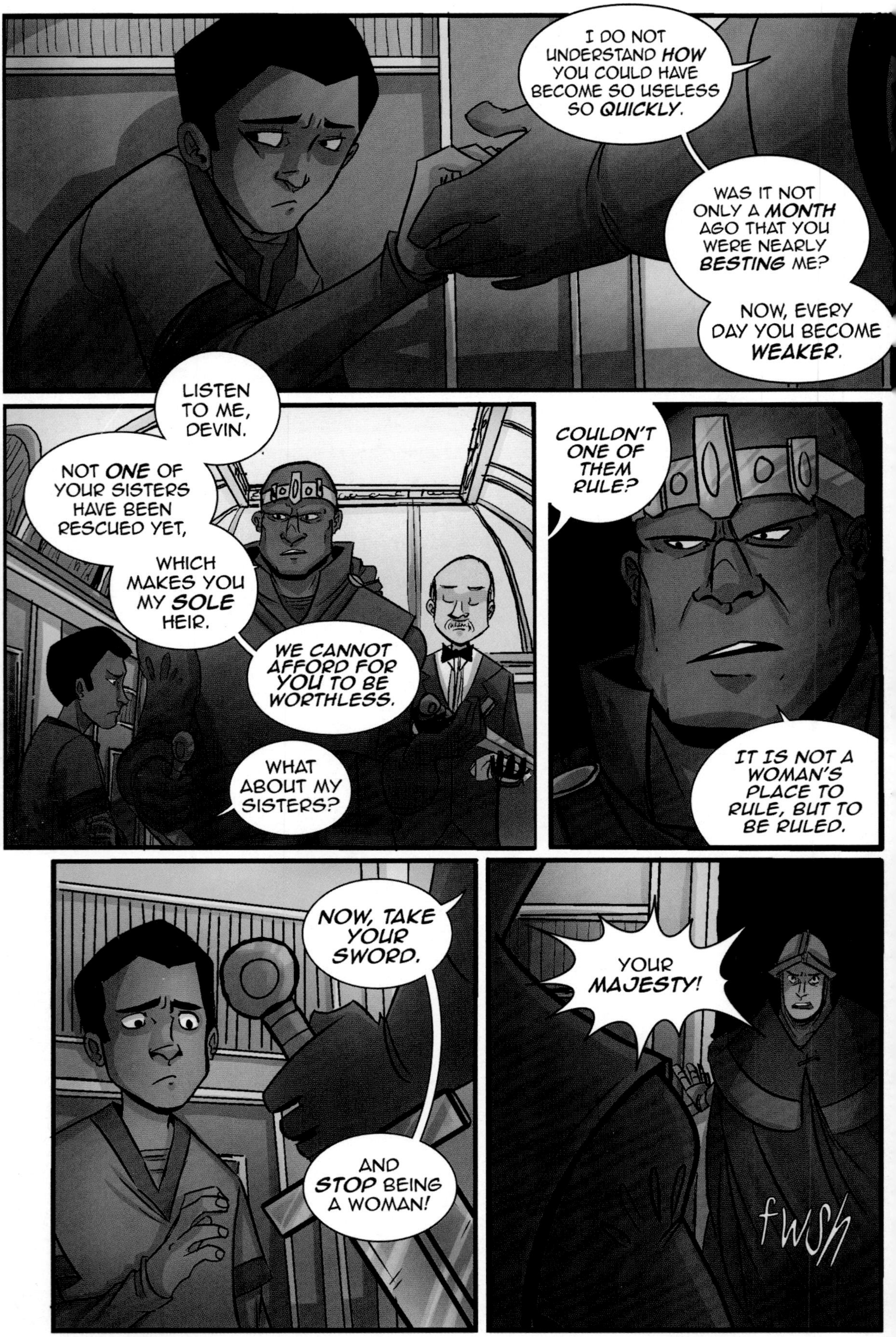
I DO NOT UNDERSTAND HOW YOU COULD HAVE BECOME SO USELESS SO QUICKLY.
WAS IT NOT ONLY A MONTH AGO THAT YOU WERE NEARLY BESTING ME?
NOW, EVERY DAY YOU BECOME WEAKER.
LISTEN TO ME, DEVIN.
NOT ONE OF YOUR SISTERS HAVE BEEN RESCUED YET,
WHICH MAKES YOU MY SOLE HEIR.
WE CANNOT AFFORD FOR YOU TO BE WORTHLESS.
WHAT ABOUT MY SISTERS?
COULDN'T ONE OF THEM RULE?
IT IS NOT A WOMAN'S PLACE TO RULE, BUT TO BE RULED.
NOW, TAKE YOUR SWORD.
AND STOP BEING A WOMAN!
YOUR MAJESTY!
fwsh

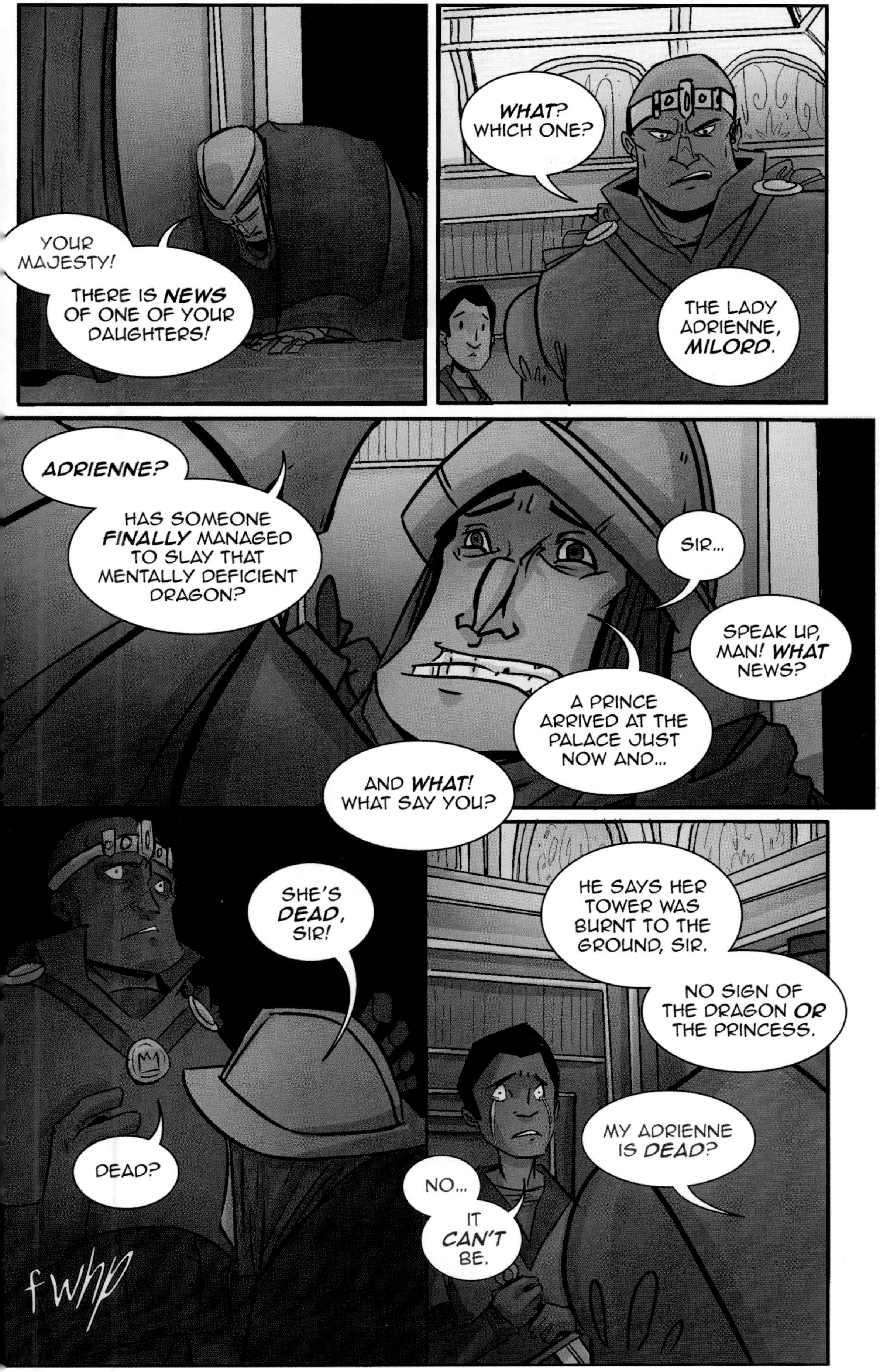
YOUR MAJESTY!
THERE IS NEWS OF ONE OF YOUR DAUGHTERS!
WHAT? WHICH ONE?
THE LADY ADRIENNE, MILORD.
ADRIENNE?
HAS SOMEONE FINALLY MANAGED TO SLAY THAT MENTALLY DEFICIENT DRAGON?
SIR...
SPEAK UP, MAN! WHAT NEWS?
A PRINCE ARRIVED AT THE PALACE JUST NOW AND...
AND WHAT! WHAT SAY YOU?
SHE'S DEAD, SIR!
DEAD?
fwhp
HE SAYS HER TOWER WAS BURNT TO THE GROUND, SIR.
NO SIGN OF THE DRAGON OR THE PRINCESS.
MY ADRIENNE IS DEAD?
NO...
IT CAN'T BE.

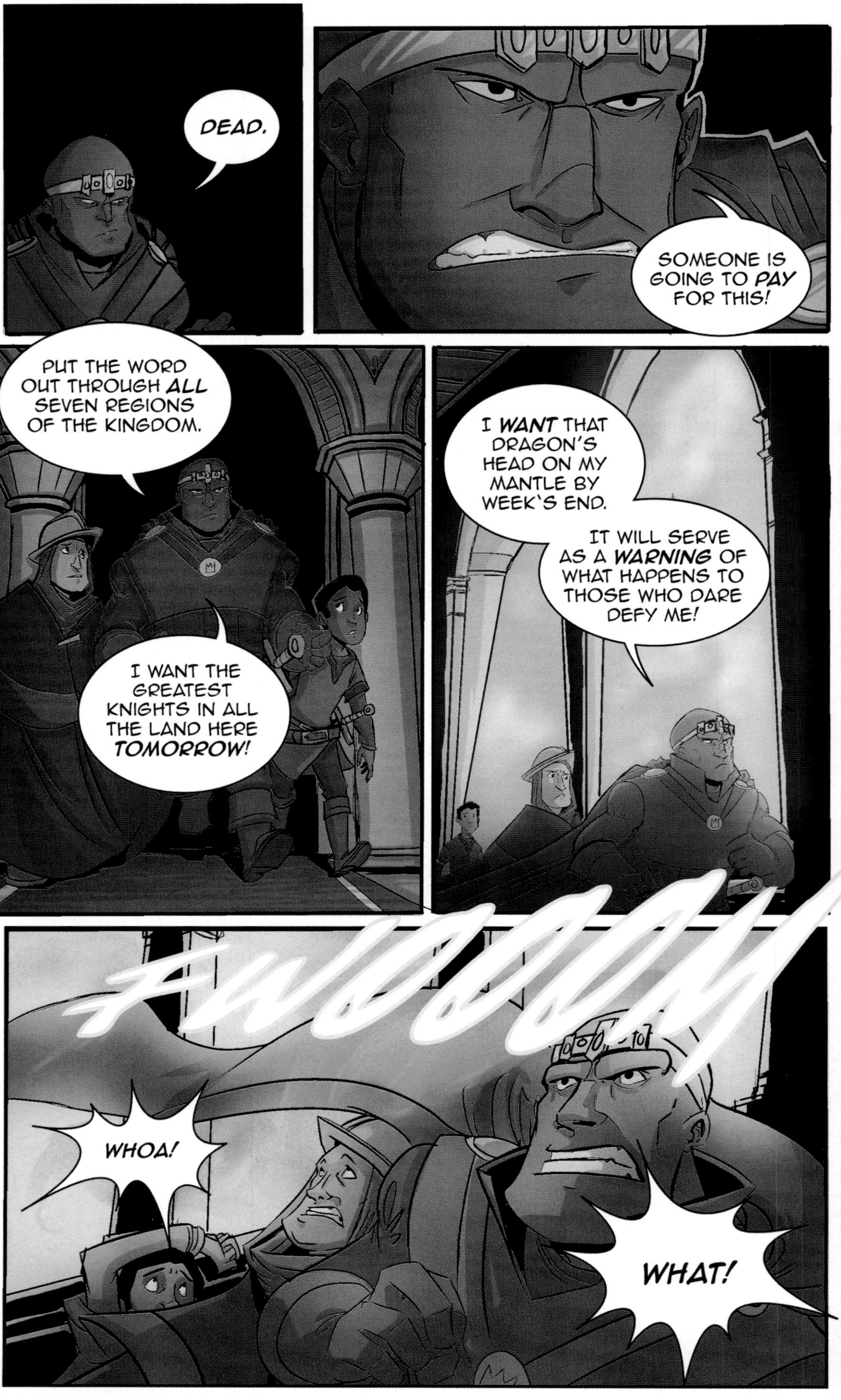
DEAD.
SOMEONE IS GOING TO *PAY* FOR THIS!
PUT THE WORD OUT THROUGH ***ALL*** SEVEN REGIONS OF THE KINGDOM.
I WANT THE GREATEST KNIGHTS IN ALL THE LAND HERE ***TOMORROW!***
I ***WANT*** THAT DRAGON'S HEAD ON MY MANTLE BY WEEK'S END.
IT WILL SERVE AS A ***WARNING*** OF WHAT HAPPENS TO THOSE WHO DARE DEFY ME!
FWOOOM
WHOA!
WHAT!

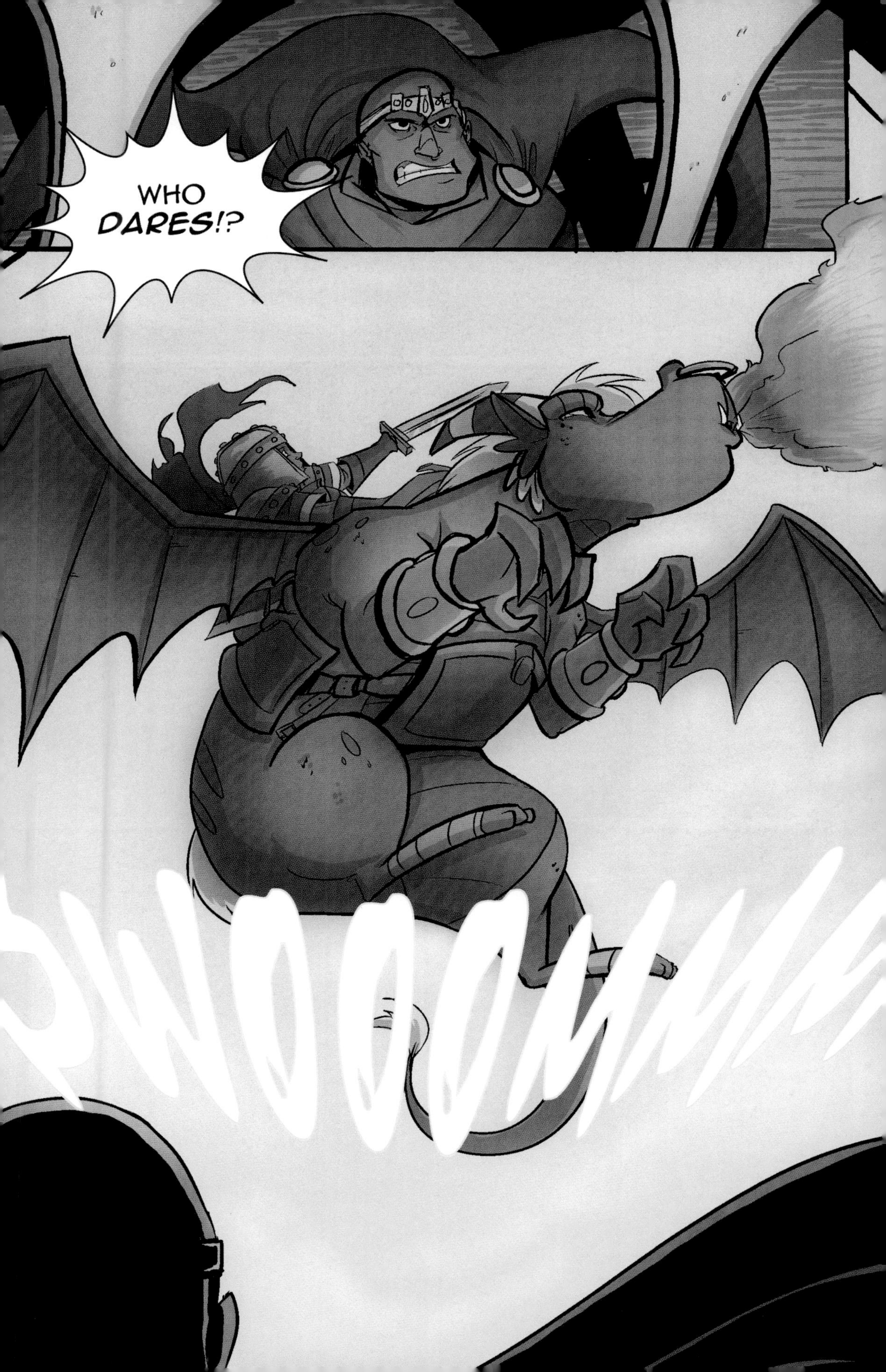
WHO DARES!?

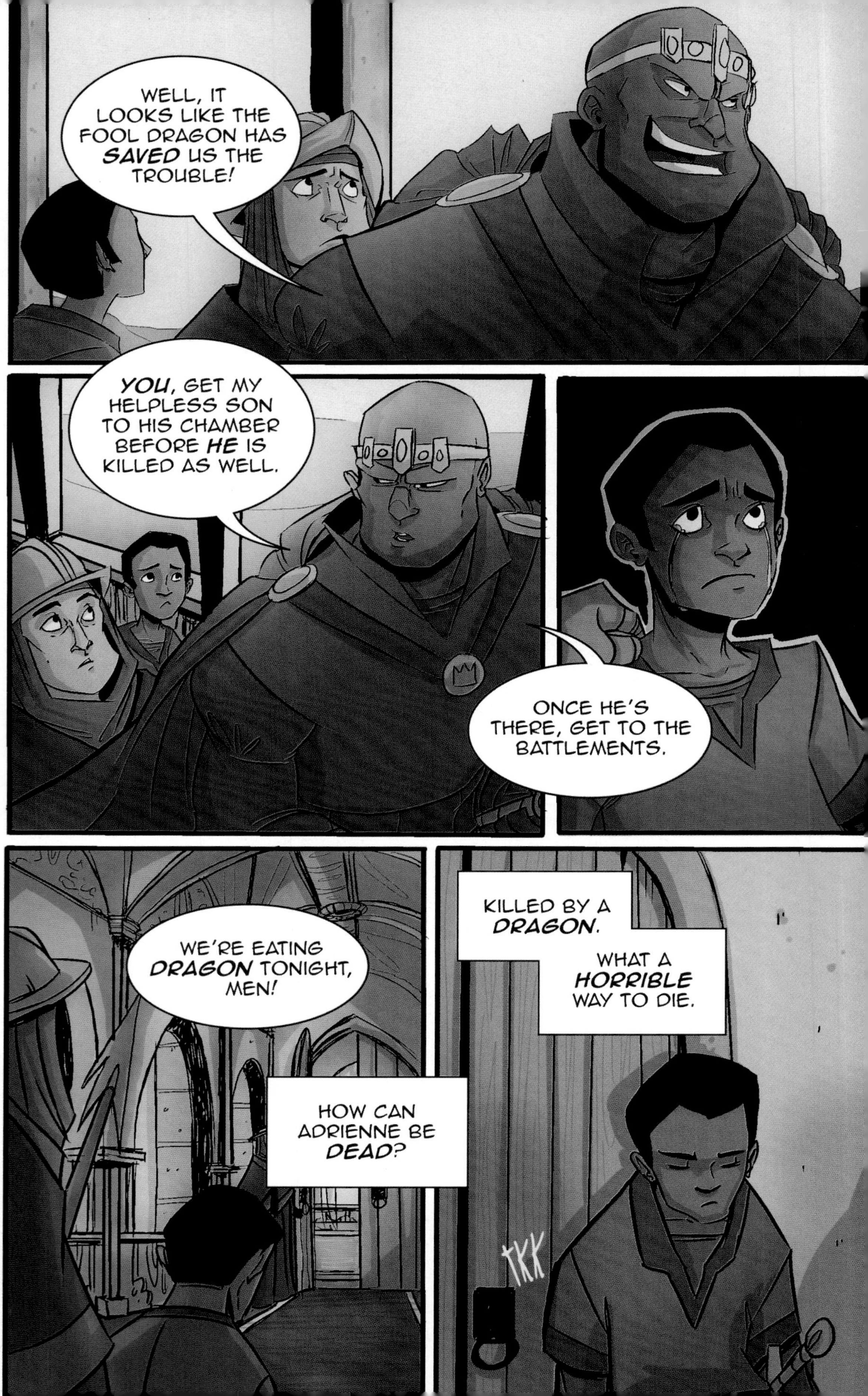
WELL, IT LOOKS LIKE THE FOOL DRAGON HAS SAVED US THE TROUBLE!
YOU, GET MY HELPLESS SON TO HIS CHAMBER BEFORE HE IS KILLED AS WELL.
ONCE HE'S THERE, GET TO THE BATTLEMENTS.
WE'RE EATING DRAGON TONIGHT, MEN!
HOW CAN ADRIENNE BE DEAD?
KILLED BY A DRAGON.
WHAT A HORRIBLE WAY TO DIE.
TKK

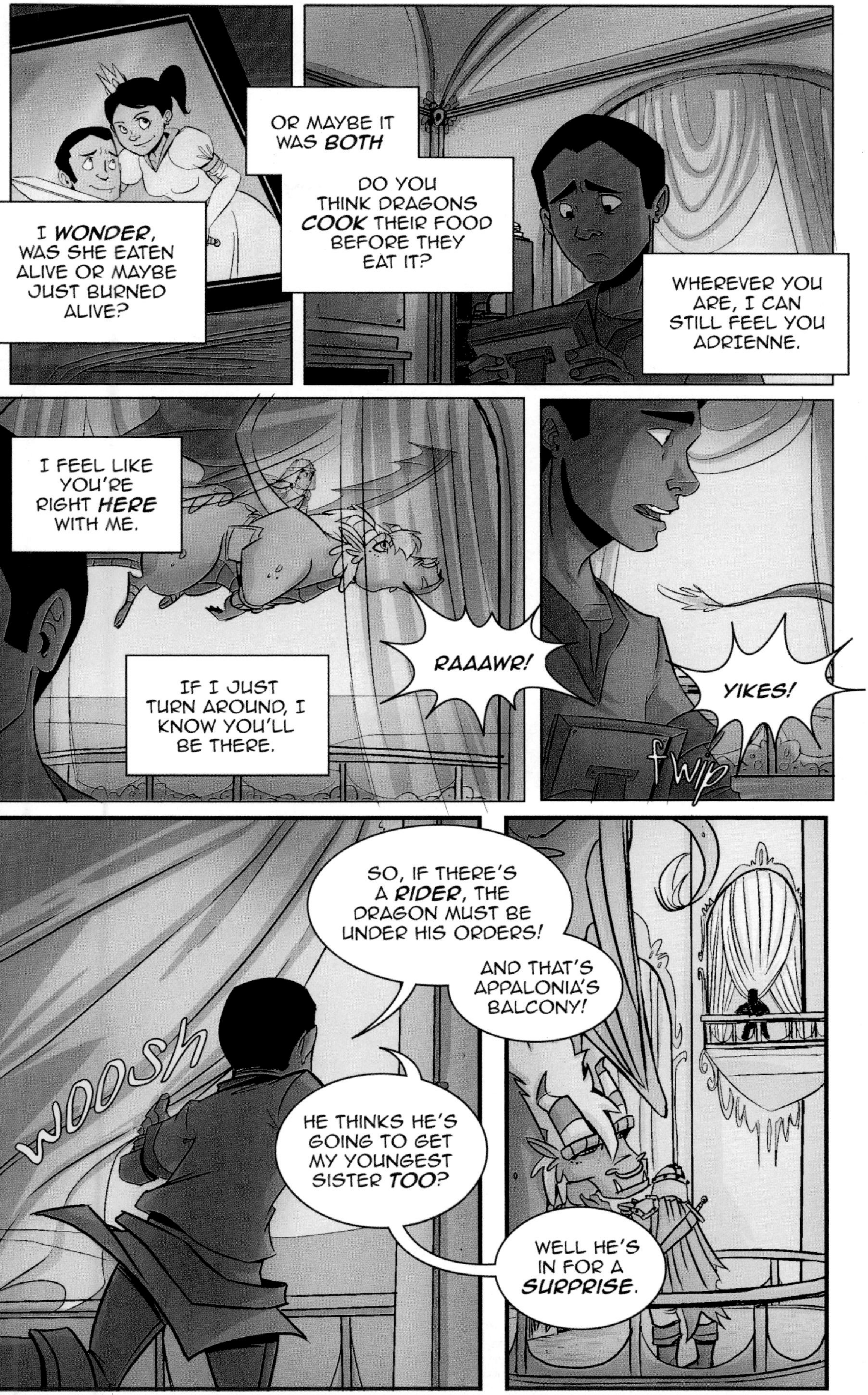
I WONDER, WAS SHE EATEN ALIVE OR MAYBE JUST BURNED ALIVE?
OR MAYBE IT WAS BOTH
DO YOU THINK DRAGONS COOK THEIR FOOD BEFORE THEY EAT IT?
WHEREVER YOU ARE, I CAN STILL FEEL YOU ADRIENNE.
I FEEL LIKE YOU'RE RIGHT HERE WITH ME.
IF I JUST TURN AROUND, I KNOW YOU'LL BE THERE.
RAAAWR!
YIKES!
fwip
SO, IF THERE'S A RIDER, THE DRAGON MUST BE UNDER HIS ORDERS!
AND THAT'S APPALONIA'S BALCONY!
WOOSH
HE THINKS HE'S GOING TO GET MY YOUNGEST SISTER TOO?
WELL HE'S IN FOR A SURPRISE.

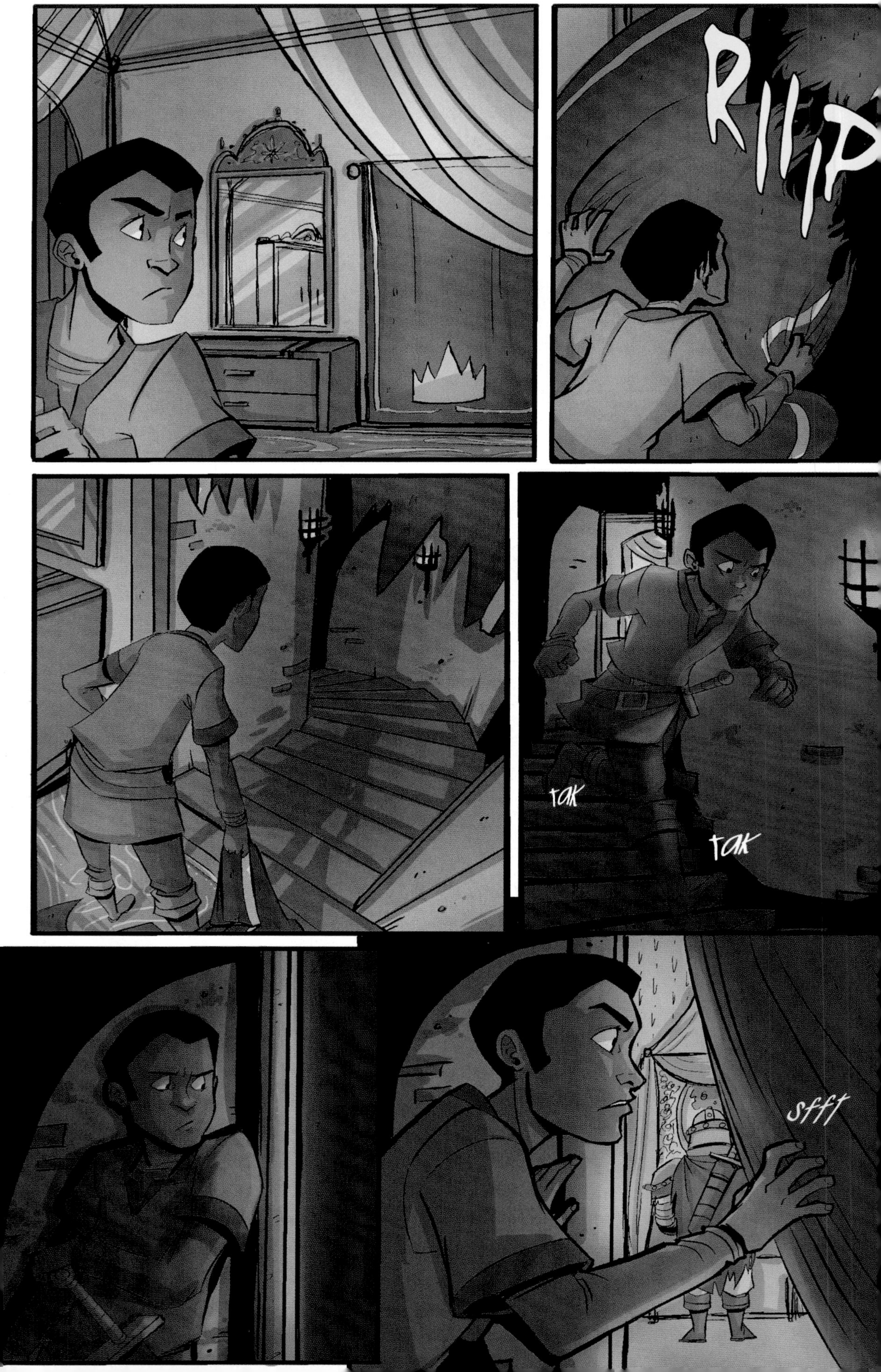
RIIIP
tak
tak
sfft

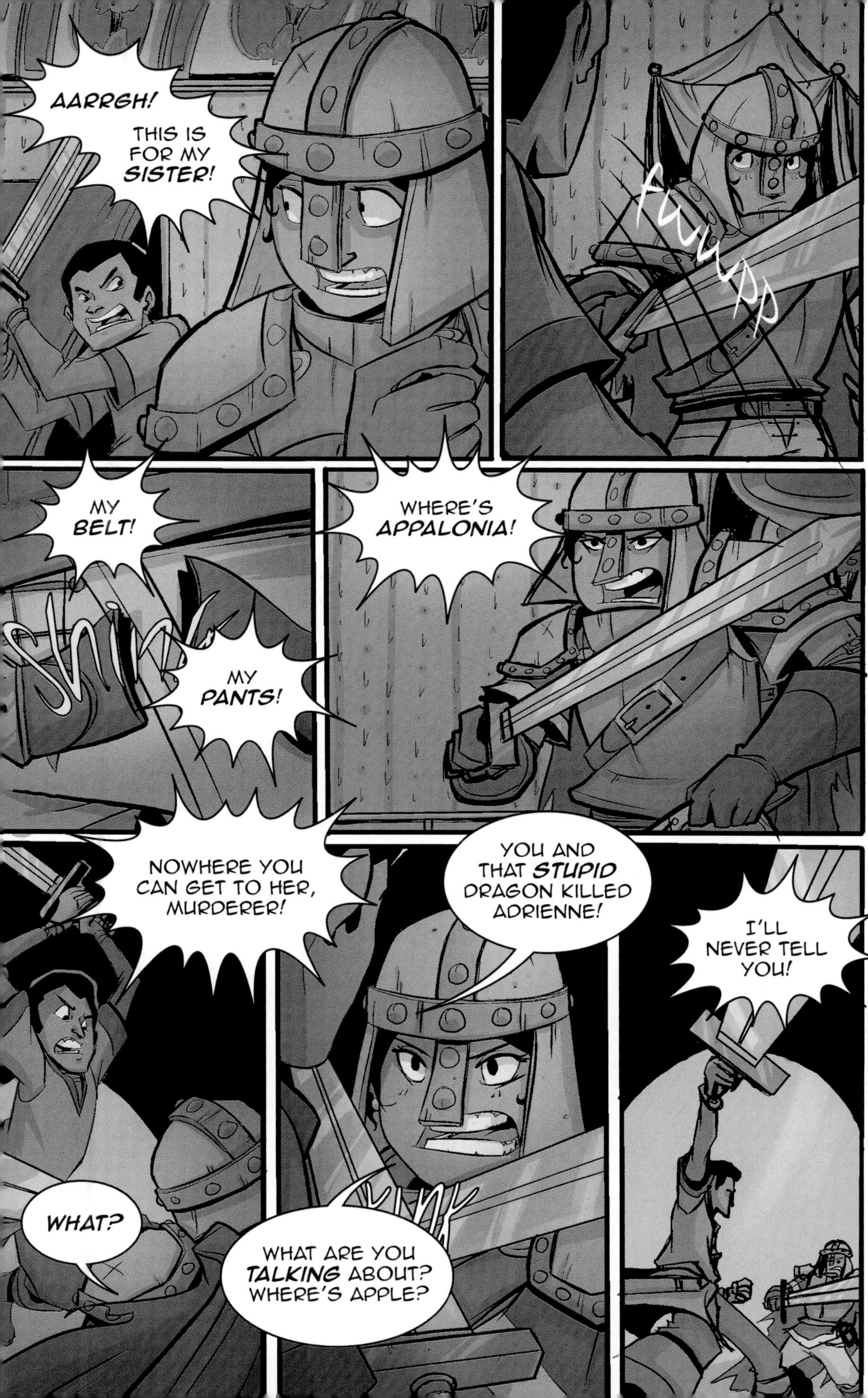
AARRGH!
THIS IS FOR MY SISTER!
FWUPP
MY BELT!
SHINK
MY PANTS!
WHERE'S APPALONIA!
NOWHERE YOU CAN GET TO HER, MURDERER!
YOU AND THAT STUPID DRAGON KILLED ADRIENNE!
I'LL NEVER TELL YOU!
WHAT?
WHAT ARE YOU TALKING ABOUT? WHERE'S APPLE?

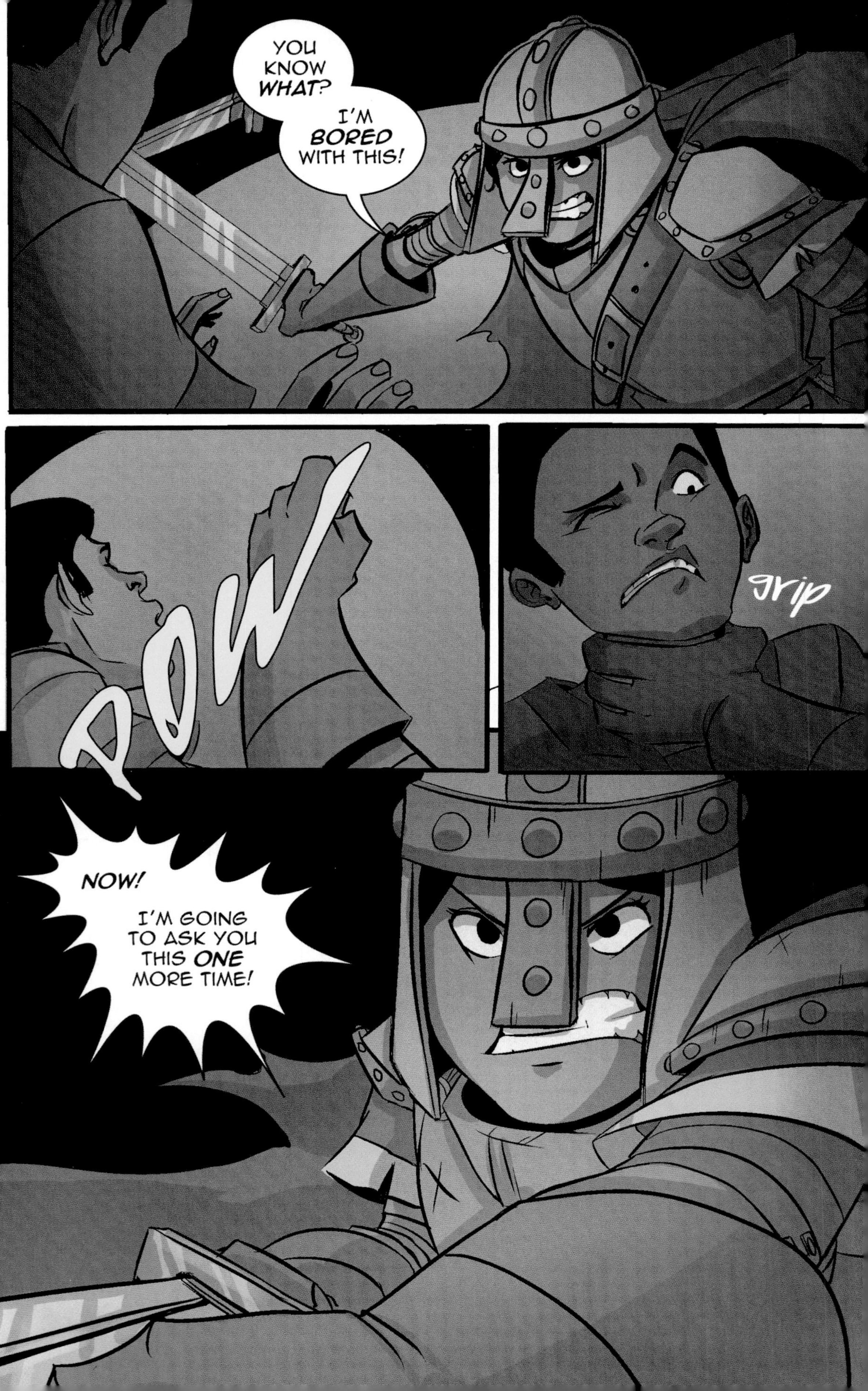
YOU KNOW WHAT?
I'M BORED WITH THIS!
POW
grip
NOW!
I'M GOING TO ASK YOU THIS ONE MORE TIME!

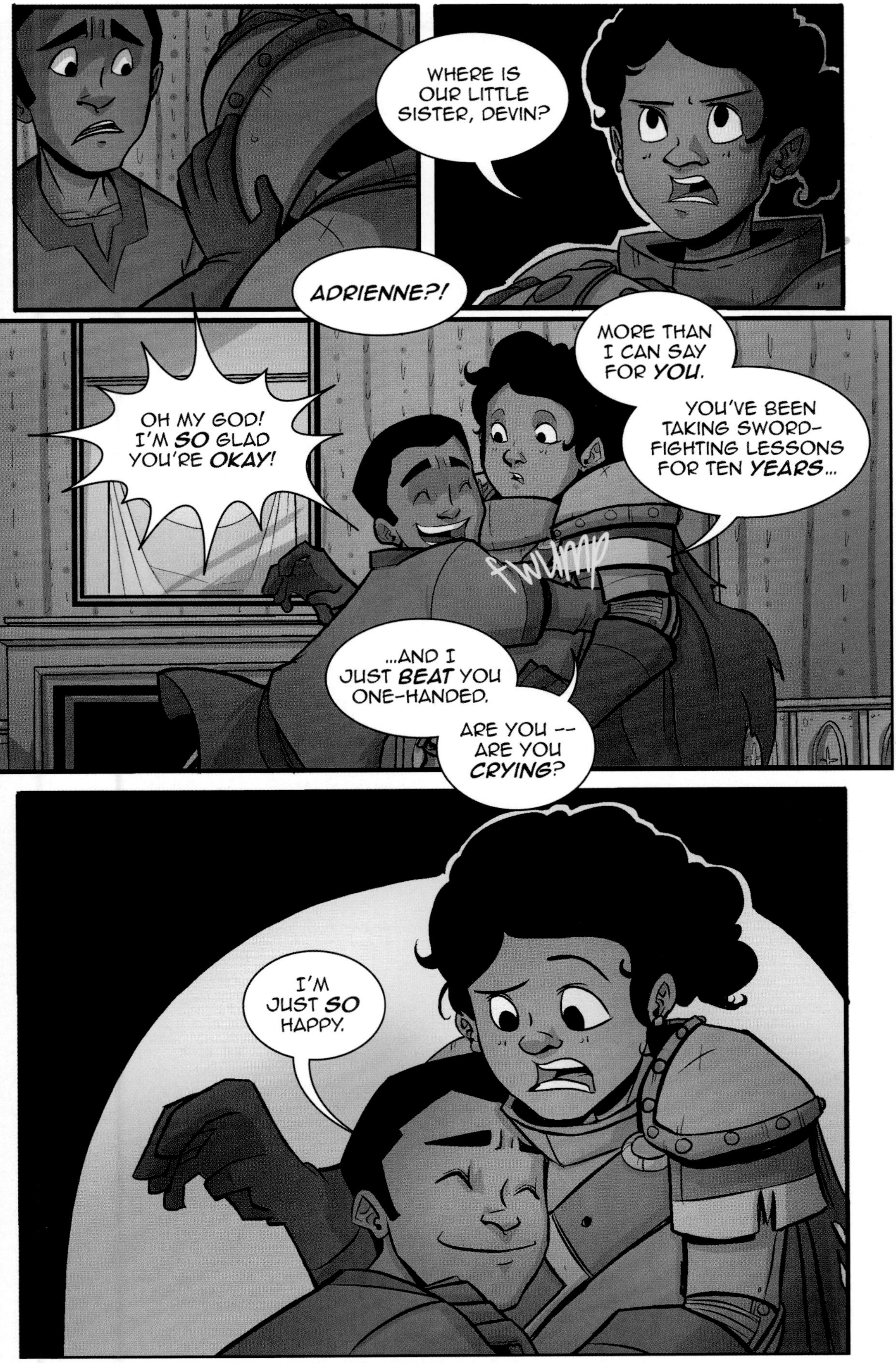
WHERE IS OUR LITTLE SISTER, DEVIN?
ADRIENNE?!
OH MY GOD! I'M SO GLAD YOU'RE OKAY!
MORE THAN I CAN SAY FOR YOU.
YOU'VE BEEN TAKING SWORD-FIGHTING LESSONS FOR TEN YEARS...
fwump
...AND I JUST BEAT YOU ONE-HANDED.
ARE YOU -- ARE YOU CRYING?
I'M JUST SO HAPPY.

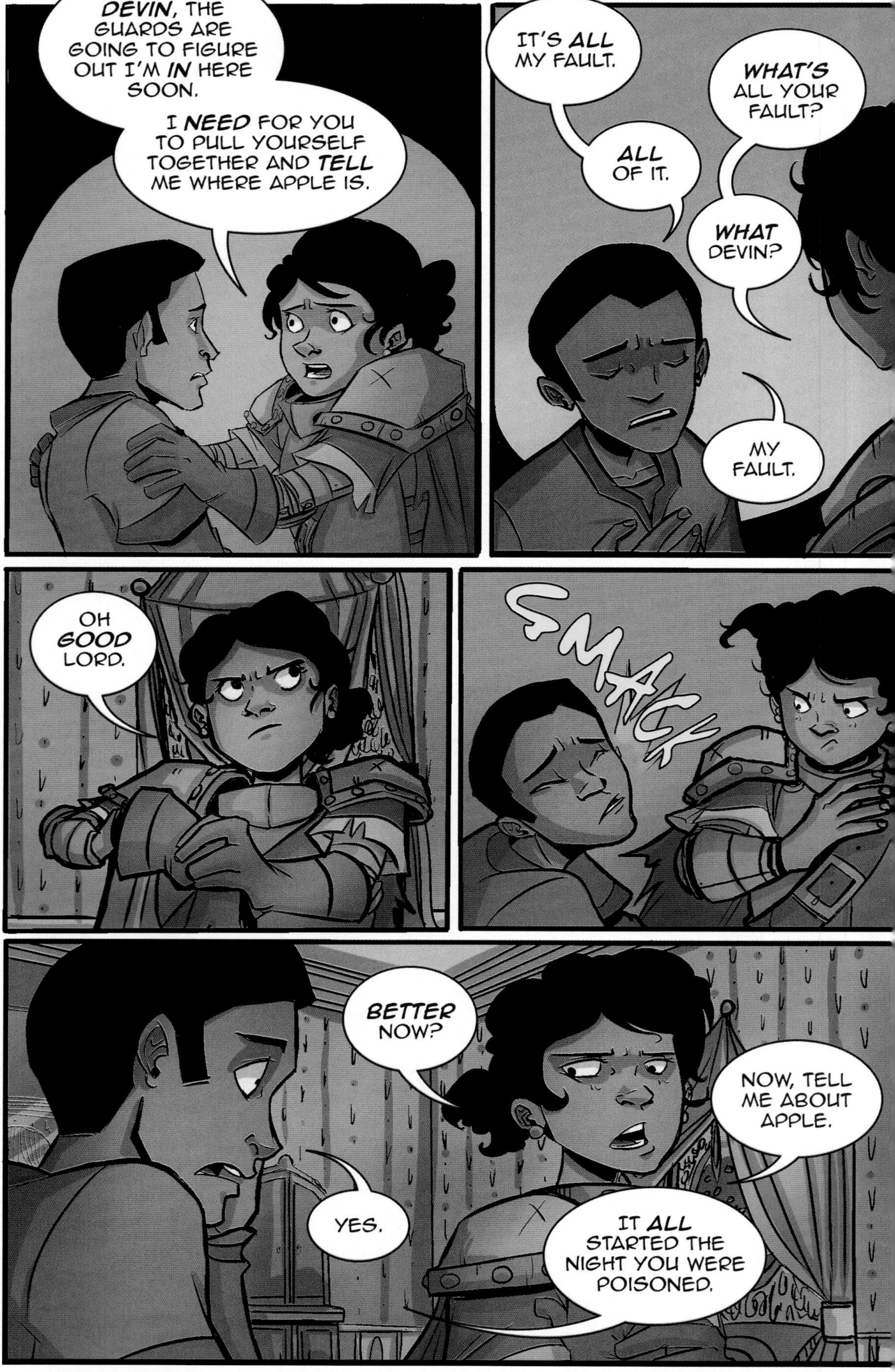
DEVIN, THE GUARDS ARE GOING TO FIGURE OUT I'M IN HERE SOON.
I NEED FOR YOU TO PULL YOURSELF TOGETHER AND TELL ME WHERE APPLE IS.
IT'S ALL MY FAULT.
WHAT'S ALL YOUR FAULT?
ALL OF IT.
WHAT DEVIN?
MY FAULT.
OH GOOD LORD.
SMACK
BETTER NOW?
YES.
NOW, TELL ME ABOUT APPLE.
IT ALL STARTED THE NIGHT YOU WERE POISONED.

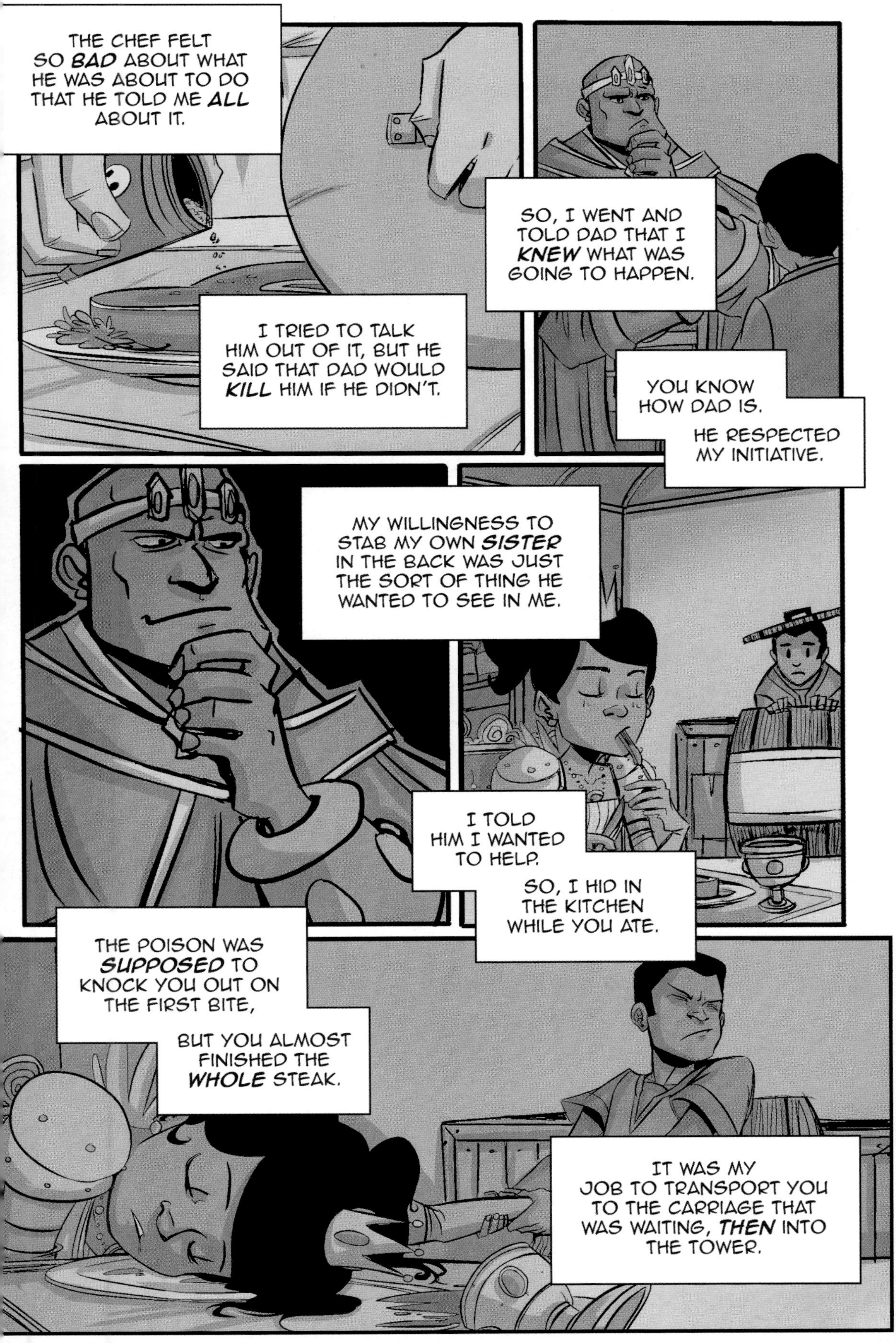
THE CHEF FELT SO BAD ABOUT WHAT HE WAS ABOUT TO DO THAT HE TOLD ME ALL ABOUT IT.
I TRIED TO TALK HIM OUT OF IT, BUT HE SAID THAT DAD WOULD KILL HIM IF HE DIDN'T.
SO, I WENT AND TOLD DAD THAT I KNEW WHAT WAS GOING TO HAPPEN.
YOU KNOW HOW DAD IS.
HE RESPECTED MY INITIATIVE.
MY WILLINGNESS TO STAB MY OWN SISTER IN THE BACK WAS JUST THE SORT OF THING HE WANTED TO SEE IN ME.
I TOLD HIM I WANTED TO HELP.
SO, I HID IN THE KITCHEN WHILE YOU ATE.
THE POISON WAS SUPPOSED TO KNOCK YOU OUT ON THE FIRST BITE,
BUT YOU ALMOST FINISHED THE WHOLE STEAK.
IT WAS MY JOB TO TRANSPORT YOU TO THE CARRIAGE THAT WAS WAITING, THEN INTO THE TOWER.

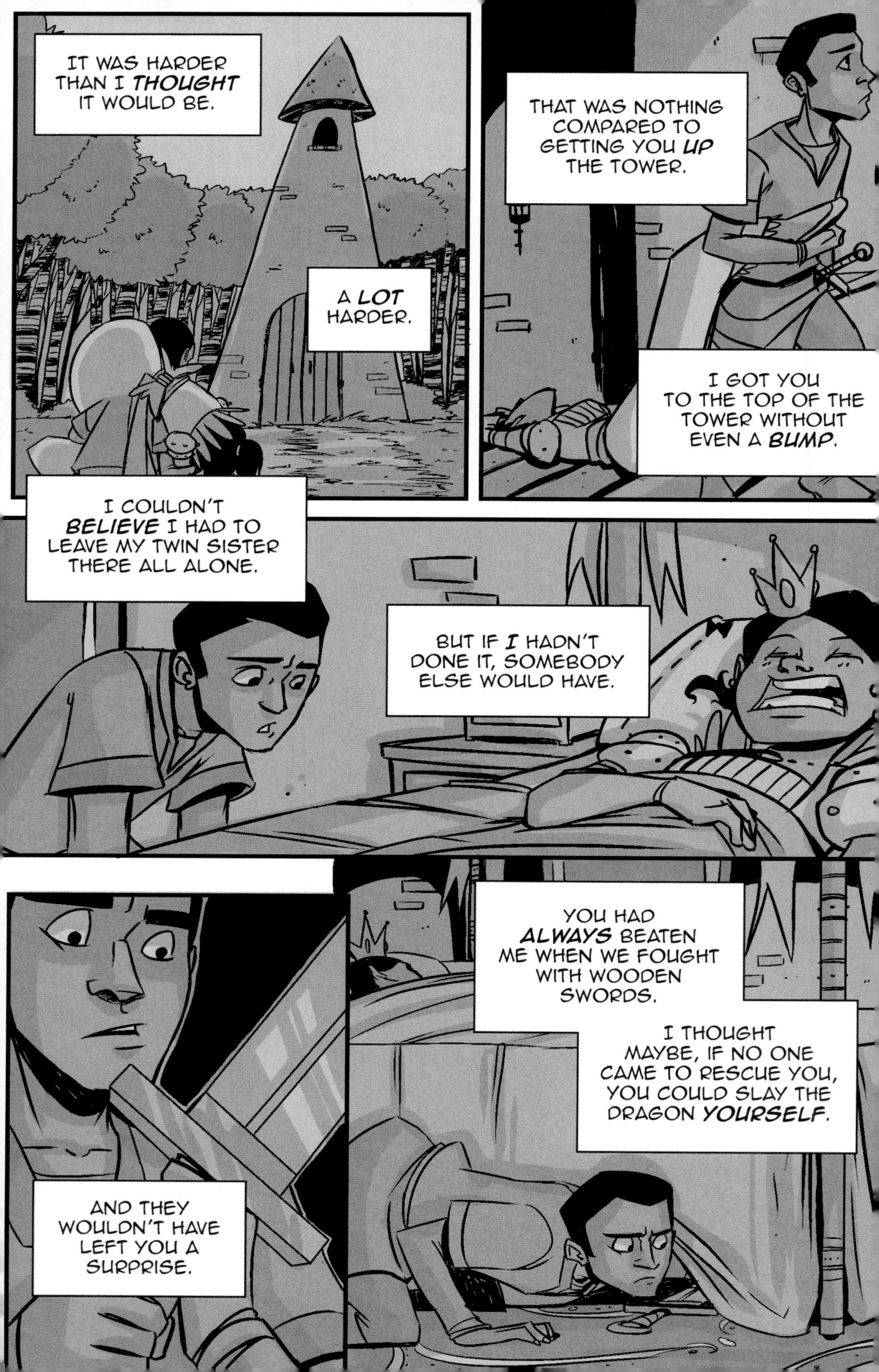
IT WAS HARDER THAN I THOUGHT IT WOULD BE.
A LOT HARDER.
THAT WAS NOTHING COMPARED TO GETTING YOU UP THE TOWER.
I GOT YOU TO THE TOP OF THE TOWER WITHOUT EVEN A BUMP.
I COULDN'T BELIEVE I HAD TO LEAVE MY TWIN SISTER THERE ALL ALONE.
BUT IF I HADN'T DONE IT, SOMEBODY ELSE WOULD HAVE.
AND THEY WOULDN'T HAVE LEFT YOU A SURPRISE.
YOU HAD ALWAYS BEATEN ME WHEN WE FOUGHT WITH WOODEN SWORDS.
I THOUGHT MAYBE, IF NO ONE CAME TO RESCUE YOU, YOU COULD SLAY THE DRAGON YOURSELF.

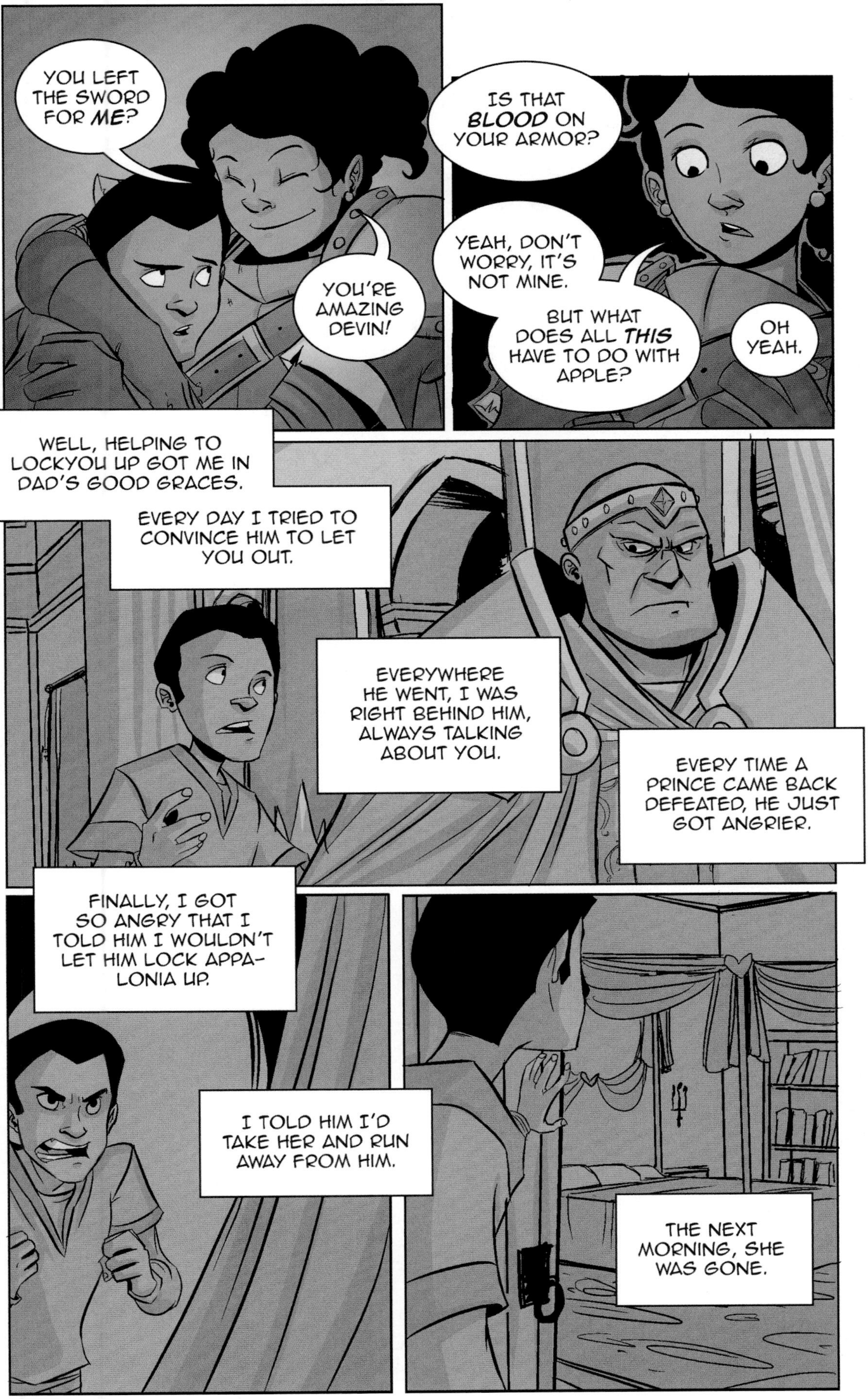
YOU LEFT THE SWORD FOR *ME*?
YOU'RE AMAZING DEVIN!
IS THAT *BLOOD* ON YOUR ARMOR?
YEAH, DON'T WORRY, IT'S NOT MINE.
BUT WHAT DOES ALL *THIS* HAVE TO DO WITH APPLE?
OH YEAH.
WELL, HELPING TO LOCKYOU UP GOT ME IN DAD'S GOOD GRACES.
EVERY DAY I TRIED TO CONVINCE HIM TO LET YOU OUT.
EVERYWHERE HE WENT, I WAS RIGHT BEHIND HIM, ALWAYS TALKING ABOUT YOU.
EVERY TIME A PRINCE CAME BACK DEFEATED, HE JUST GOT ANGRIER.
FINALLY, I GOT SO ANGRY THAT I TOLD HIM I WOULDN'T LET HIM LOCK APPA-LONIA UP.
I TOLD HIM I'D TAKE HER AND RUN AWAY FROM HIM.
THE NEXT MORNING, SHE WAS GONE.

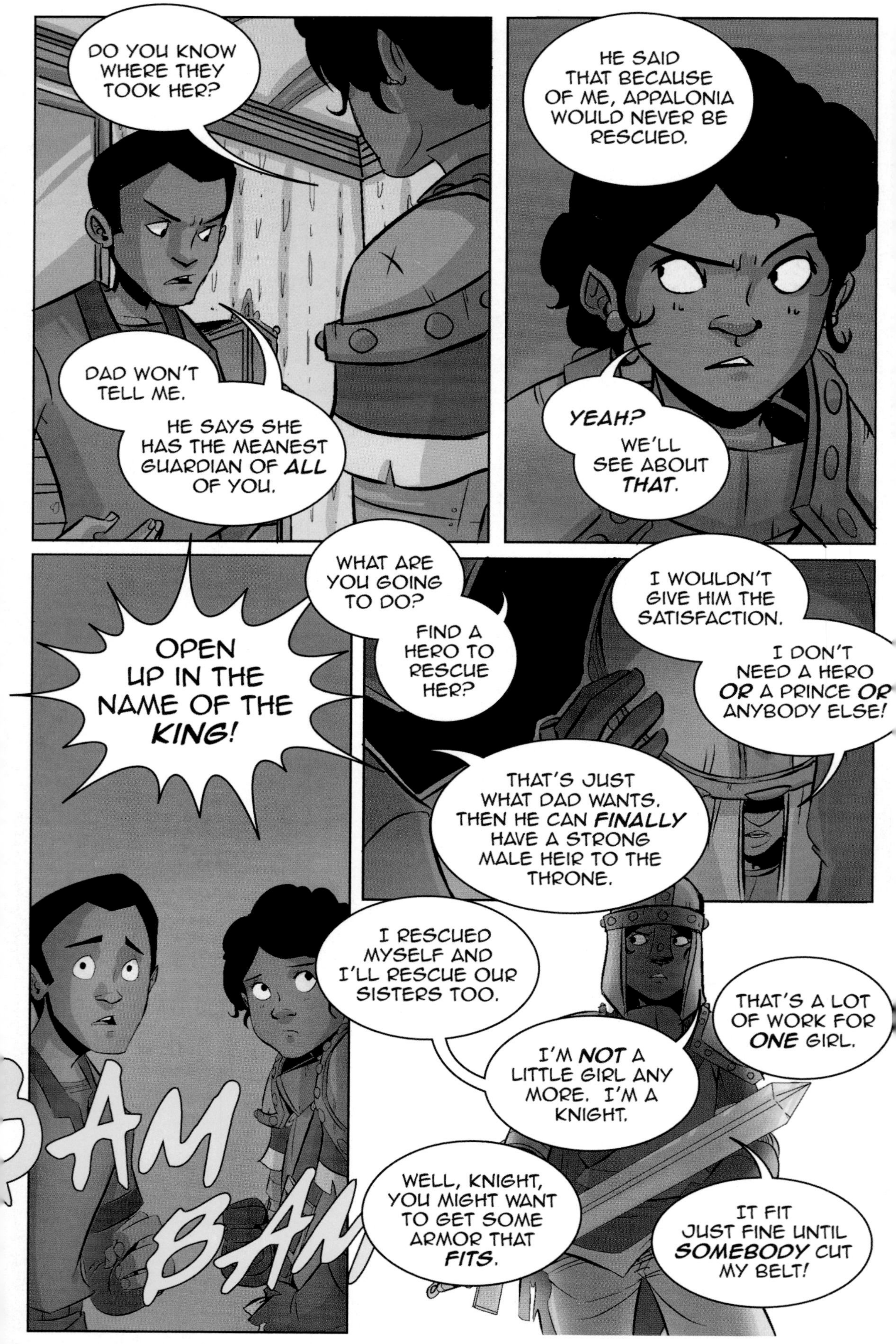
DO YOU KNOW WHERE THEY TOOK HER?
DAD WON'T TELL ME.
HE SAYS SHE HAS THE MEANEST GUARDIAN OF ALL OF YOU.
HE SAID THAT BECAUSE OF ME, APPALONIA WOULD NEVER BE RESCUED.
YEAH?
WE'LL SEE ABOUT THAT.
OPEN UP IN THE NAME OF THE KING!
WHAT ARE YOU GOING TO DO?
FIND A HERO TO RESCUE HER?
I WOULDN'T GIVE HIM THE SATISFACTION.
I DON'T NEED A HERO OR A PRINCE OR ANYBODY ELSE!
THAT'S JUST WHAT DAD WANTS. THEN HE CAN FINALLY HAVE A STRONG MALE HEIR TO THE THRONE.
I RESCUED MYSELF AND I'LL RESCUE OUR SISTERS TOO.
THAT'S A LOT OF WORK FOR ONE GIRL.
I'M NOT A LITTLE GIRL ANY MORE. I'M A KNIGHT.
WELL, KNIGHT, YOU MIGHT WANT TO GET SOME ARMOR THAT FITS.
IT FIT JUST FINE UNTIL SOMEBODY CUT MY BELT!
BAM BAM

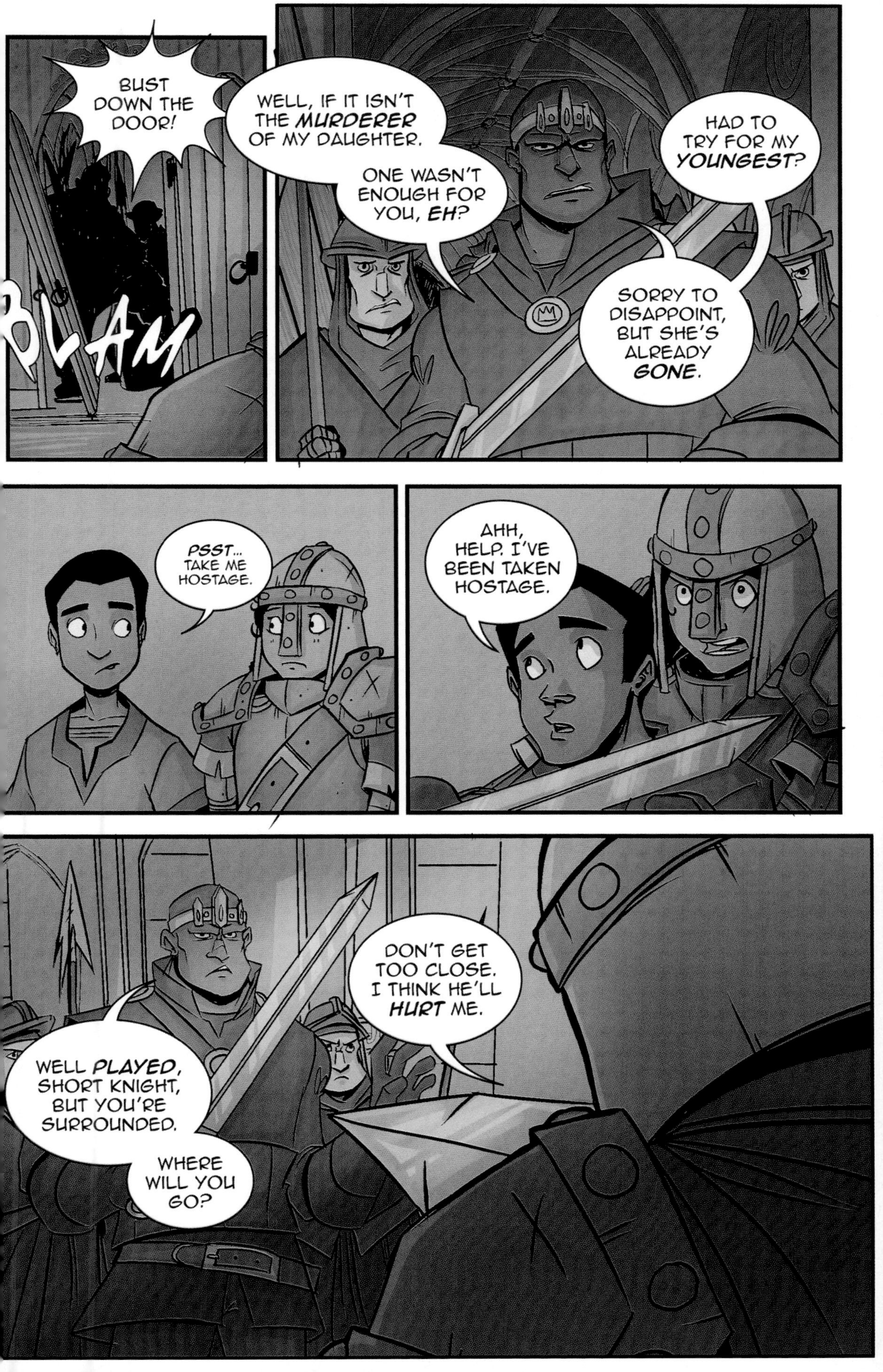
BUST DOWN THE DOOR!
BLAM
WELL, IF IT ISN'T THE *MURDERER* OF MY DAUGHTER.
ONE WASN'T ENOUGH FOR YOU, *EH*?
HAD TO TRY FOR MY *YOUNGEST*?
SORRY TO DISAPPOINT, BUT SHE'S ALREADY *GONE*.
PSST... TAKE ME HOSTAGE.
AHH, HELP. I'VE BEEN TAKEN HOSTAGE.
DON'T GET TOO CLOSE. I THINK HE'LL *HURT* ME.
WELL *PLAYED*, SHORT KNIGHT, BUT YOU'RE SURROUNDED.
WHERE WILL YOU GO?

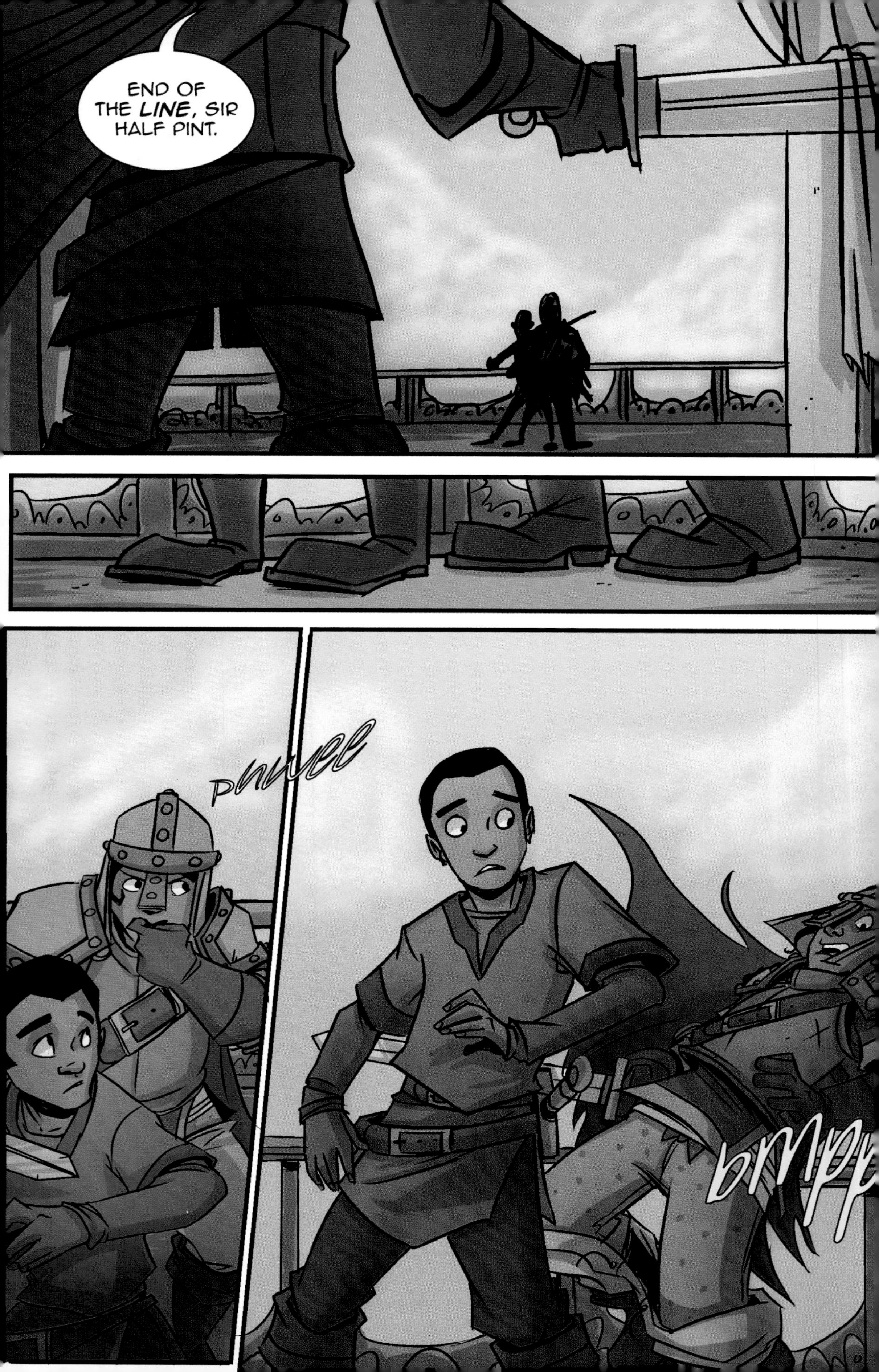
END OF THE LINE, SIR HALF PINT.
phweel
bmpp

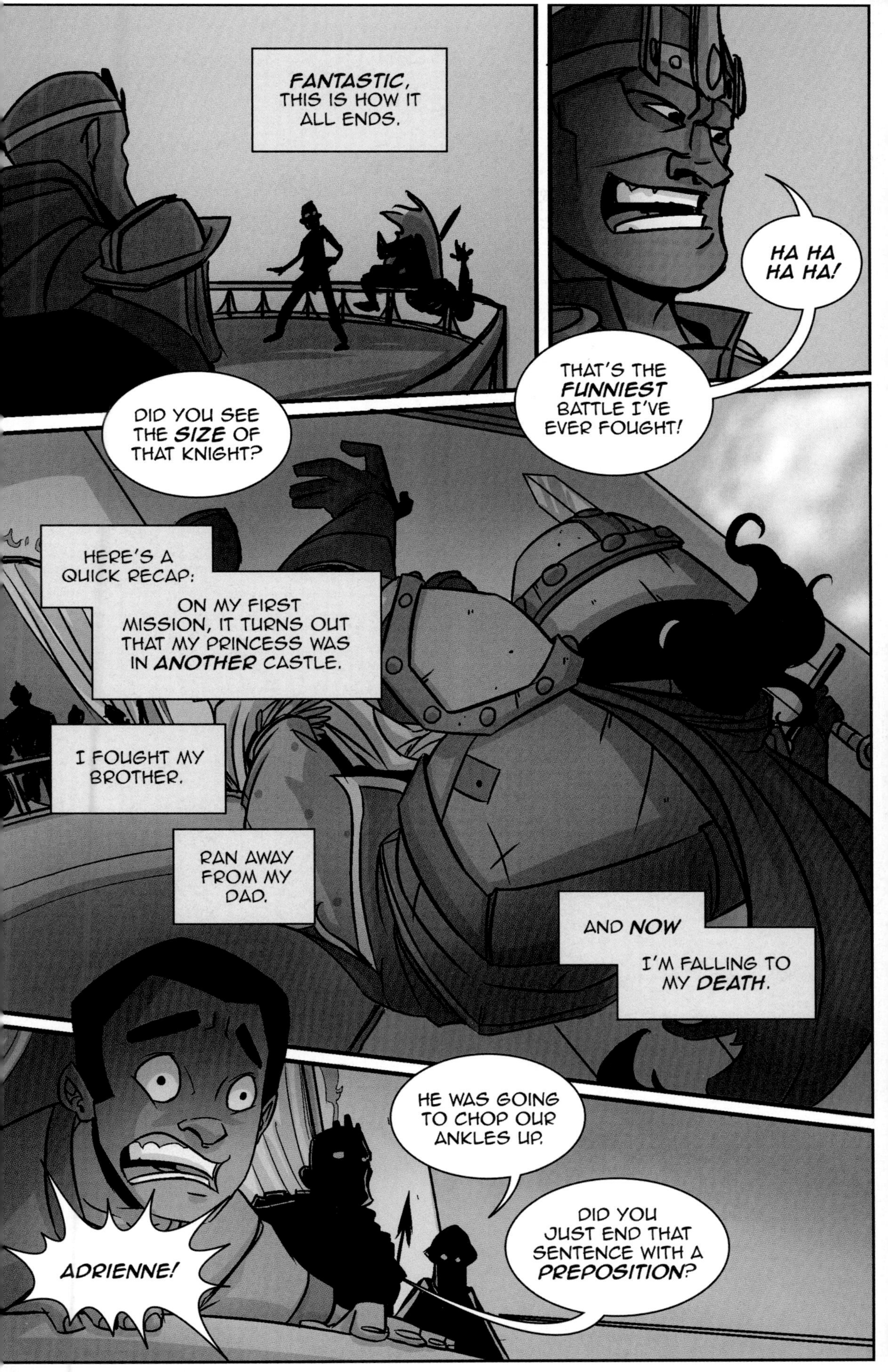

FANTASTIC, THIS IS HOW IT ALL ENDS.
HA HA HA HA!
THAT'S THE FUNNIEST BATTLE I'VE EVER FOUGHT!
DID YOU SEE THE SIZE OF THAT KNIGHT?
HERE'S A QUICK RECAP:
ON MY FIRST MISSION, IT TURNS OUT THAT MY PRINCESS WAS IN ANOTHER CASTLE.
I FOUGHT MY BROTHER.
RAN AWAY FROM MY DAD.
AND NOW
I'M FALLING TO MY DEATH.
HE WAS GOING TO CHOP OUR ANKLES UP.
DID YOU JUST END THAT SENTENCE WITH A PREPOSITION?
ADRIENNE!

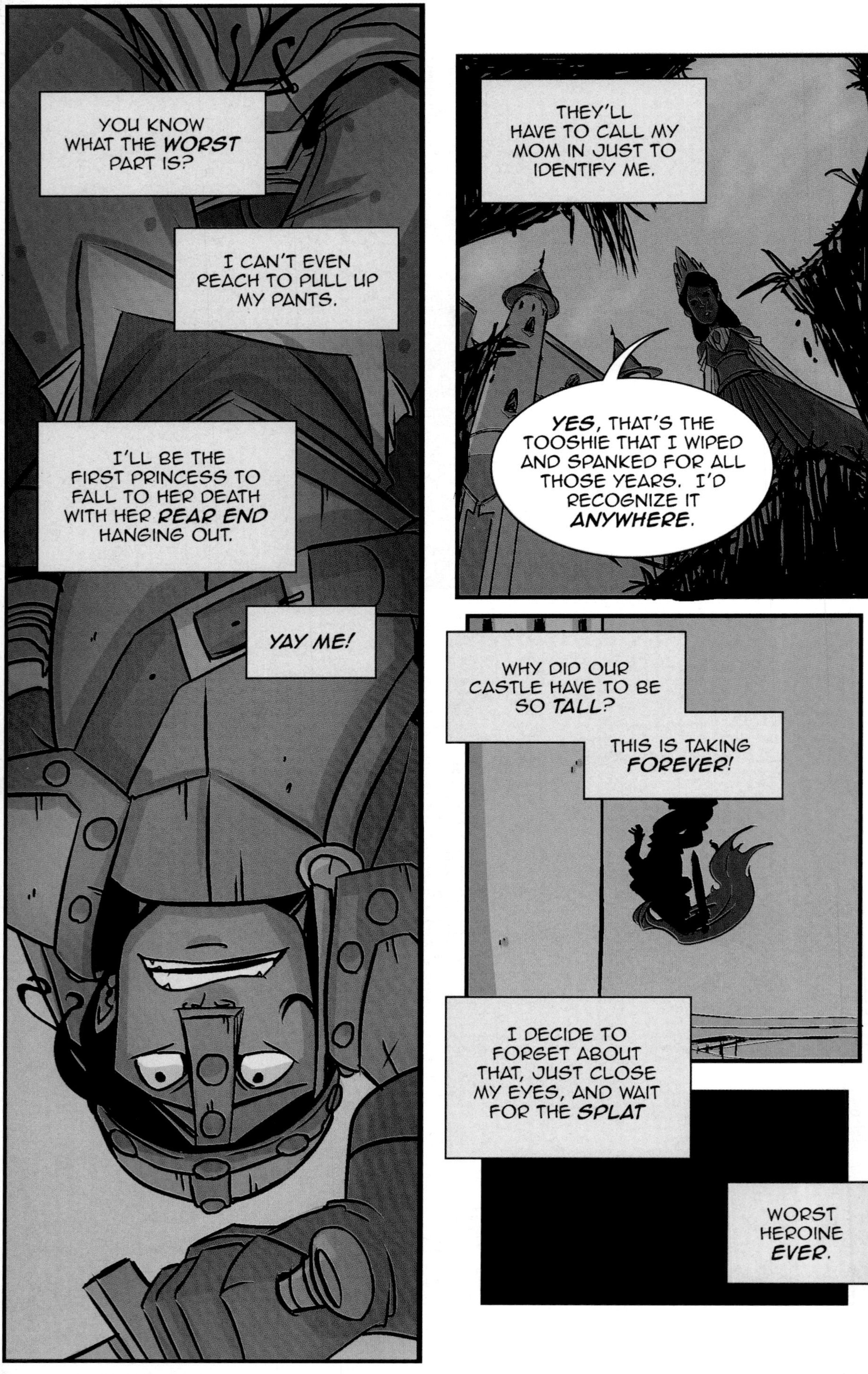
YOU KNOW WHAT THE WORST PART IS?
I CAN'T EVEN REACH TO PULL UP MY PANTS.
I'LL BE THE FIRST PRINCESS TO FALL TO HER DEATH WITH HER REAR END HANGING OUT.
YAY ME!
THEY'LL HAVE TO CALL MY MOM IN JUST TO IDENTIFY ME.
YES, THAT'S THE TOOSHIE THAT I WIPED AND SPANKED FOR ALL THOSE YEARS. I'D RECOGNIZE IT ANYWHERE.
WHY DID OUR CASTLE HAVE TO BE SO TALL?
THIS IS TAKING FOREVER!
I DECIDE TO FORGET ABOUT THAT, JUST CLOSE MY EYES, AND WAIT FOR THE SPLAT
WORST HEROINE EVER.

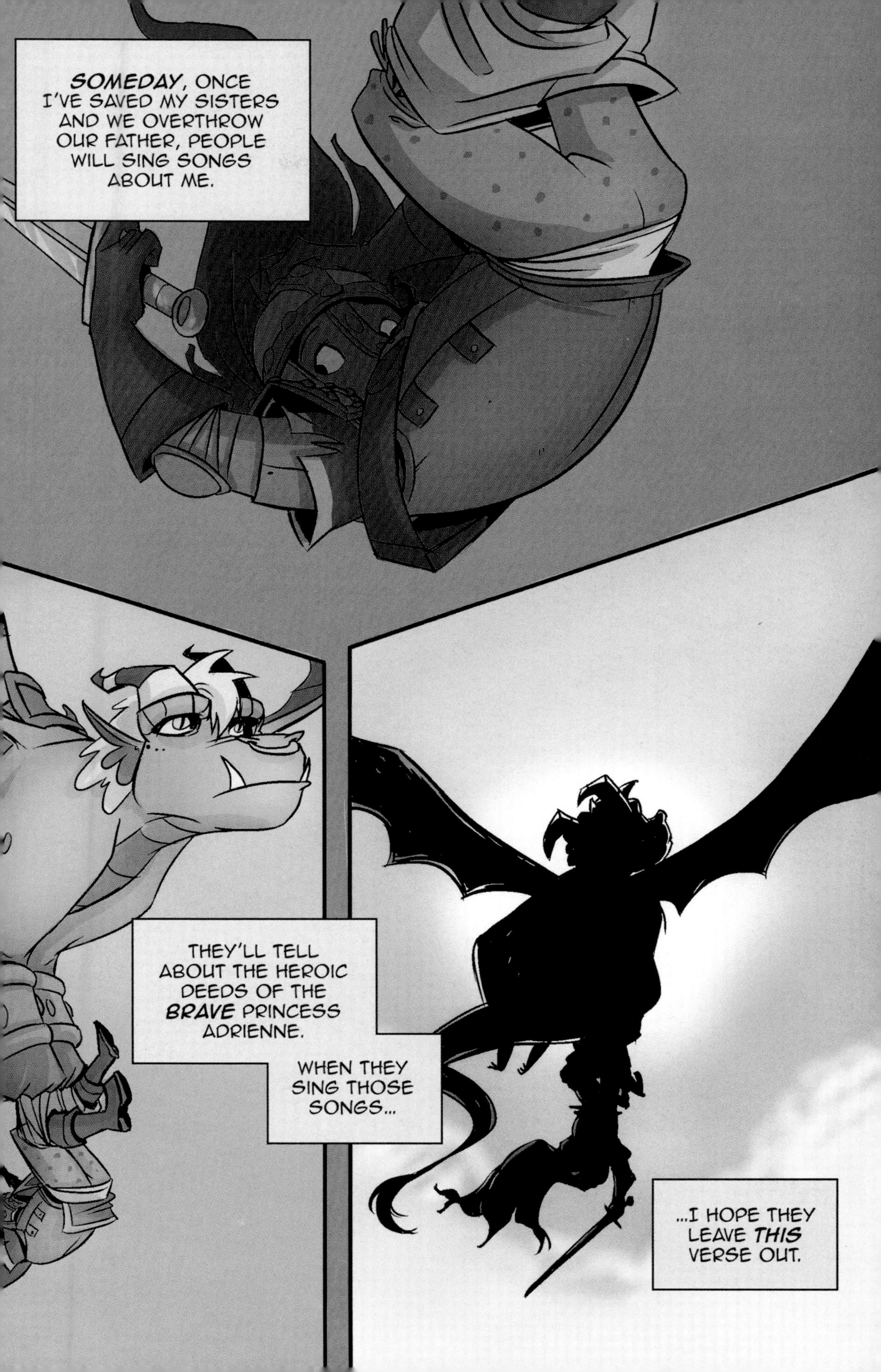
SOMEDAY, ONCE I'VE SAVED MY SISTERS AND WE OVERTHROW OUR FATHER, PEOPLE WILL SING SONGS ABOUT ME.
THEY'LL TELL ABOUT THE HEROIC DEEDS OF THE BRAVE PRINCESS ADRIENNE.
WHEN THEY SING THOSE SONGS...
...I HOPE THEY LEAVE THIS VERSE OUT.

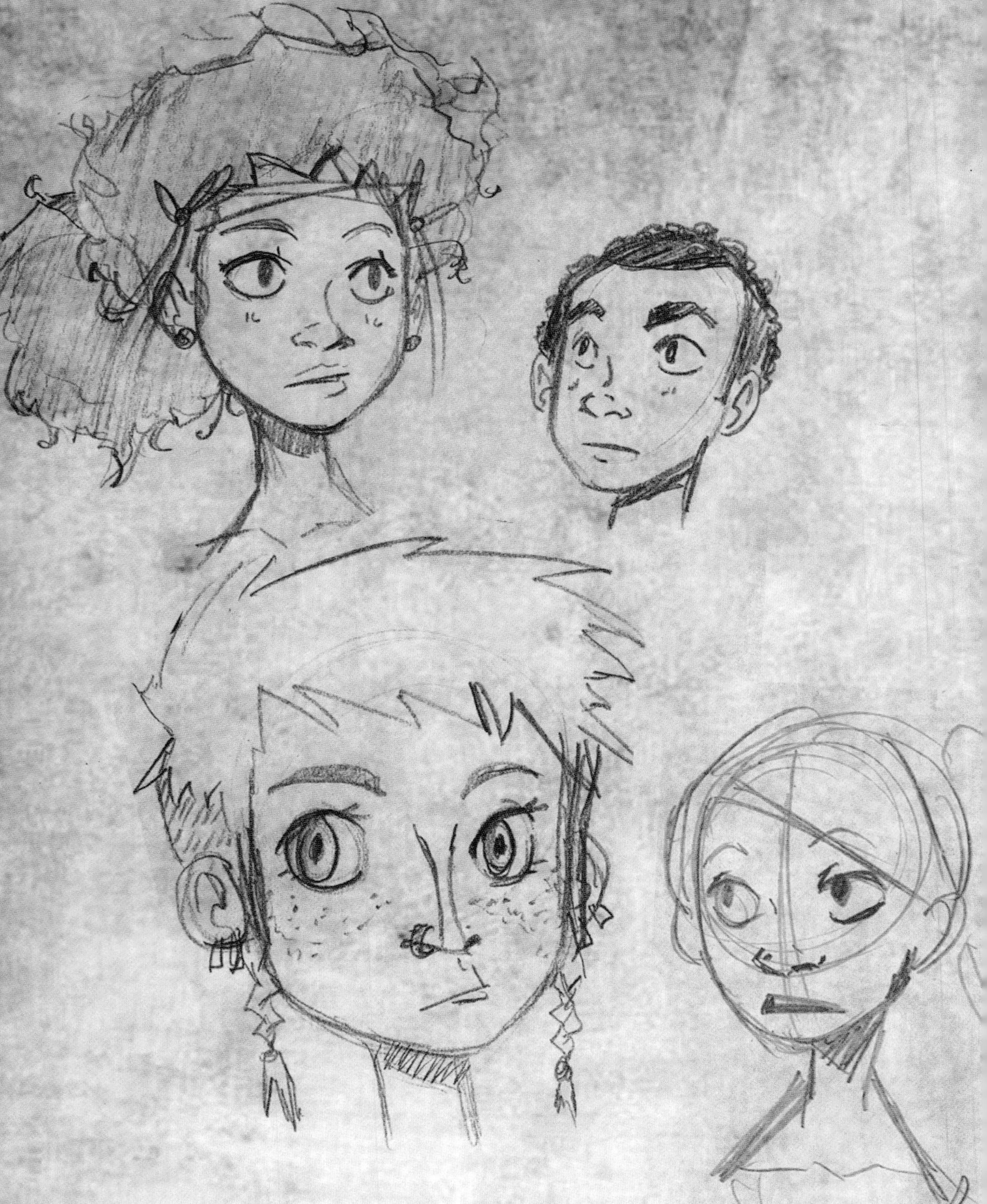

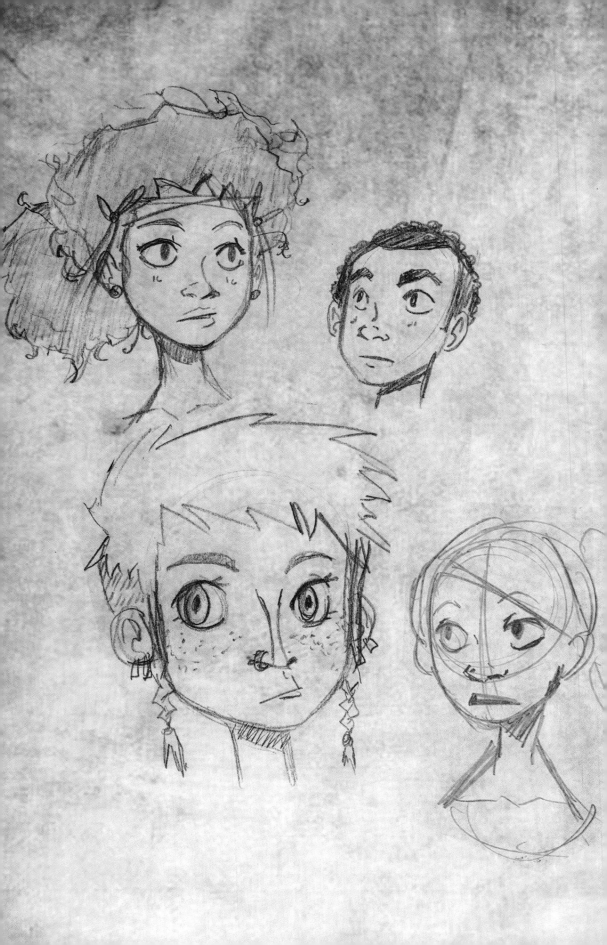

3: On Sexism in the Armor Industry

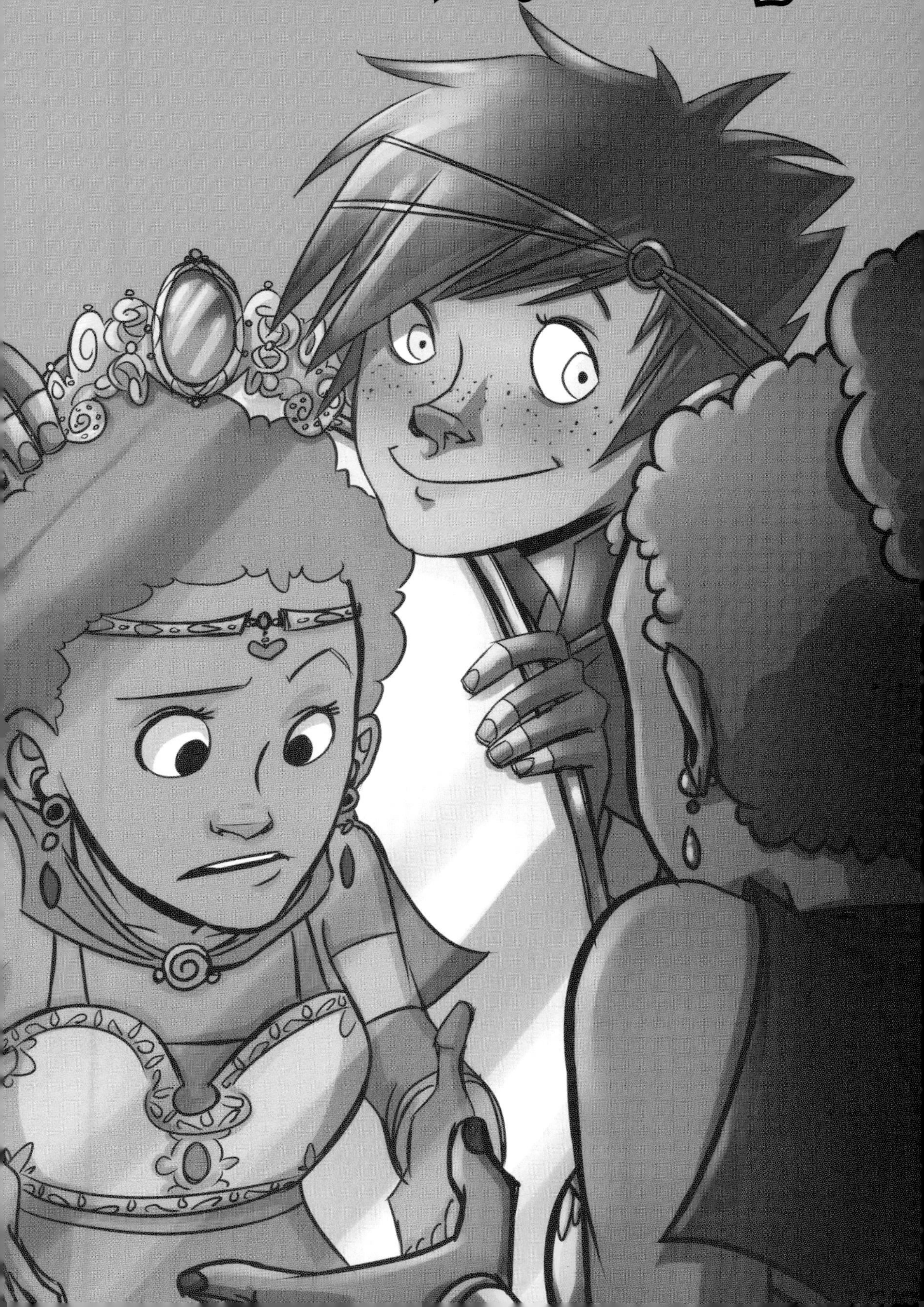

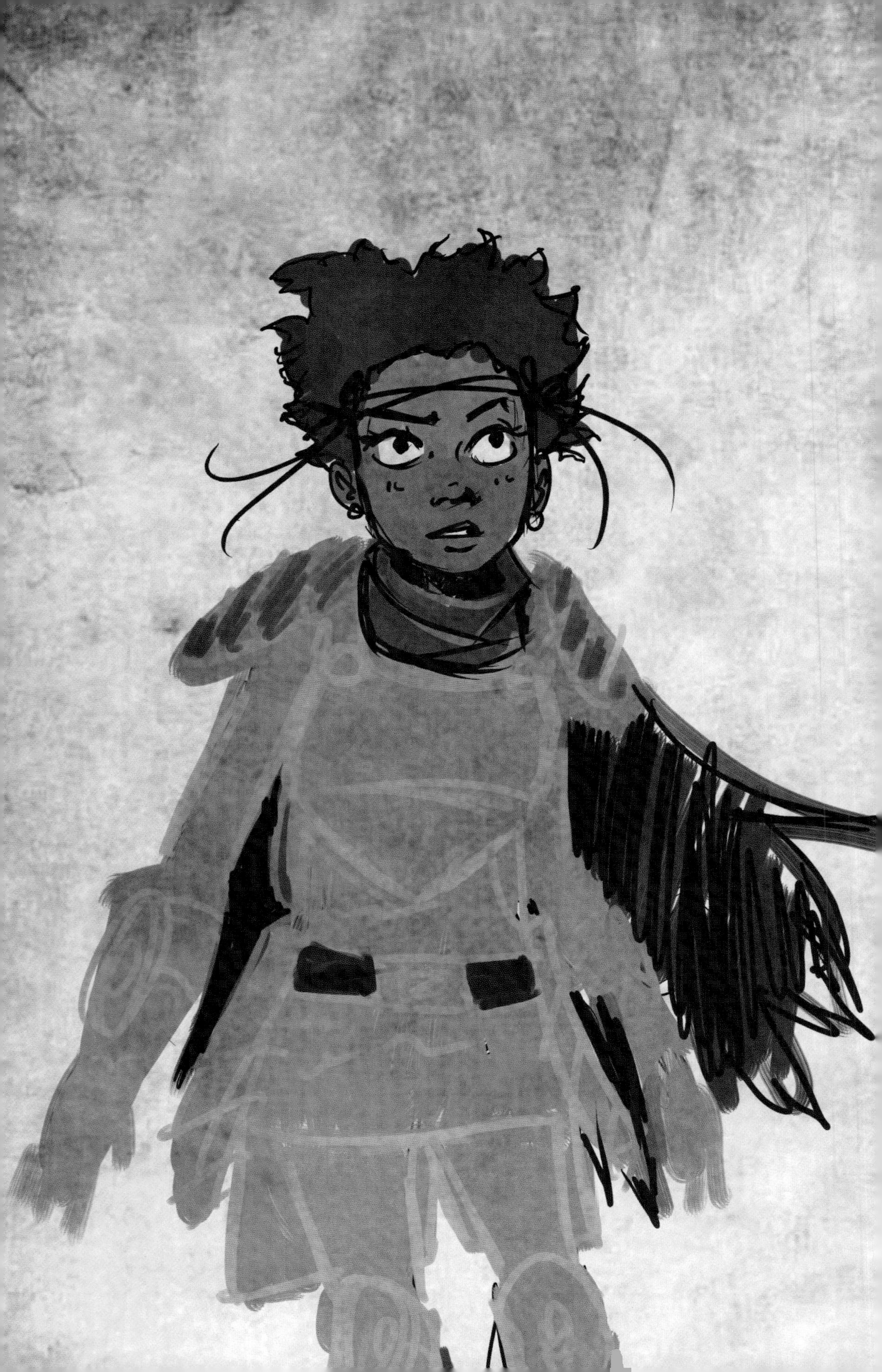

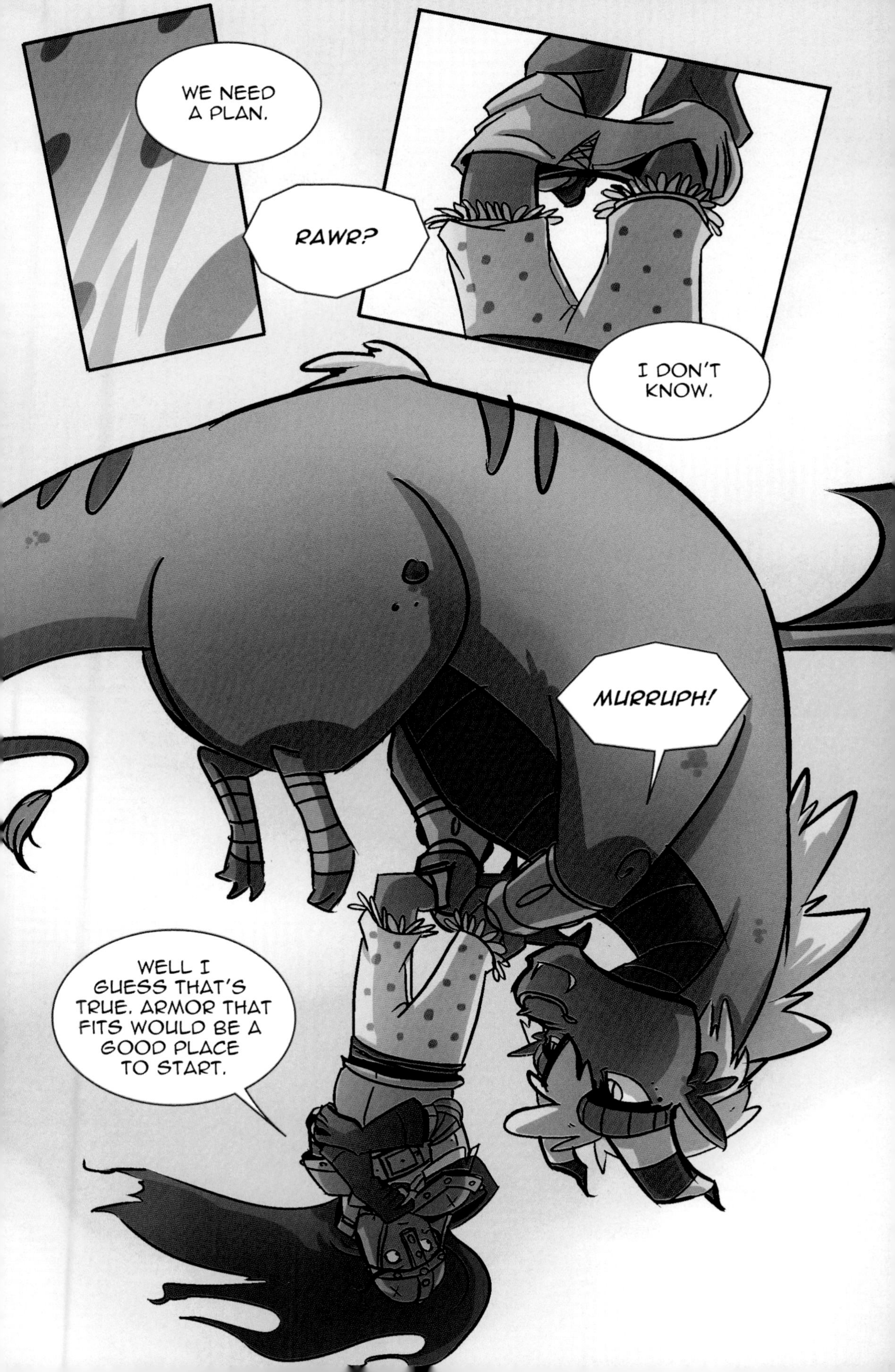
WE NEED A PLAN.
RAWR?
I DON'T KNOW.
MURRUPH!
WELL I GUESS THAT'S TRUE. ARMOR THAT FITS WOULD BE A GOOD PLACE TO START.

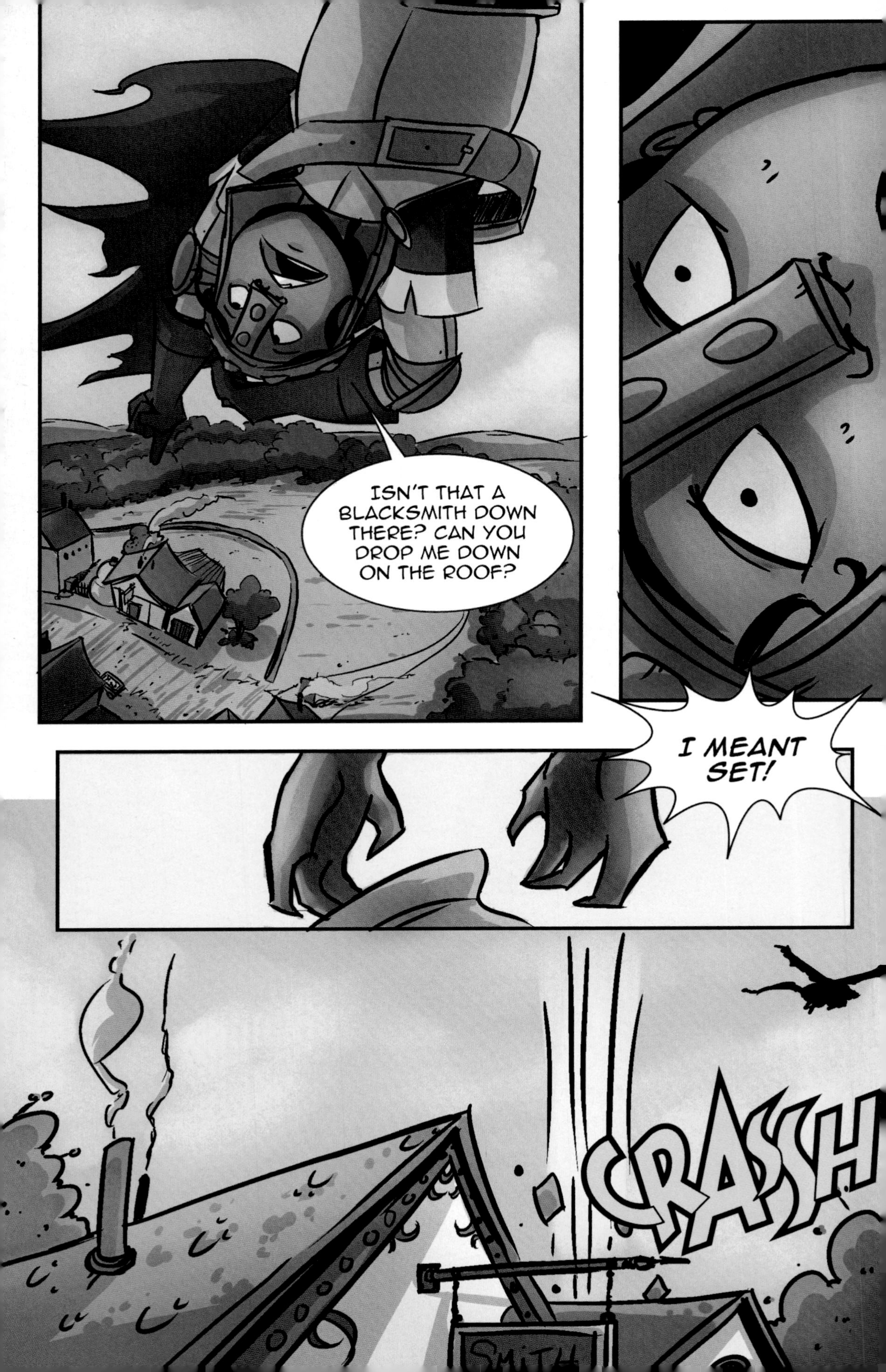
ISN'T THAT A BLACKSMITH DOWN THERE? CAN YOU DROP ME DOWN ON THE ROOF?
I MEANT SET!
CRASH
SMITH

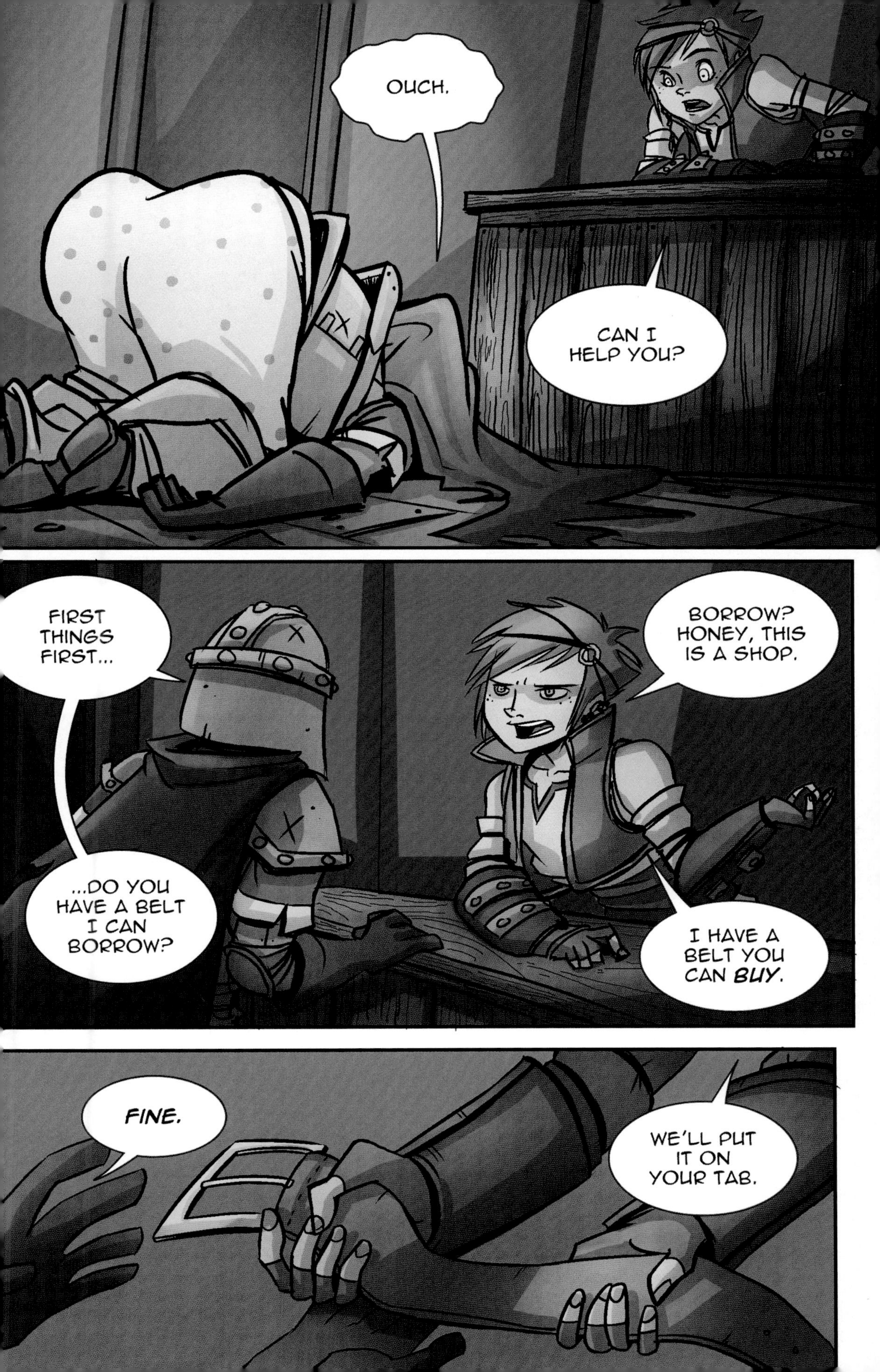
OUCH.
CAN I HELP YOU?
FIRST THINGS FIRST...
...DO YOU HAVE A BELT I CAN BORROW?
BORROW? HONEY, THIS IS A SHOP.
I HAVE A BELT YOU CAN *BUY*.
FINE.
WE'LL PUT IT ON YOUR TAB.

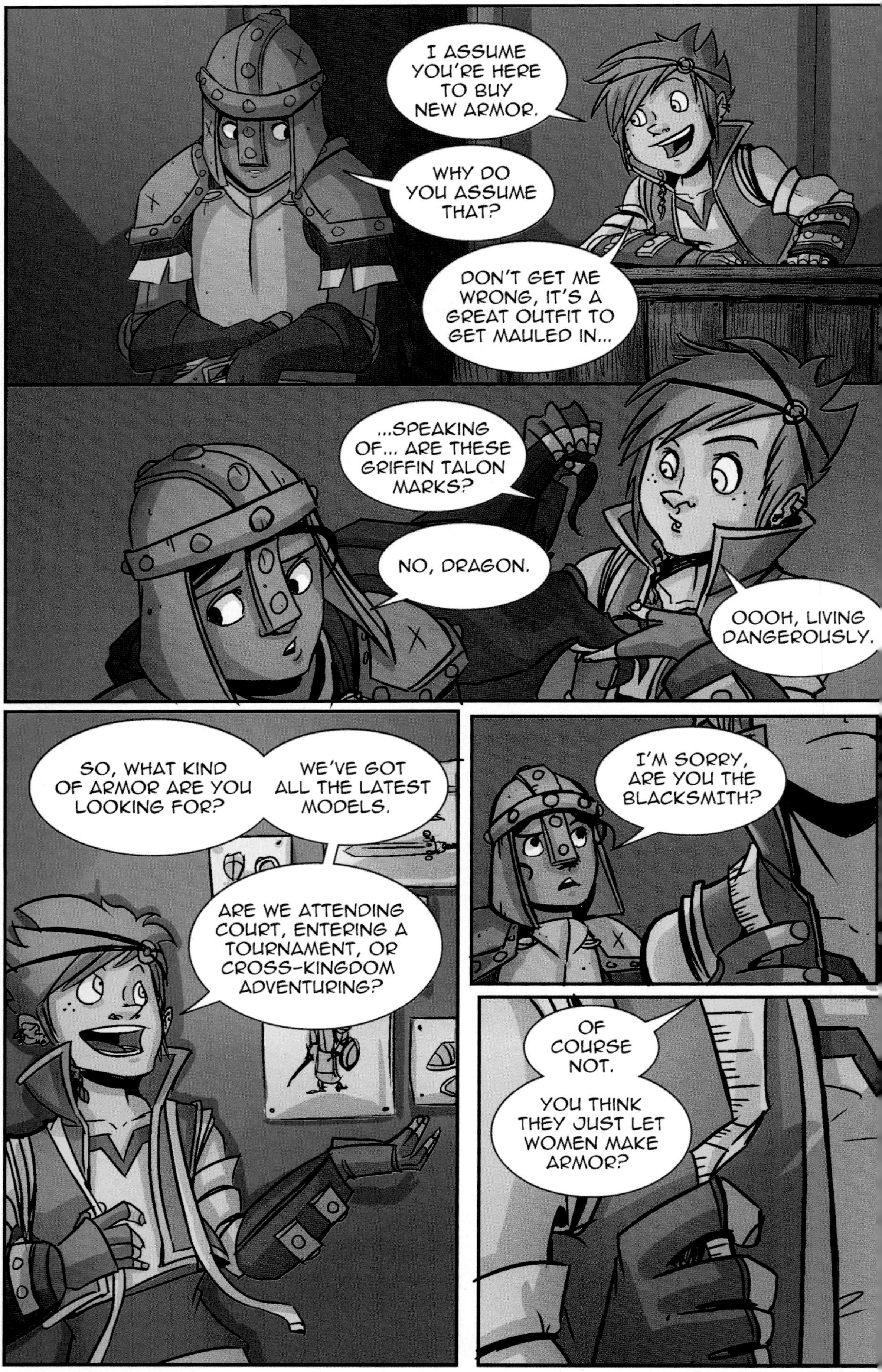
I ASSUME YOU'RE HERE TO BUY NEW ARMOR.
WHY DO YOU ASSUME THAT?
DON'T GET ME WRONG, IT'S A GREAT OUTFIT TO GET MAULED IN...
...SPEAKING OF... ARE THESE GRIFFIN TALON MARKS?
NO, DRAGON.
OOOH, LIVING DANGEROUSLY.
SO, WHAT KIND OF ARMOR ARE YOU LOOKING FOR?
WE'VE GOT ALL THE LATEST MODELS.
ARE WE ATTENDING COURT, ENTERING A TOURNAMENT, OR CROSS-KINGDOM ADVENTURING?
I'M SORRY, ARE YOU THE BLACKSMITH?
OF COURSE NOT.
YOU THINK THEY JUST LET WOMEN MAKE ARMOR?

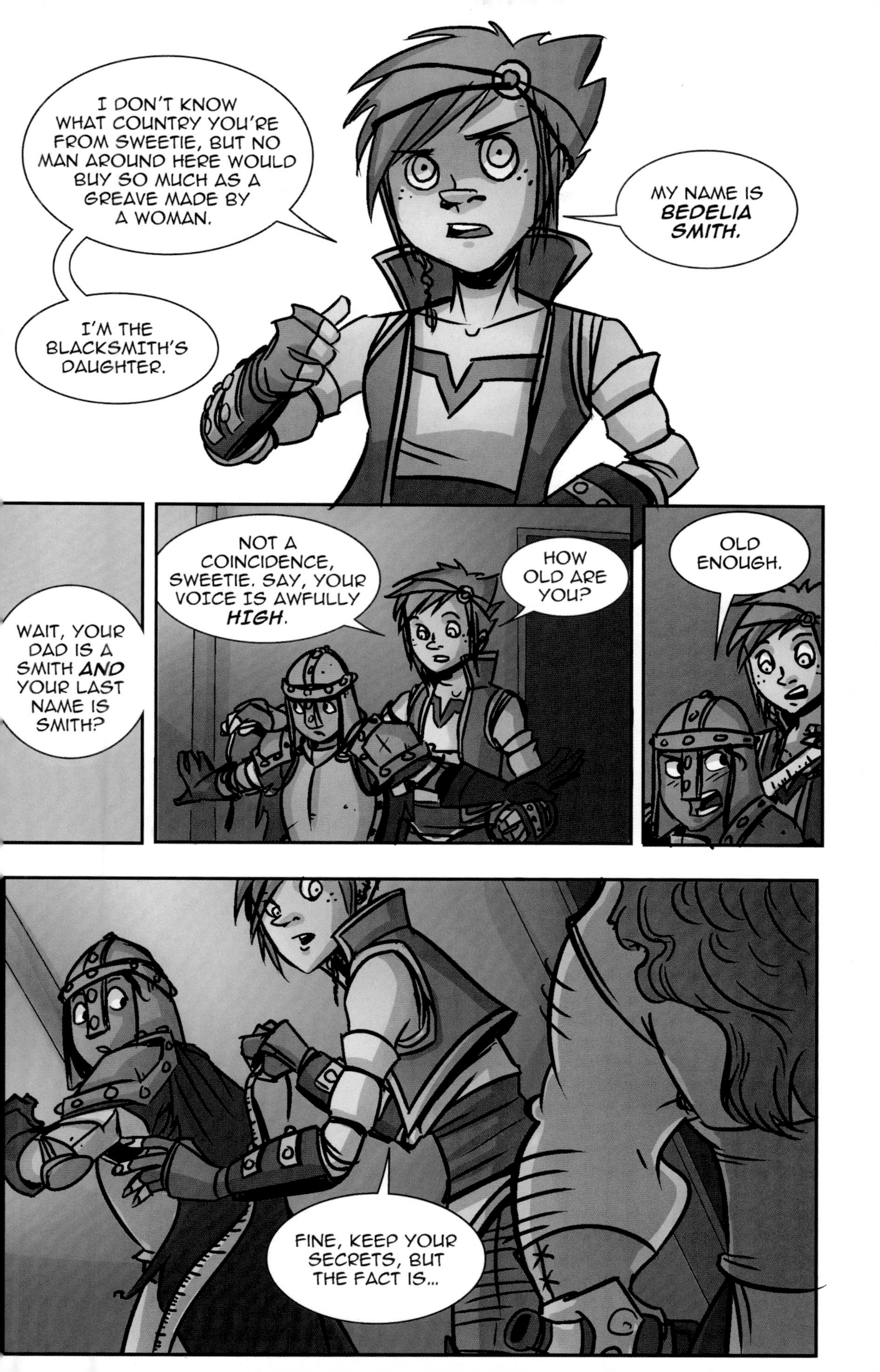

I DON'T KNOW WHAT COUNTRY YOU'RE FROM SWEETIE, BUT NO MAN AROUND HERE WOULD BUY SO MUCH AS A GREAVE MADE BY A WOMAN.
I'M THE BLACKSMITH'S DAUGHTER.
MY NAME IS *BEDELIA SMITH.*
WAIT, YOUR DAD IS A SMITH *AND* YOUR LAST NAME IS SMITH?
NOT A COINCIDENCE, SWEETIE. SAY, YOUR VOICE IS AWFULLY *HIGH*.
HOW OLD ARE YOU?
OLD ENOUGH.
FINE, KEEP YOUR SECRETS, BUT THE FACT IS...

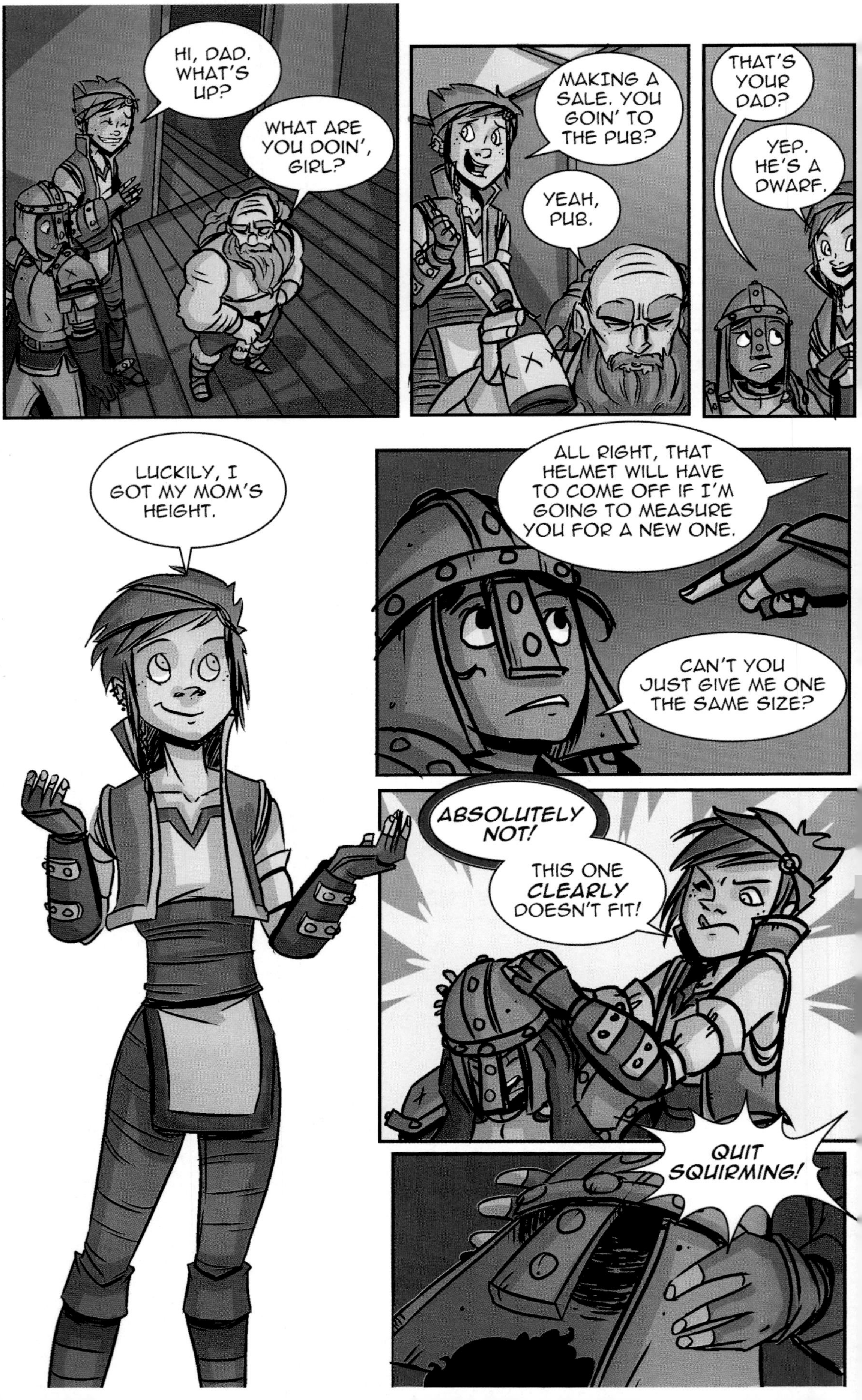
HI, DAD. WHAT'S UP?
WHAT ARE YOU DOIN', GIRL?
MAKING A SALE. YOU GOIN' TO THE PUB?
YEAH, PUB.
THAT'S YOUR DAD?
YEP. HE'S A DWARF.
LUCKILY, I GOT MY MOM'S HEIGHT.
ALL RIGHT, THAT HELMET WILL HAVE TO COME OFF IF I'M GOING TO MEASURE YOU FOR A NEW ONE.
CAN'T YOU JUST GIVE ME ONE THE SAME SIZE?
ABSOLUTELY NOT!
THIS ONE CLEARLY DOESN'T FIT!
QUIT SQUIRMING!

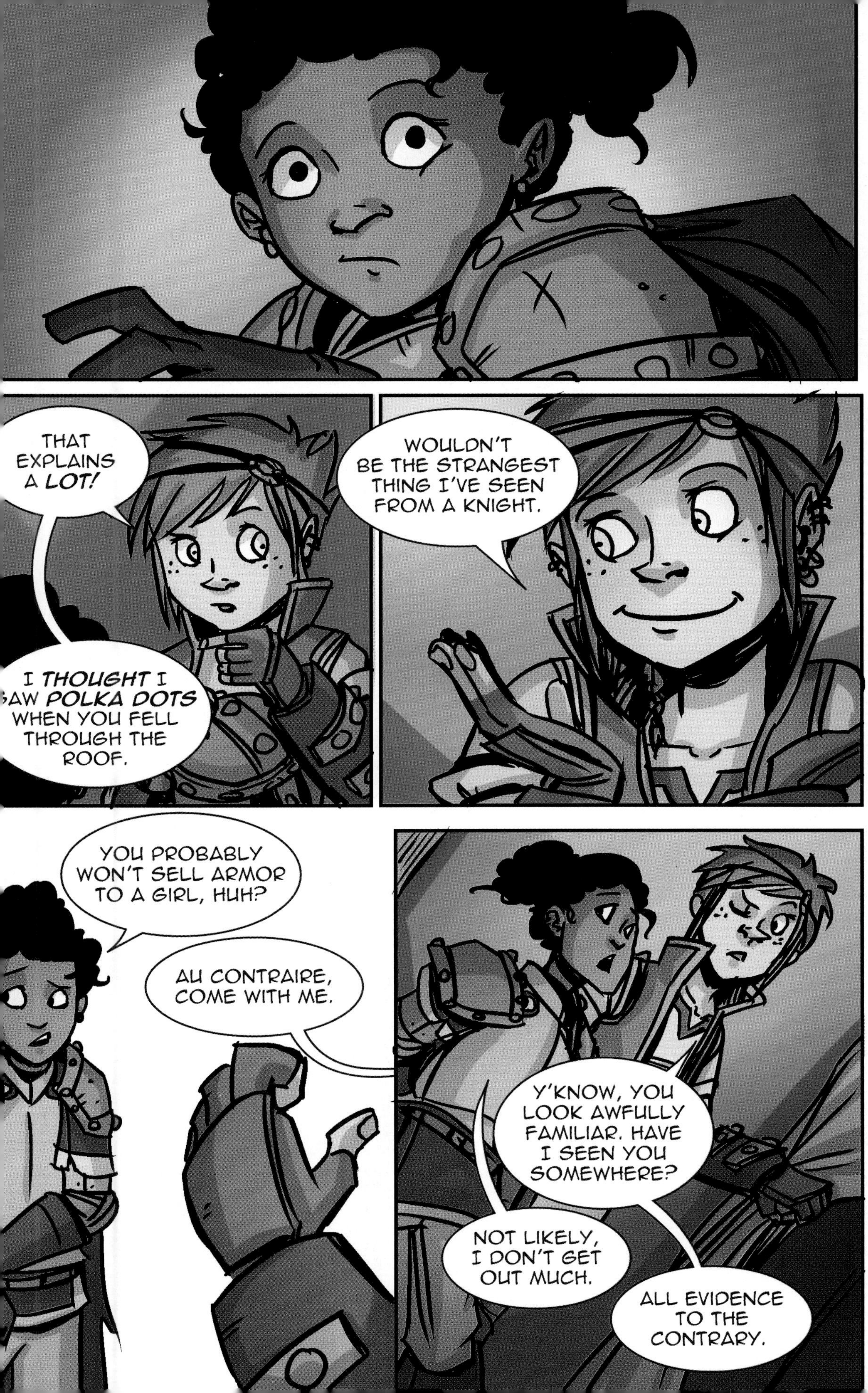
THAT EXPLAINS A *LOT!*
I *THOUGHT* I SAW *POLKA DOTS* WHEN YOU FELL THROUGH THE ROOF.
WOULDN'T BE THE STRANGEST THING I'VE SEEN FROM A KNIGHT.
YOU PROBABLY WON'T SELL ARMOR TO A GIRL, HUH?
AU CONTRAIRE, COME WITH ME.
Y'KNOW, YOU LOOK AWFULLY FAMILIAR. HAVE I SEEN YOU SOMEWHERE?
NOT LIKELY, I DON'T GET OUT MUCH.
ALL EVIDENCE TO THE CONTRARY.

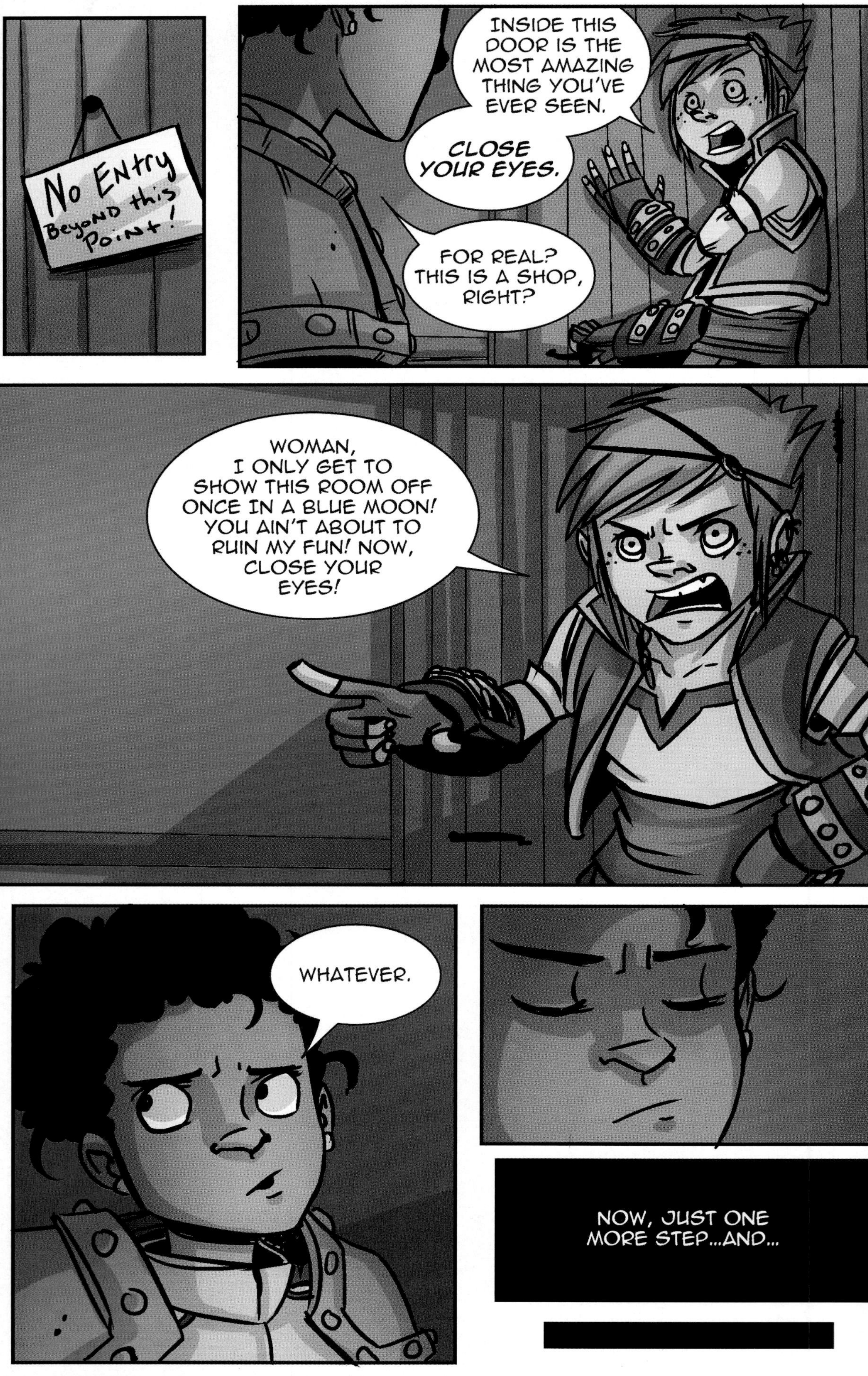
No Entry Beyond this Point!
INSIDE THIS DOOR IS THE MOST AMAZING THING YOU'VE EVER SEEN.
CLOSE YOUR EYES.
FOR REAL? THIS IS A SHOP, RIGHT?
WOMAN, I ONLY GET TO SHOW THIS ROOM OFF ONCE IN A BLUE MOON! YOU AIN'T ABOUT TO RUIN MY FUN! NOW, CLOSE YOUR EYES!
WHATEVER.
NOW, JUST ONE MORE STEP...AND...

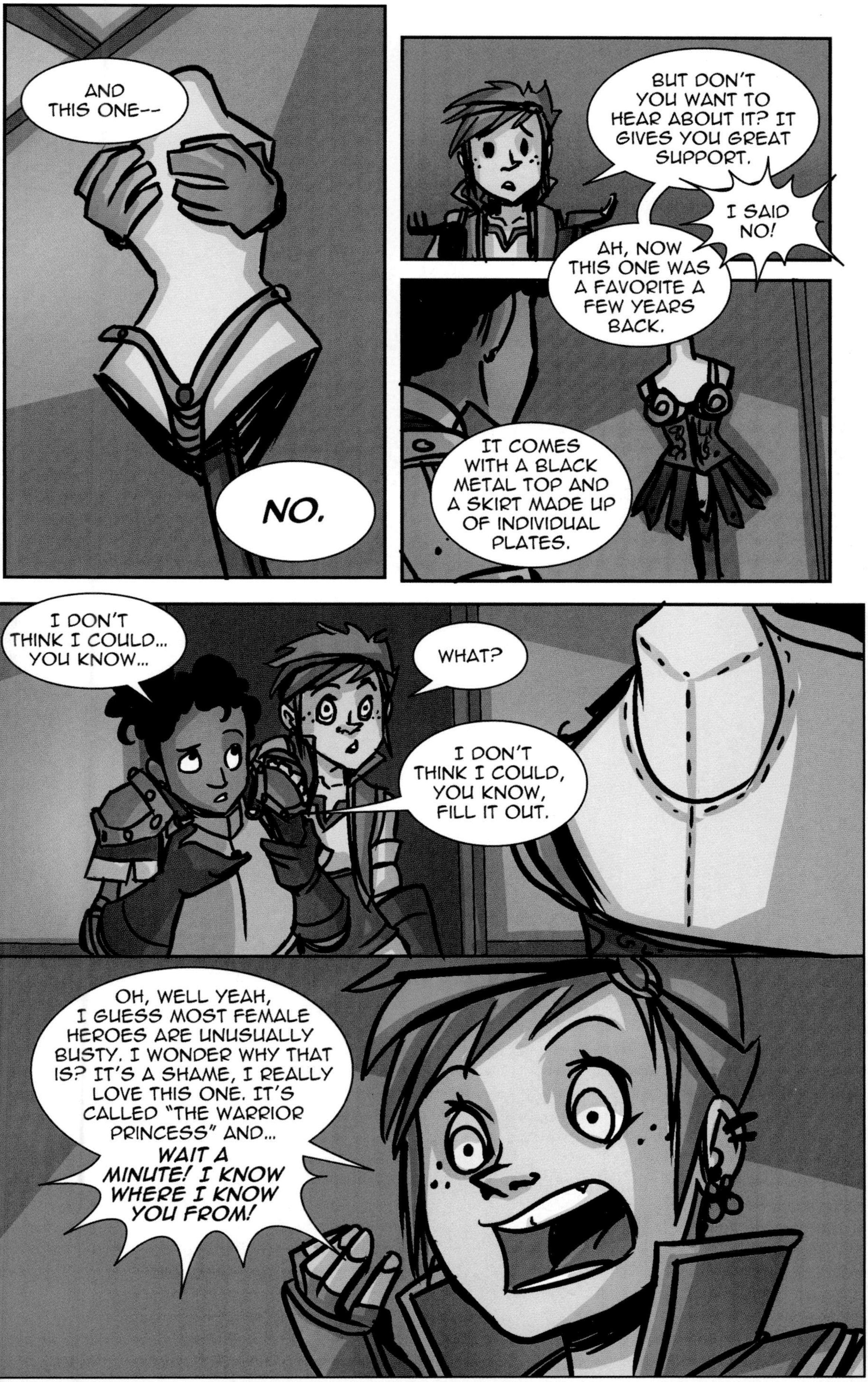
AND THIS ONE--
NO.
BUT DON'T YOU WANT TO HEAR ABOUT IT? IT GIVES YOU GREAT SUPPORT.
I SAID NO!
AH, NOW THIS ONE WAS A FAVORITE A FEW YEARS BACK.
IT COMES WITH A BLACK METAL TOP AND A SKIRT MADE UP OF INDIVIDUAL PLATES.
I DON'T THINK I COULD... YOU KNOW...
WHAT?
I DON'T THINK I COULD, YOU KNOW, FILL IT OUT.
OH, WELL YEAH, I GUESS MOST FEMALE HEROES ARE UNUSUALLY BUSTY. I WONDER WHY THAT IS? IT'S A SHAME, I REALLY LOVE THIS ONE. IT'S CALLED "THE WARRIOR PRINCESS" AND... WAIT A MINUTE! I KNOW WHERE I KNOW YOU FROM!

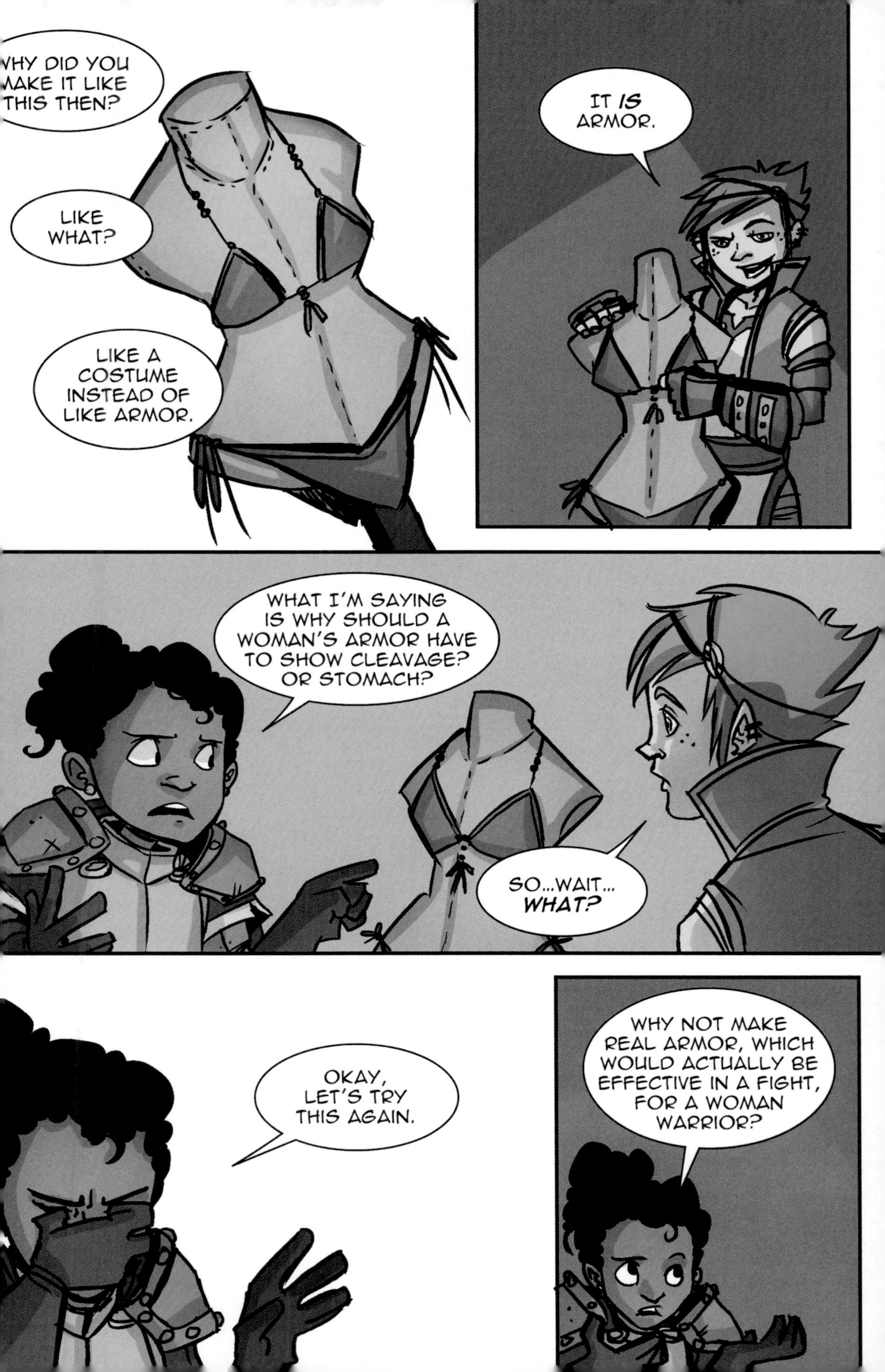
WHY DID YOU MAKE IT LIKE THIS THEN?
LIKE WHAT?
LIKE A COSTUME INSTEAD OF LIKE ARMOR.
IT *IS* ARMOR.
WHAT I'M SAYING IS WHY SHOULD A WOMAN'S ARMOR HAVE TO SHOW CLEAVAGE? OR STOMACH?
SO...WAIT... ***WHAT?***
OKAY, LET'S TRY THIS AGAIN.
WHY NOT MAKE REAL ARMOR, WHICH WOULD ACTUALLY BE EFFECTIVE IN A FIGHT, FOR A WOMAN WARRIOR?

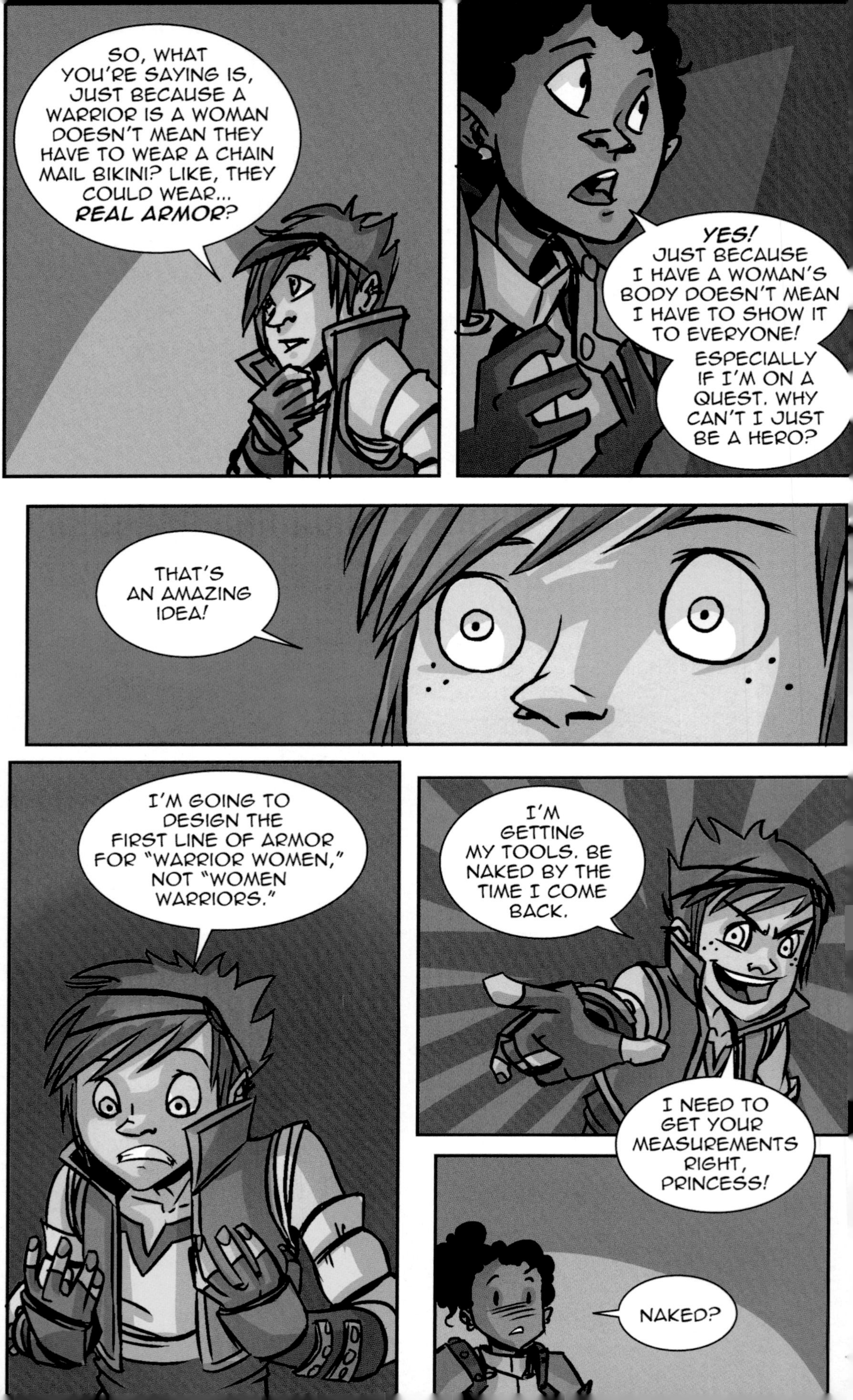

SO, WHAT YOU'RE SAYING IS, JUST BECAUSE A WARRIOR IS A WOMAN DOESN'T MEAN THEY HAVE TO WEAR A CHAIN MAIL BIKINI? LIKE, THEY COULD WEAR... *REAL ARMOR*?
YES! JUST BECAUSE I HAVE A WOMAN'S BODY DOESN'T MEAN I HAVE TO SHOW IT TO EVERYONE!
ESPECIALLY IF I'M ON A QUEST. WHY CAN'T I JUST BE A HERO?
THAT'S AN AMAZING IDEA!
I'M GOING TO DESIGN THE FIRST LINE OF ARMOR FOR "WARRIOR WOMEN," NOT "WOMEN WARRIORS."
I'M GETTING MY TOOLS. BE NAKED BY THE TIME I COME BACK.
I NEED TO GET YOUR MEASUREMENTS RIGHT, PRINCESS!
NAKED?

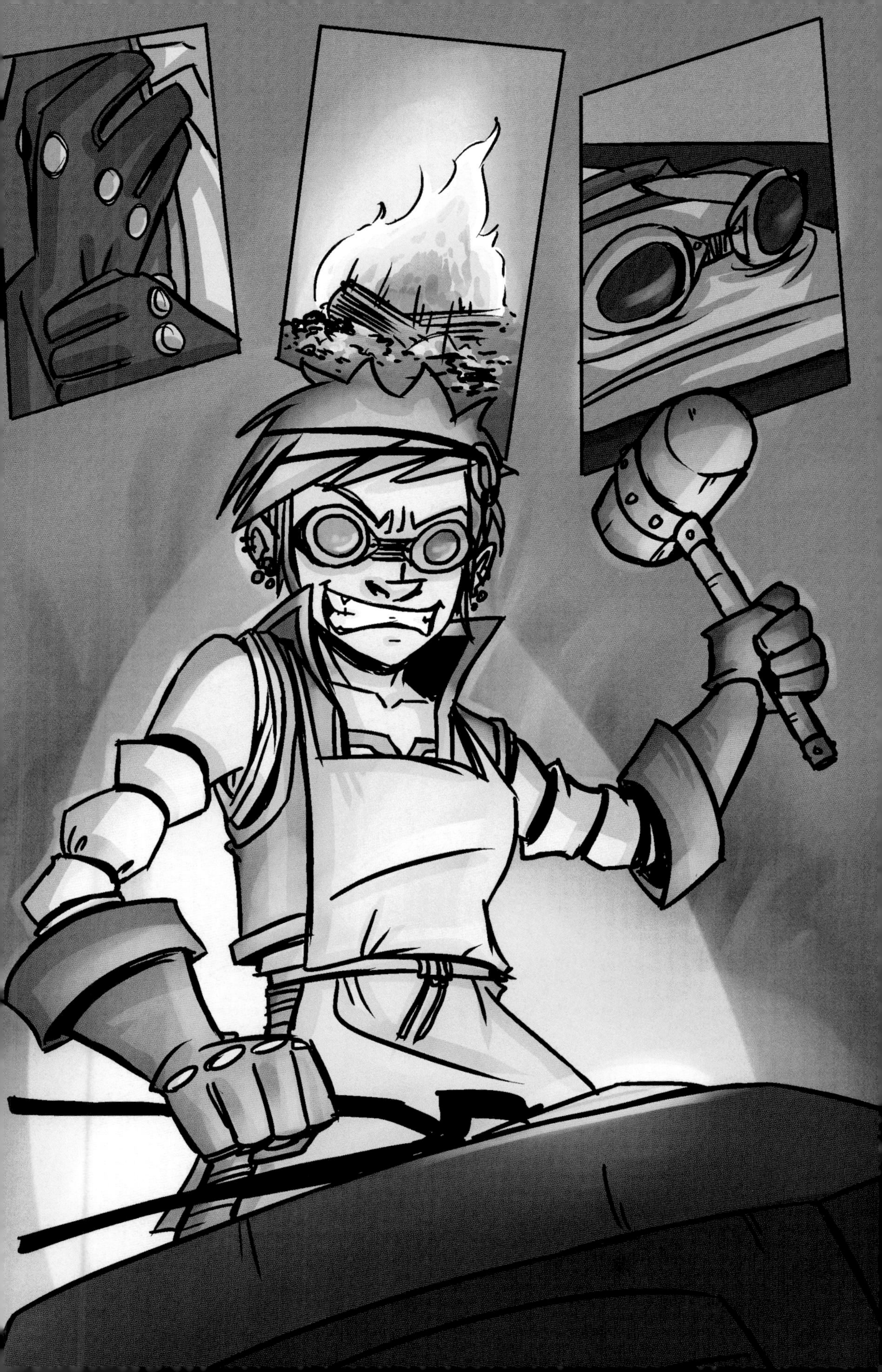

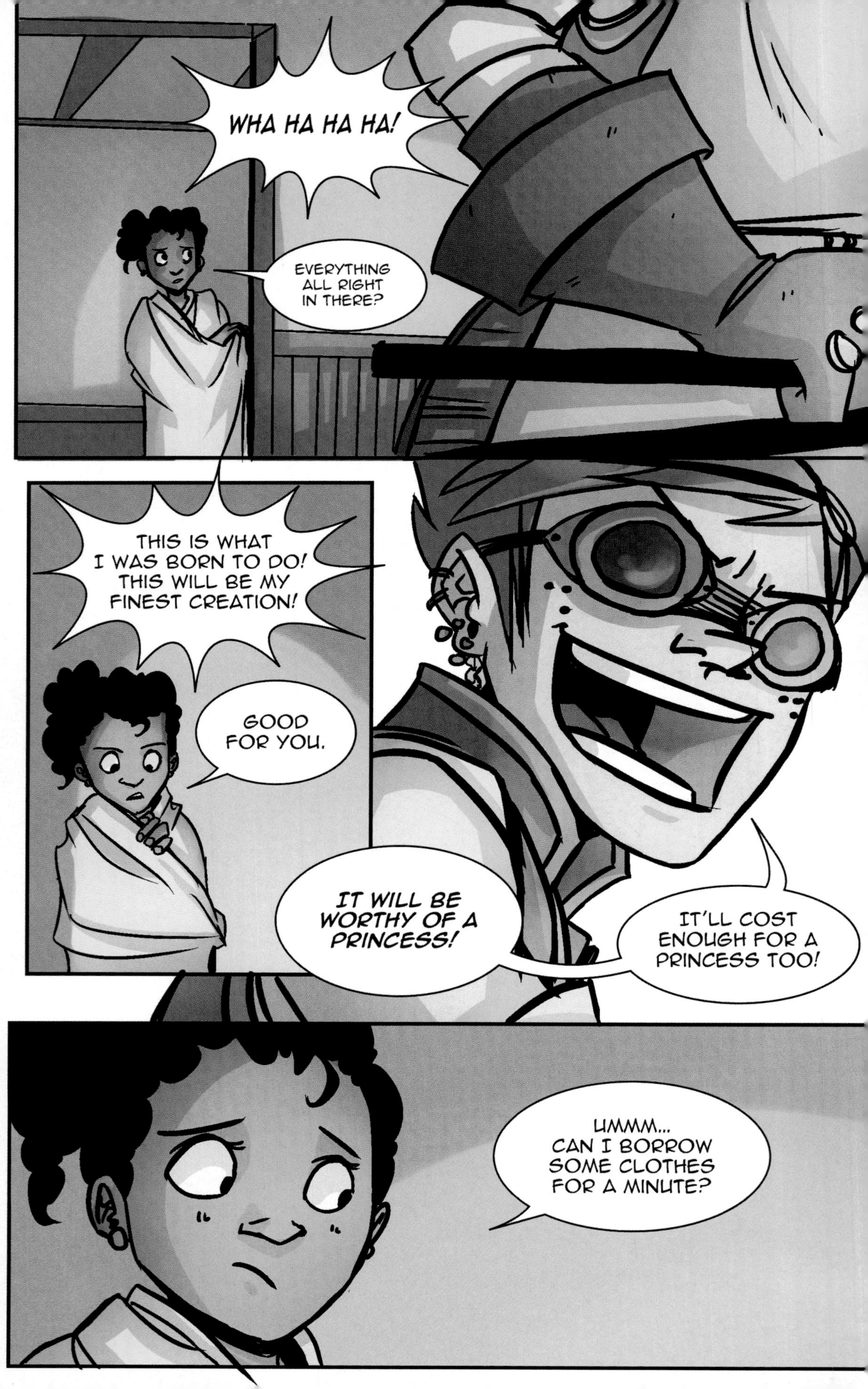
WHA HA HA HA!
EVERYTHING ALL RIGHT IN THERE?
THIS IS WHAT I WAS BORN TO DO! THIS WILL BE MY FINEST CREATION!
GOOD FOR YOU.
IT WILL BE WORTHY OF A PRINCESS!
IT'LL COST ENOUGH FOR A PRINCESS TOO!
UMMM... CAN I BORROW SOME CLOTHES FOR A MINUTE?

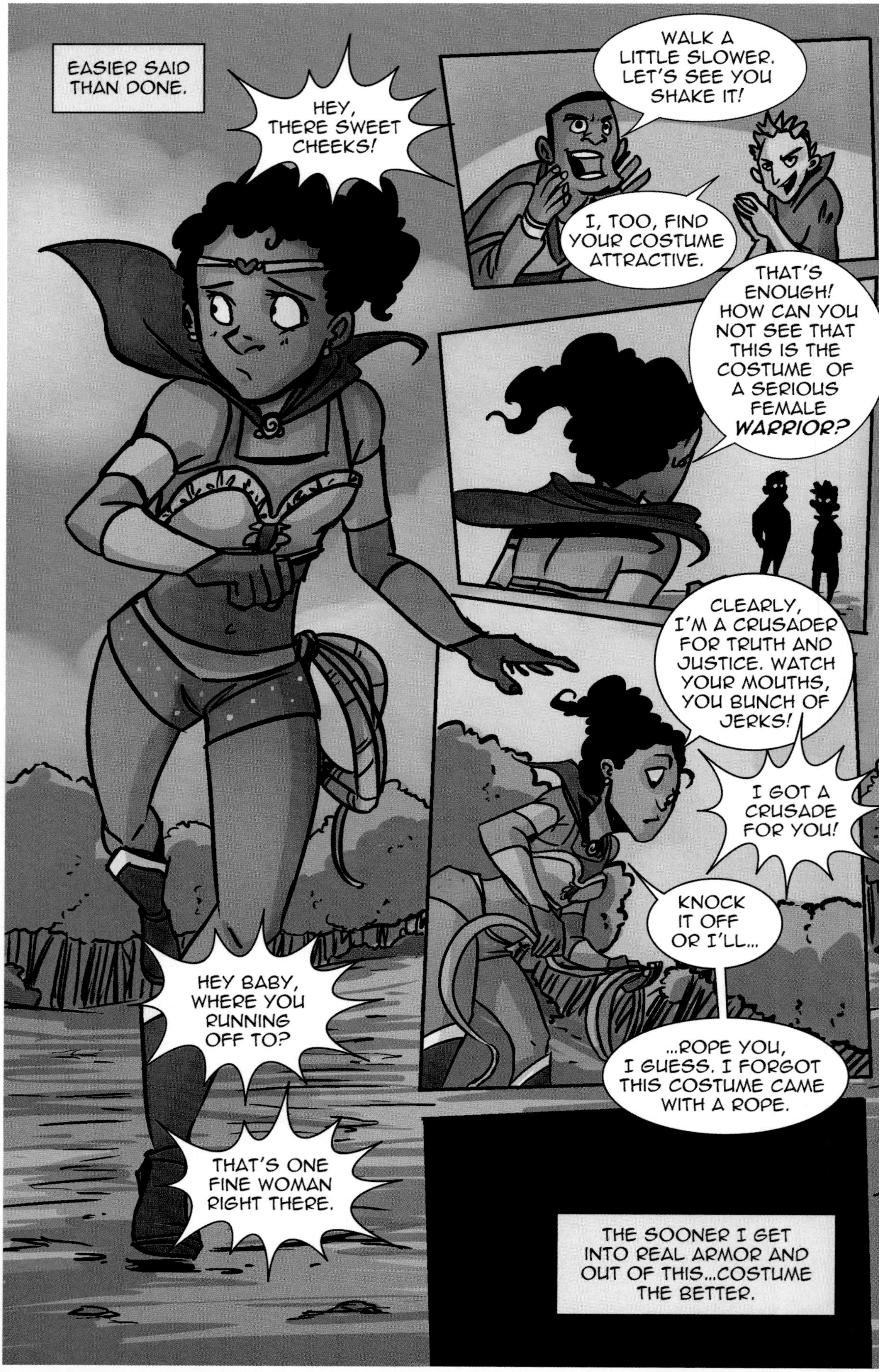
EASIER SAID THAN DONE.
HEY, THERE SWEET CHEEKS!
WALK A LITTLE SLOWER. LET'S SEE YOU SHAKE IT!
I, TOO, FIND YOUR COSTUME ATTRACTIVE.
THAT'S ENOUGH! HOW CAN YOU NOT SEE THAT THIS IS THE COSTUME OF A SERIOUS FEMALE WARRIOR?
CLEARLY, I'M A CRUSADER FOR TRUTH AND JUSTICE. WATCH YOUR MOUTHS, YOU BUNCH OF JERKS!
I GOT A CRUSADE FOR YOU!
KNOCK IT OFF OR I'LL...
...ROPE YOU, I GUESS. I FORGOT THIS COSTUME CAME WITH A ROPE.
HEY BABY, WHERE YOU RUNNING OFF TO?
THAT'S ONE FINE WOMAN RIGHT THERE.
THE SOONER I GET INTO REAL ARMOR AND OUT OF THIS...COSTUME THE BETTER.

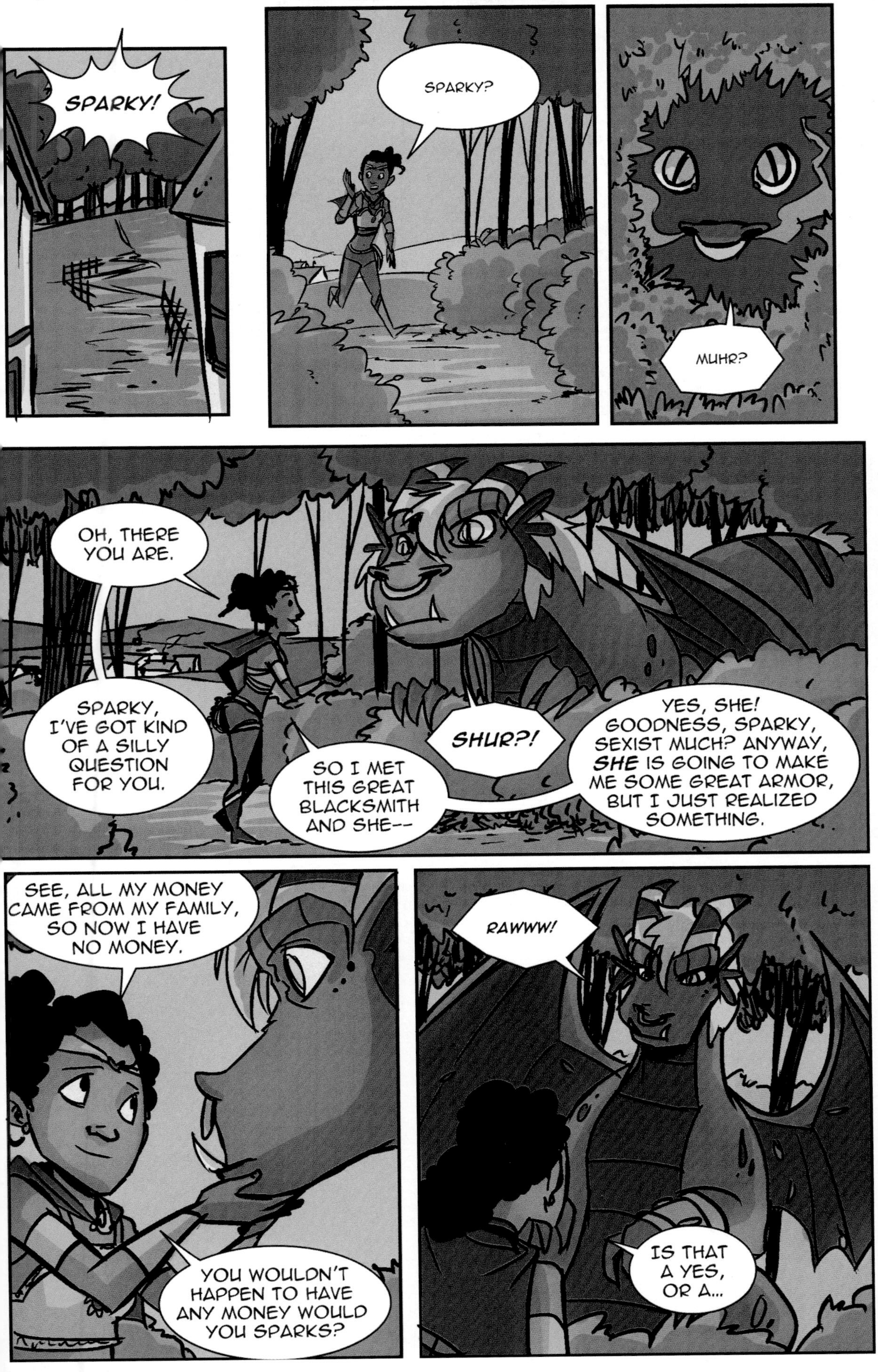
SPARKY!
SPARKY?
MUHR?
OH, THERE YOU ARE.
SPARKY, I'VE GOT KIND OF A SILLY QUESTION FOR YOU.
SO I MET THIS GREAT BLACKSMITH AND SHE--
SHUR?!
YES, SHE! GOODNESS, SPARKY, SEXIST MUCH? ANYWAY, SHE IS GOING TO MAKE ME SOME GREAT ARMOR, BUT I JUST REALIZED SOMETHING.
SEE, ALL MY MONEY CAME FROM MY FAMILY, SO NOW I HAVE NO MONEY.
YOU WOULDN'T HAPPEN TO HAVE ANY MONEY WOULD YOU SPARKS?
RAWWW!
IS THAT A YES, OR A...

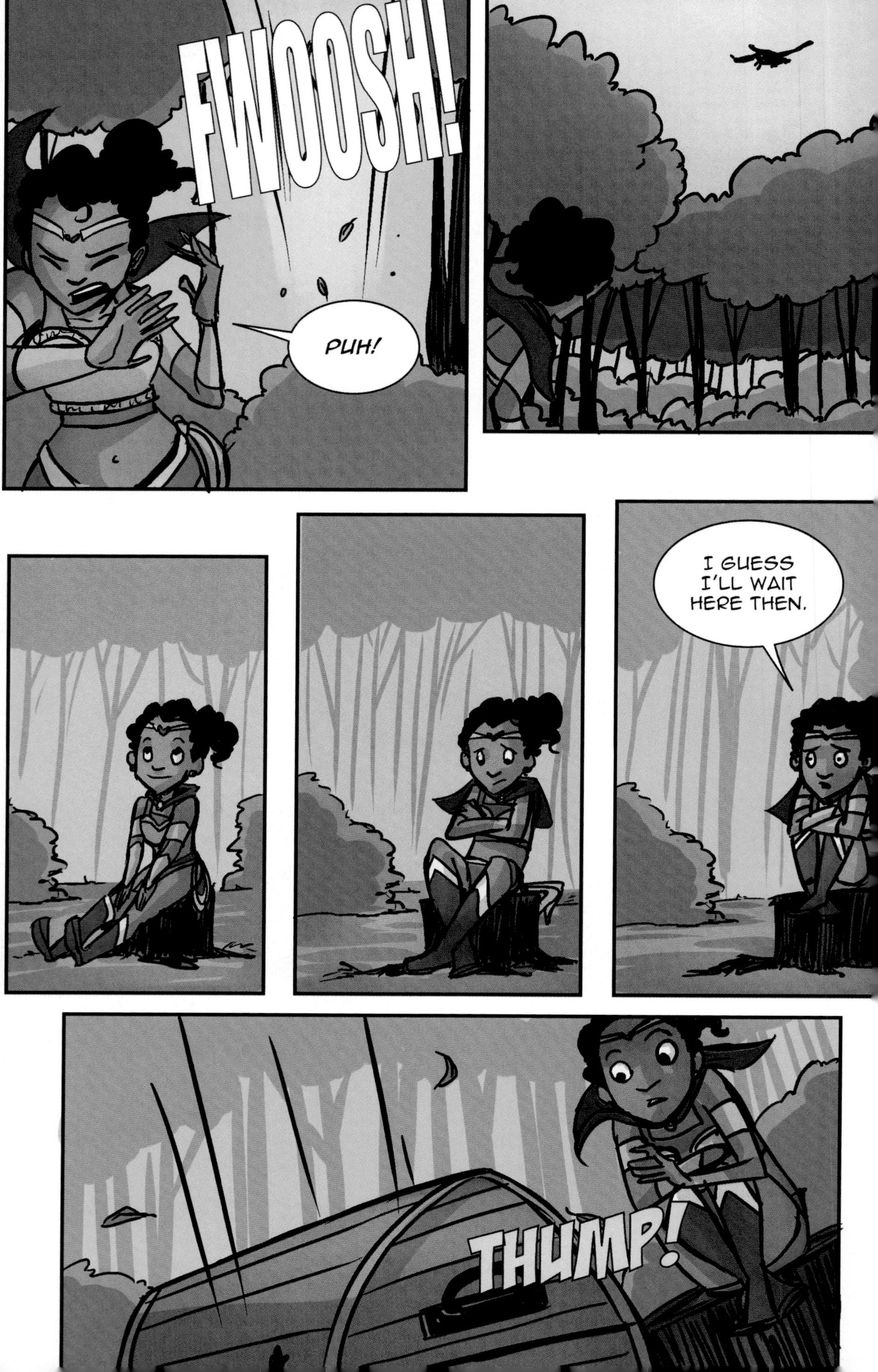
FWOOSH!
PUH!
I GUESS I'LL WAIT HERE THEN.
THUMP!

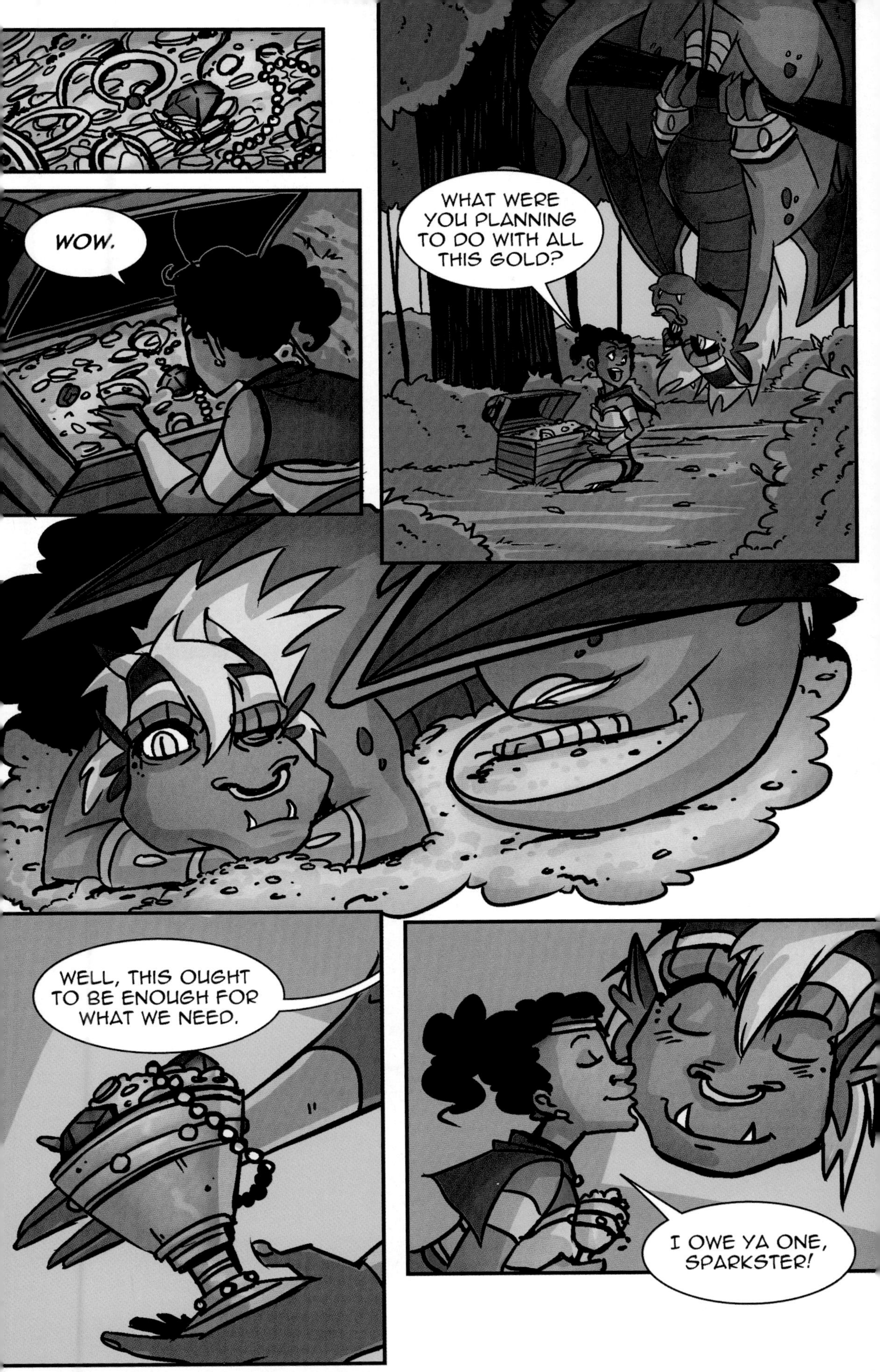
WOW.
WHAT WERE YOU PLANNING TO DO WITH ALL THIS GOLD?
WELL, THIS OUGHT TO BE ENOUGH FOR WHAT WE NEED.
I OWE YA ONE, SPARKSTER!

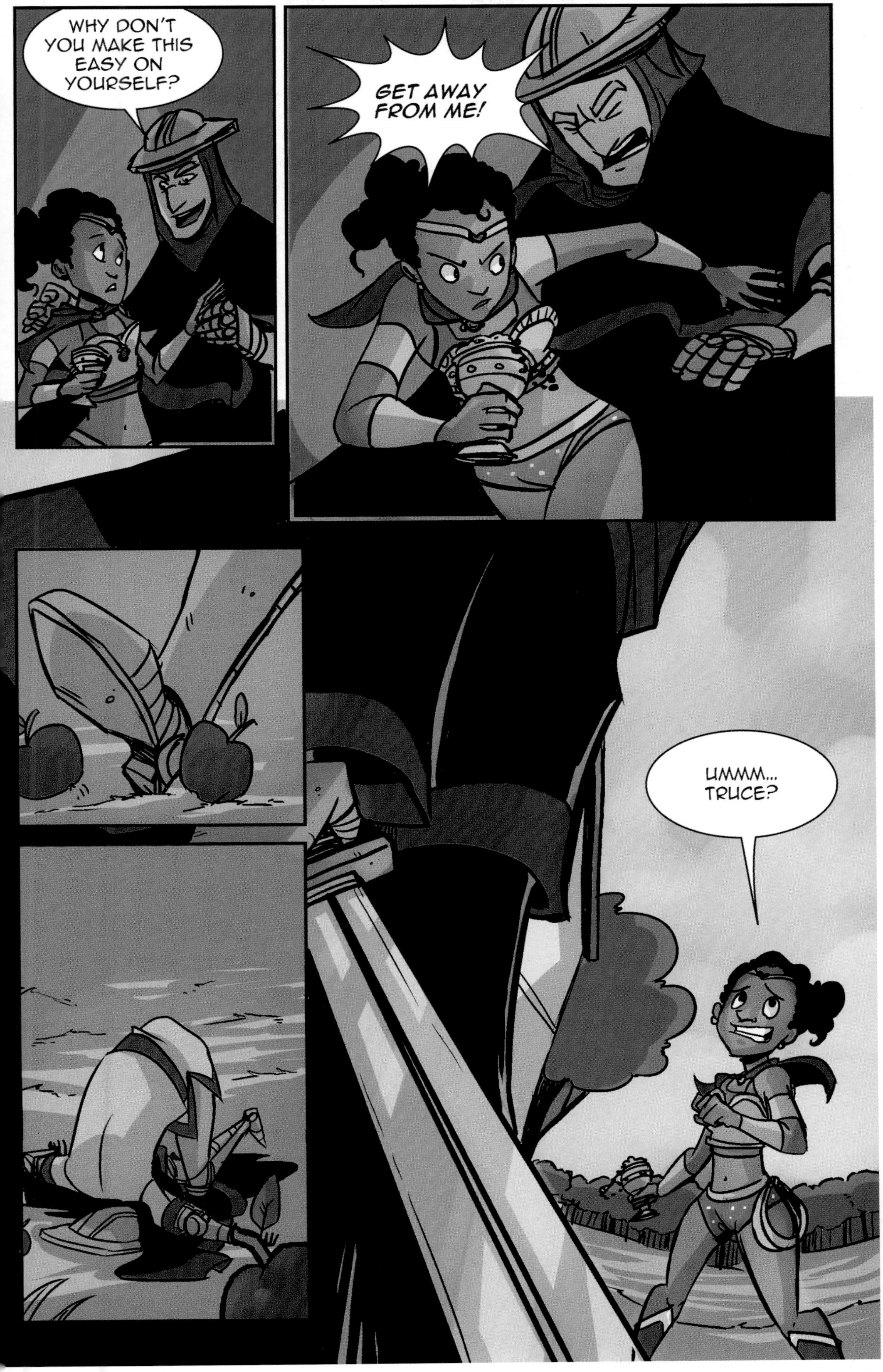
WHY DON'T YOU MAKE THIS EASY ON YOURSELF?
GET AWAY FROM ME!
UMMM... TRUCE?

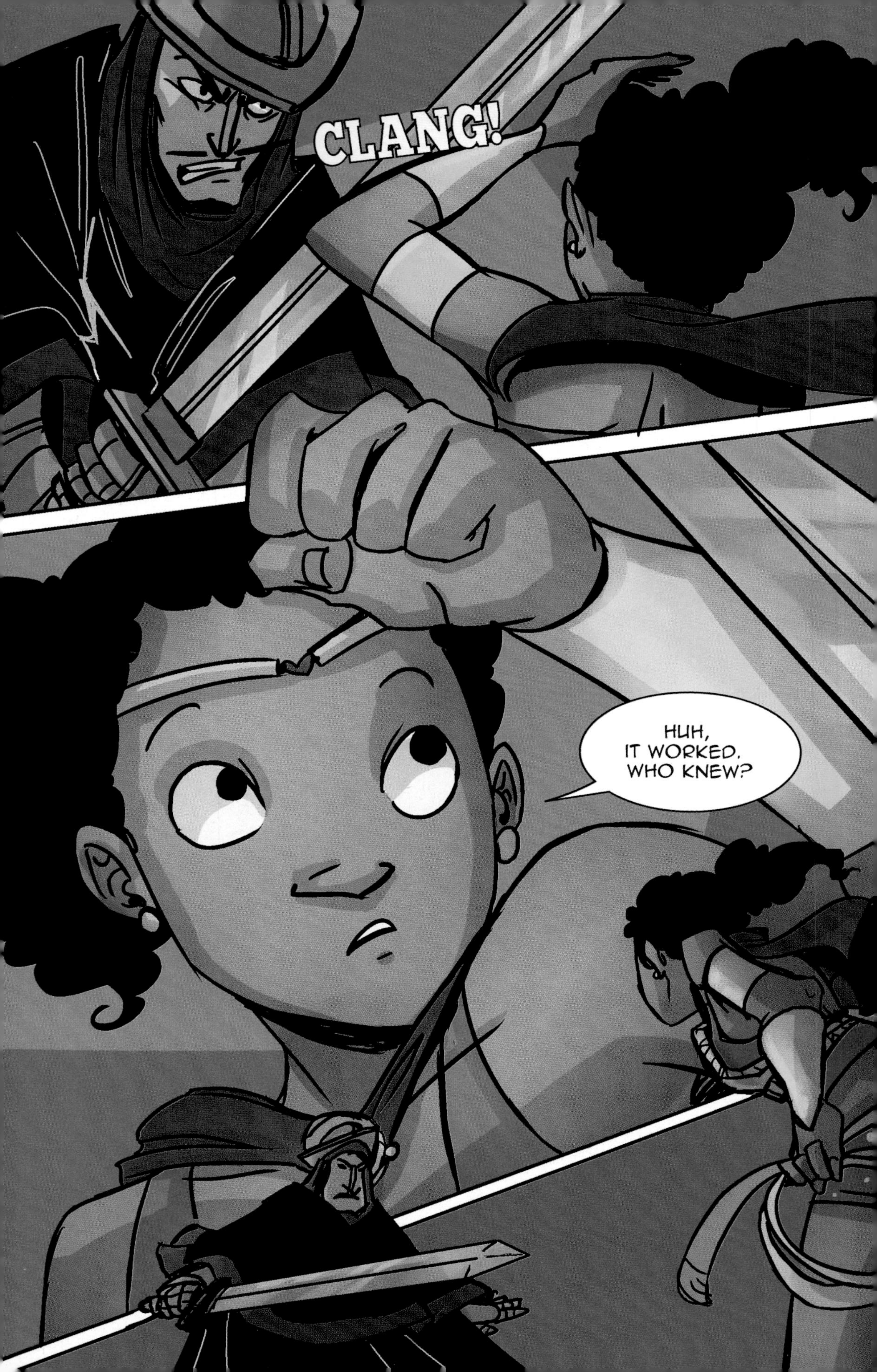
CLANG!
HUH, IT WORKED. WHO KNEW?

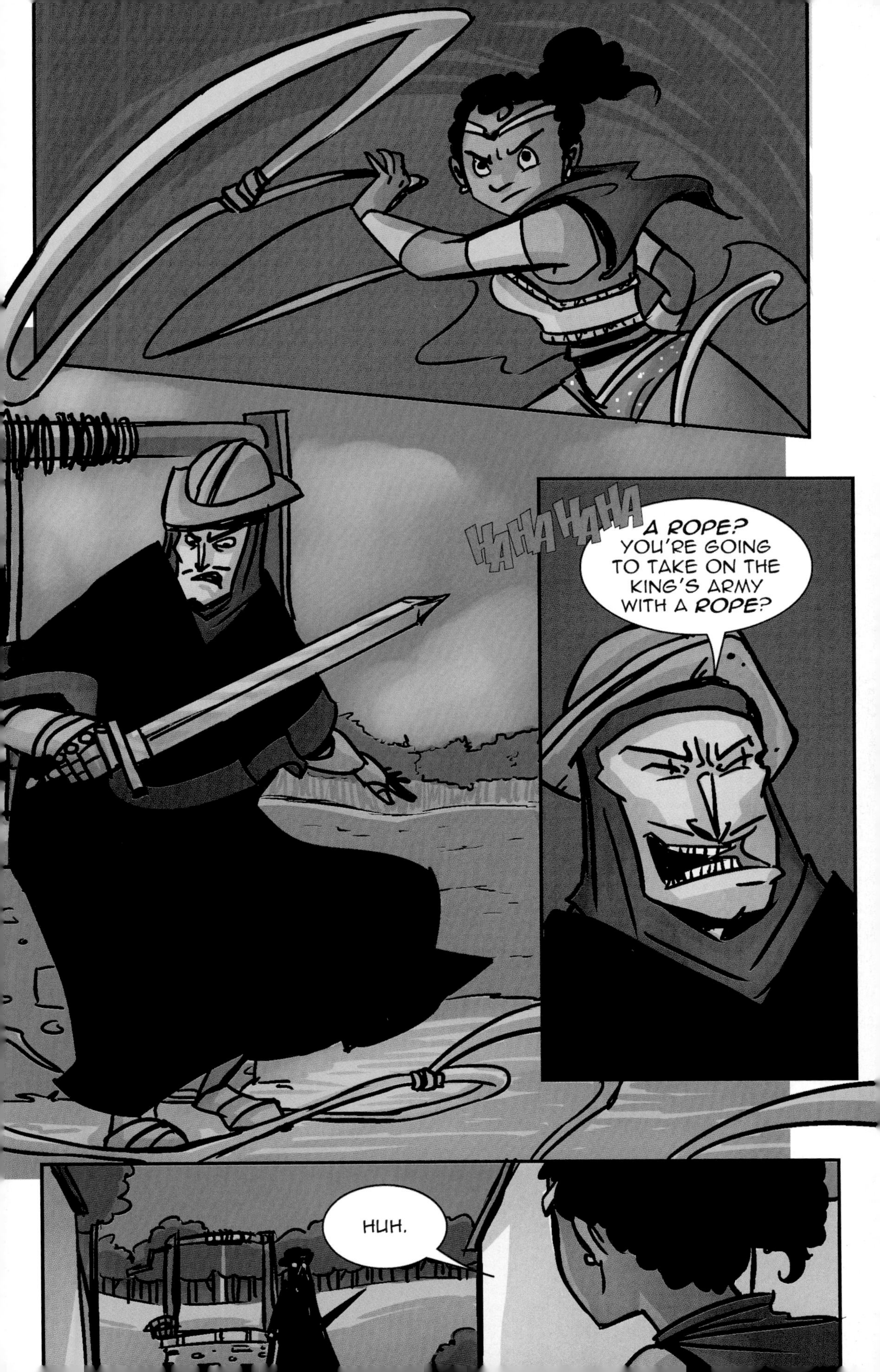
HAHA HAHA
A ROPE? YOU'RE GOING TO TAKE ON THE KING'S ARMY WITH A ROPE?
HUH.

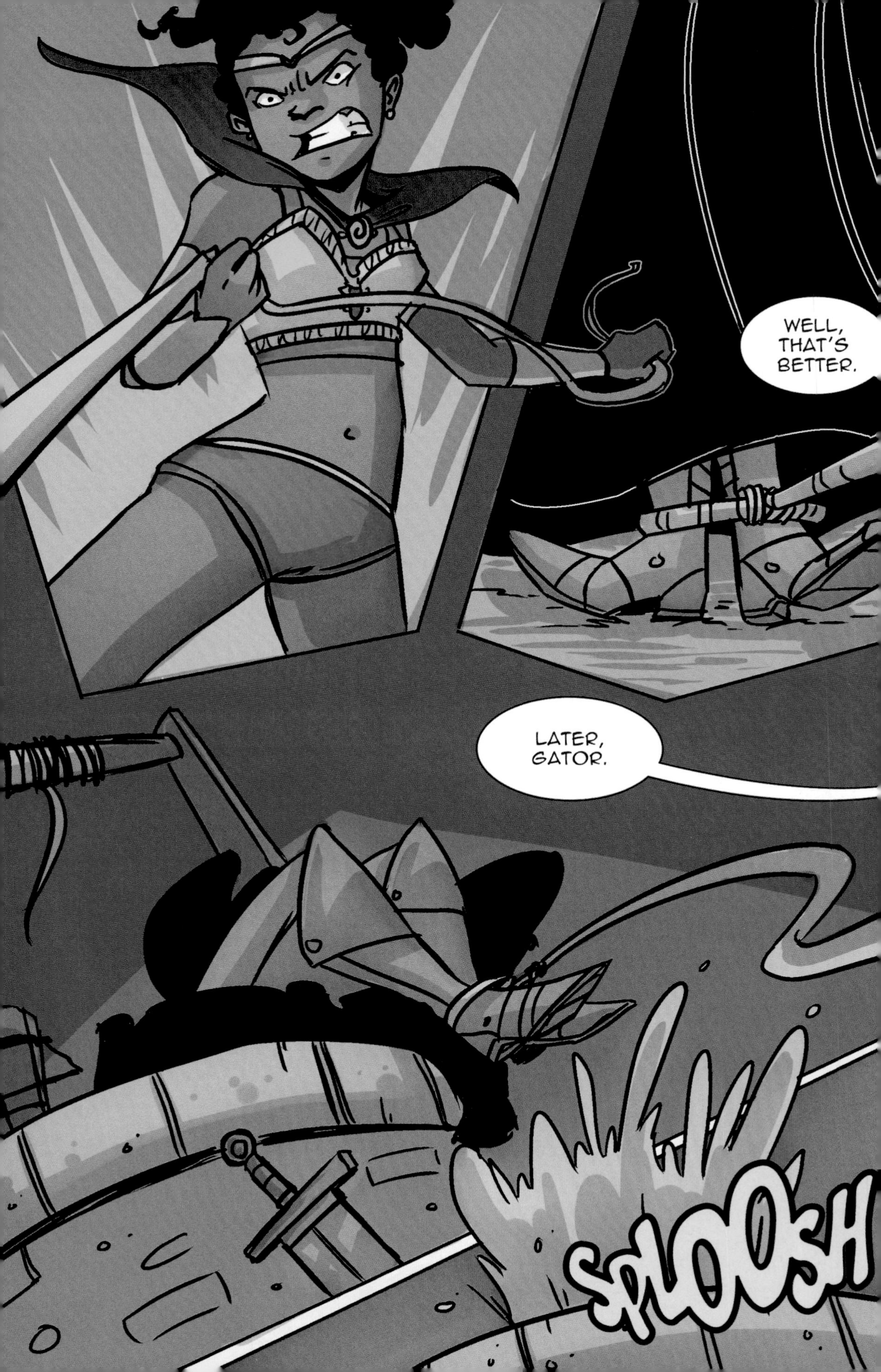
WELL, THAT'S BETTER.
LATER, GATOR.
SPLOOSH

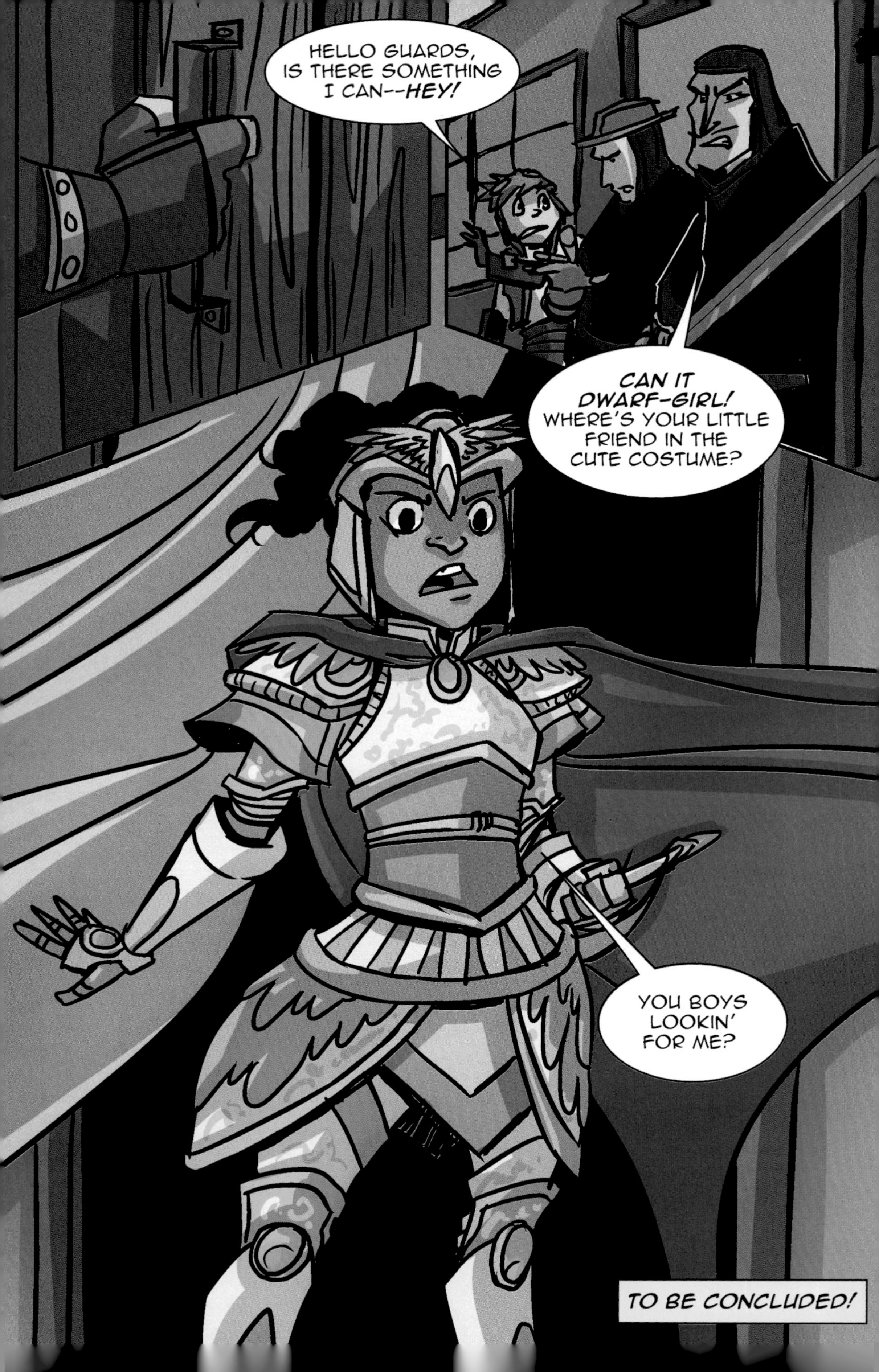
HELLO GUARDS, IS THERE SOMETHING I CAN--HEY!
CAN IT DWARF-GIRL! WHERE'S YOUR LITTLE FRIEND IN THE CUTE COSTUME?
YOU BOYS LOOKIN' FOR ME?
TO BE CONCLUDED!

4: Correct Dueling Procedure in Case of Fire

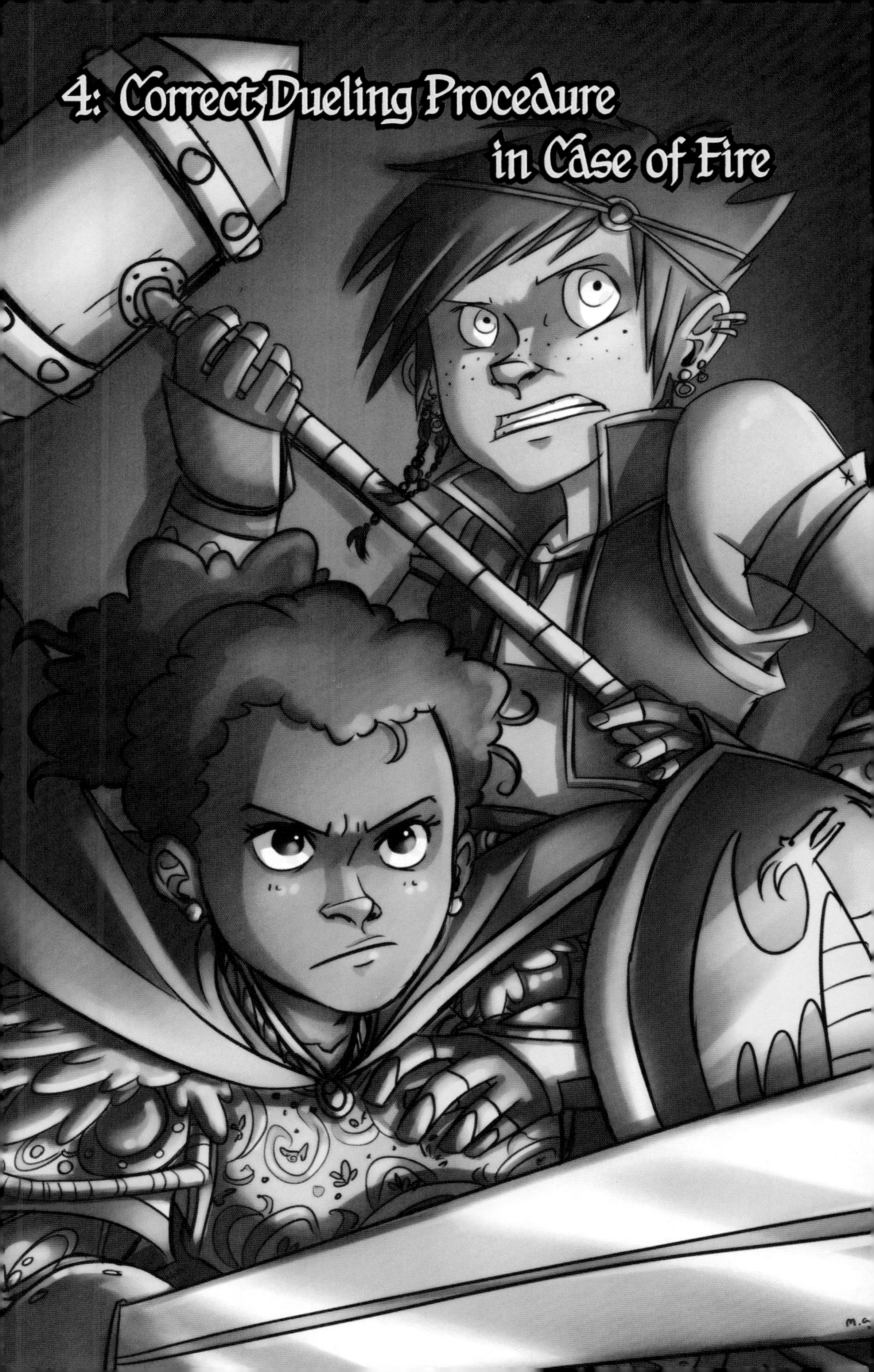

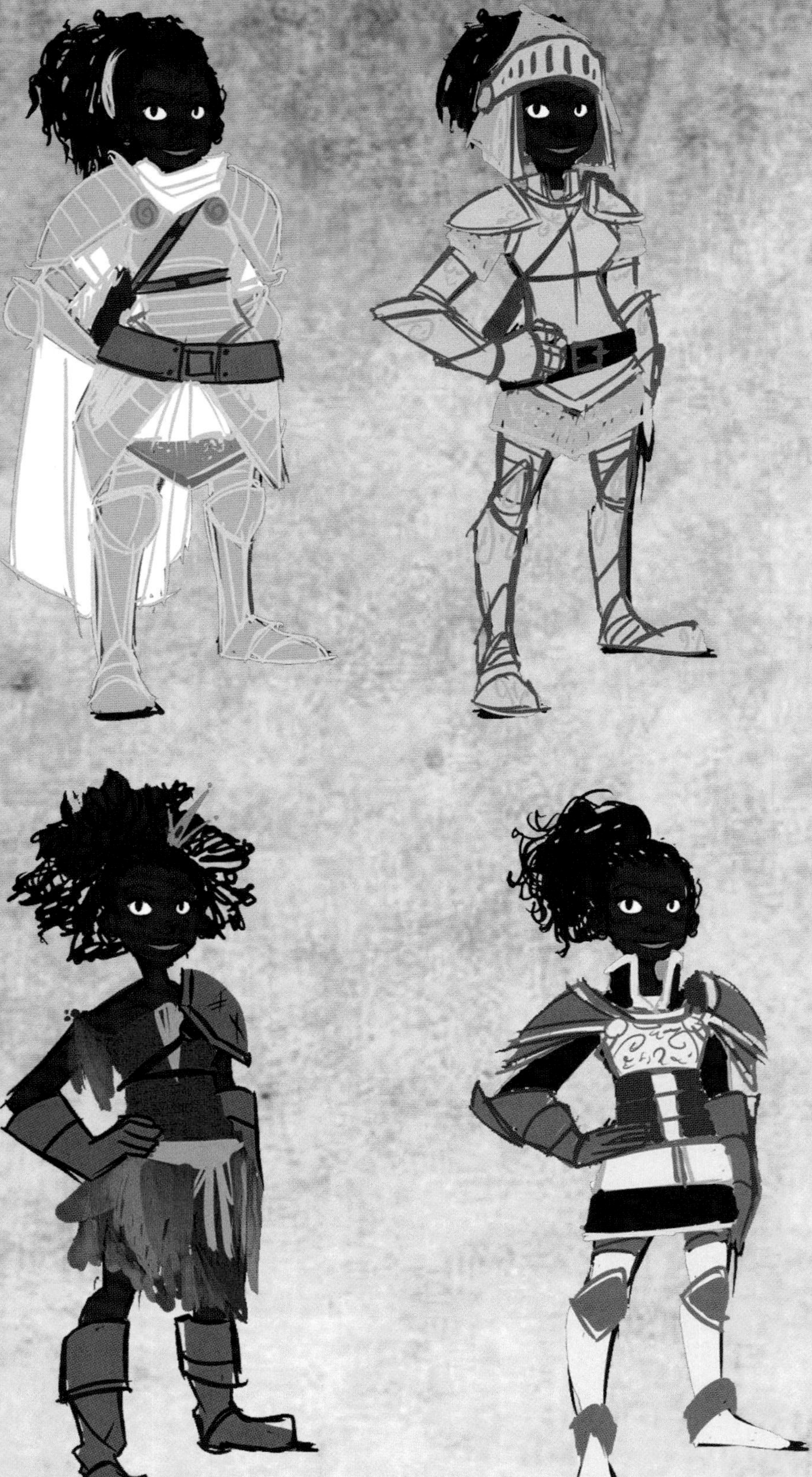

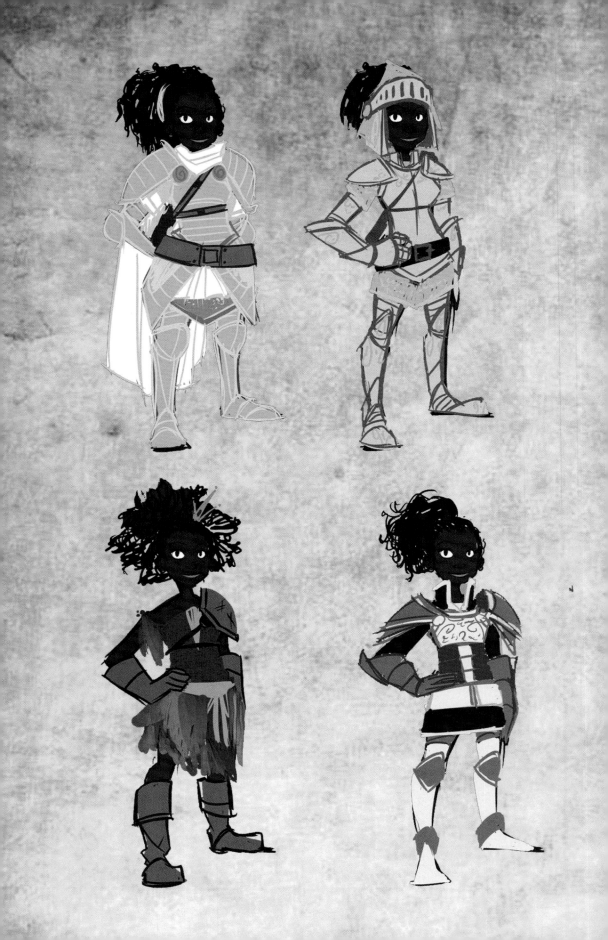

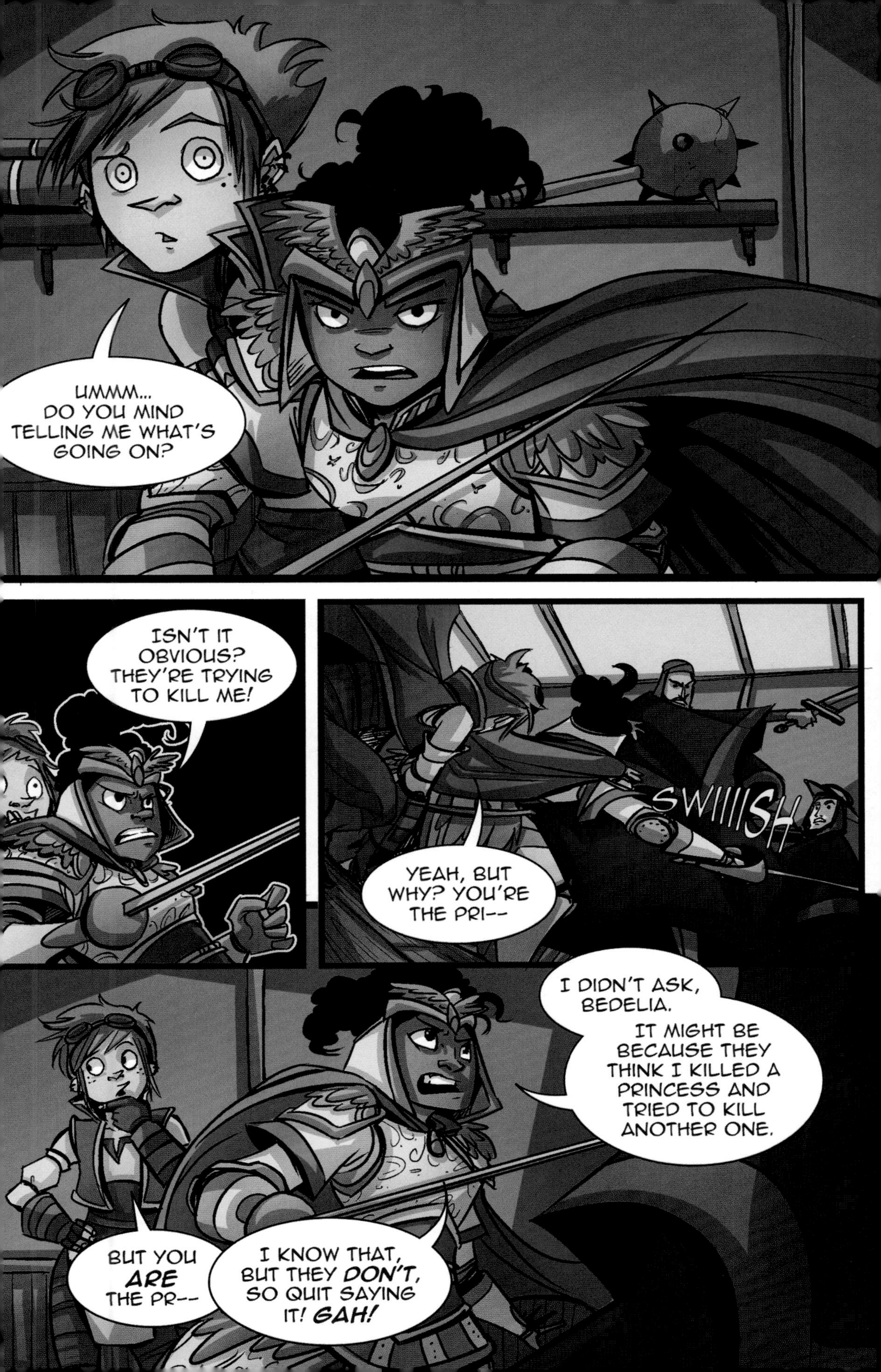
UMMM...
DO YOU MIND TELLING ME WHAT'S GOING ON?
ISN'T IT OBVIOUS? THEY'RE TRYING TO KILL ME!
YEAH, BUT WHY? YOU'RE THE PRI--
SWIIIISH
I DIDN'T ASK, BEDELIA.
IT MIGHT BE BECAUSE THEY THINK I KILLED A PRINCESS AND TRIED TO KILL ANOTHER ONE.
BUT YOU *ARE* THE PR--
I KNOW THAT, BUT THEY *DON'T*, SO QUIT SAYING IT! *GAH!*

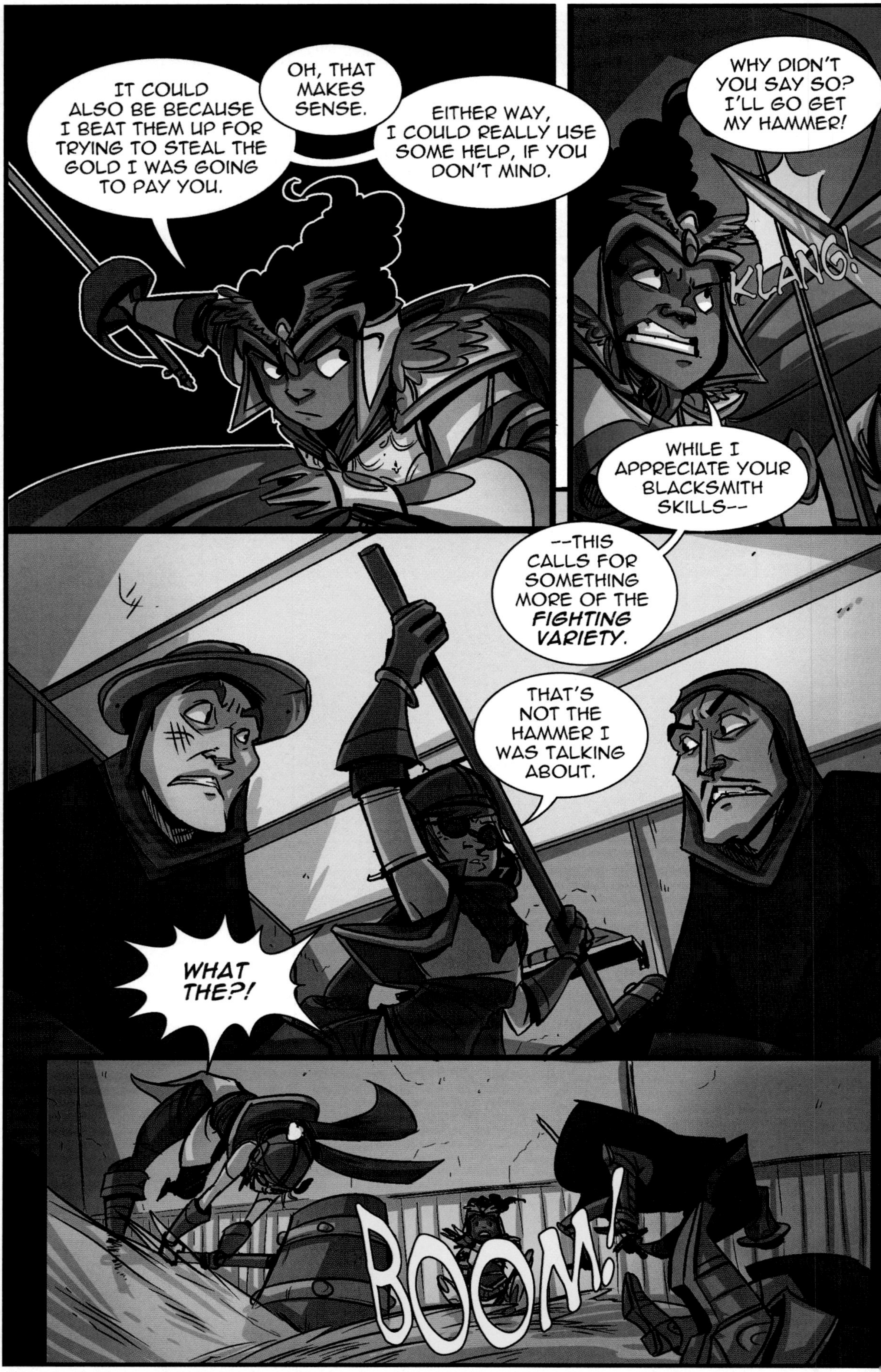
IT COULD ALSO BE BECAUSE I BEAT THEM UP FOR TRYING TO STEAL THE GOLD I WAS GOING TO PAY YOU.
OH, THAT MAKES SENSE.
EITHER WAY, I COULD REALLY USE SOME HELP, IF YOU DON'T MIND.
WHY DIDN'T YOU SAY SO? I'LL GO GET MY HAMMER!
KLANG!
WHILE I APPRECIATE YOUR BLACKSMITH SKILLS--
--THIS CALLS FOR SOMETHING MORE OF THE FIGHTING VARIETY.
THAT'S NOT THE HAMMER I WAS TALKING ABOUT.
WHAT THE?!
BOOM!

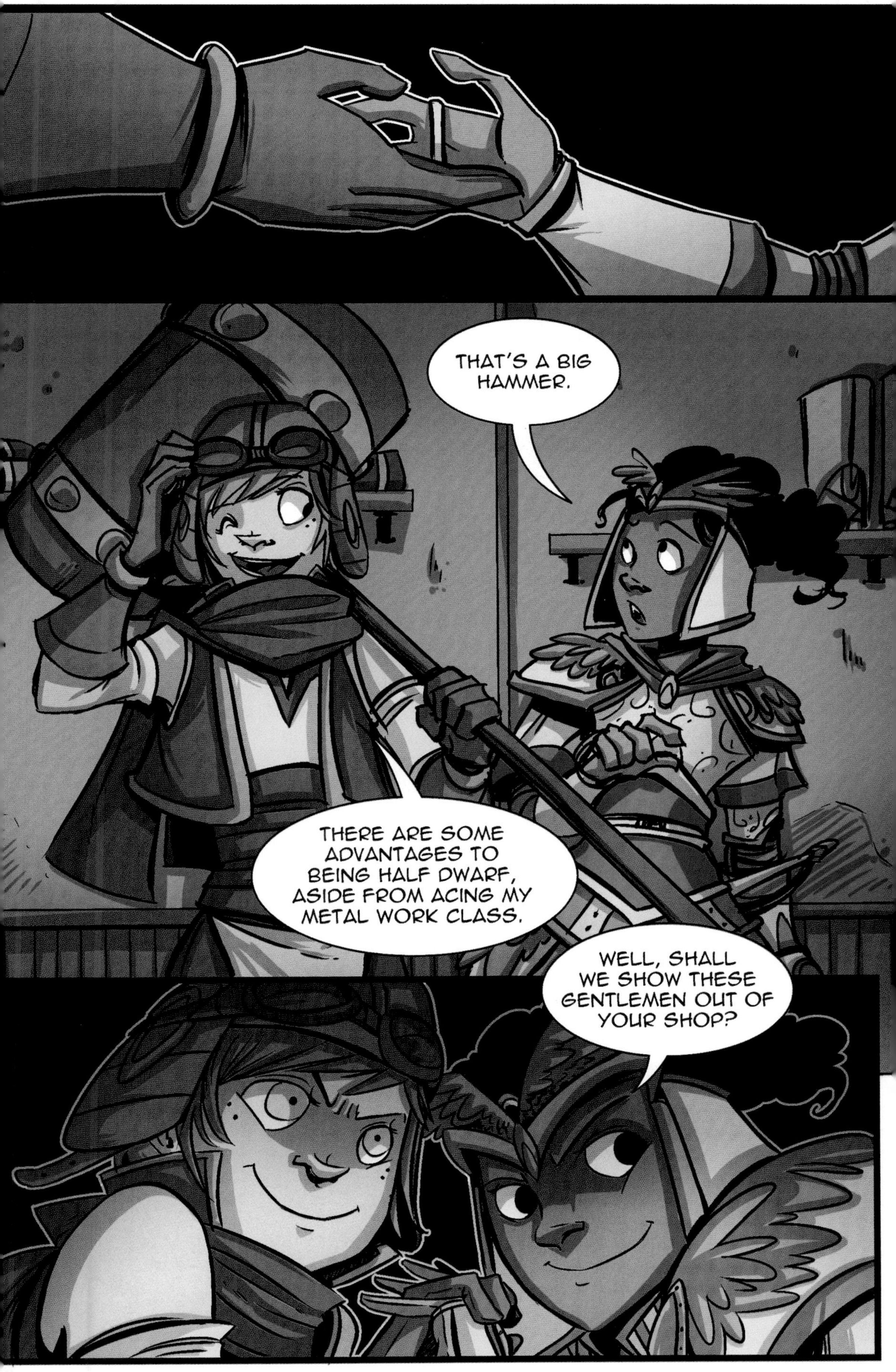
THAT'S A BIG HAMMER.
THERE ARE SOME ADVANTAGES TO BEING HALF DWARF, ASIDE FROM ACING MY METAL WORK CLASS.
WELL, SHALL WE SHOW THESE GENTLEMEN OUT OF YOUR SHOP?

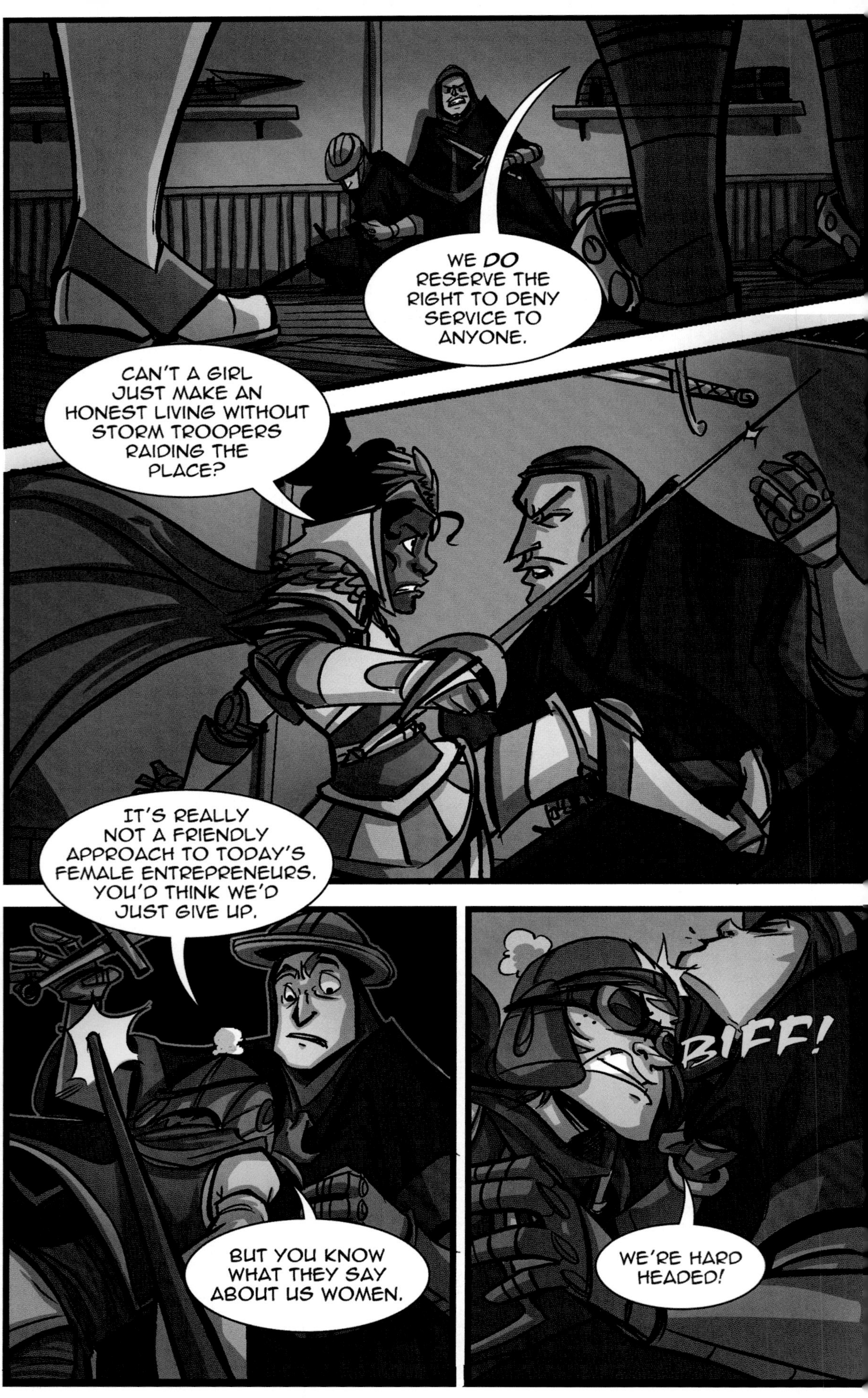
WE *DO* RESERVE THE RIGHT TO DENY SERVICE TO ANYONE.
CAN'T A GIRL JUST MAKE AN HONEST LIVING WITHOUT STORM TROOPERS RAIDING THE PLACE?
IT'S REALLY NOT A FRIENDLY APPROACH TO TODAY'S FEMALE ENTREPRENEURS. YOU'D THINK WE'D JUST GIVE UP.
BUT YOU KNOW WHAT THEY SAY ABOUT US WOMEN.
BIFF!
WE'RE HARD HEADED!

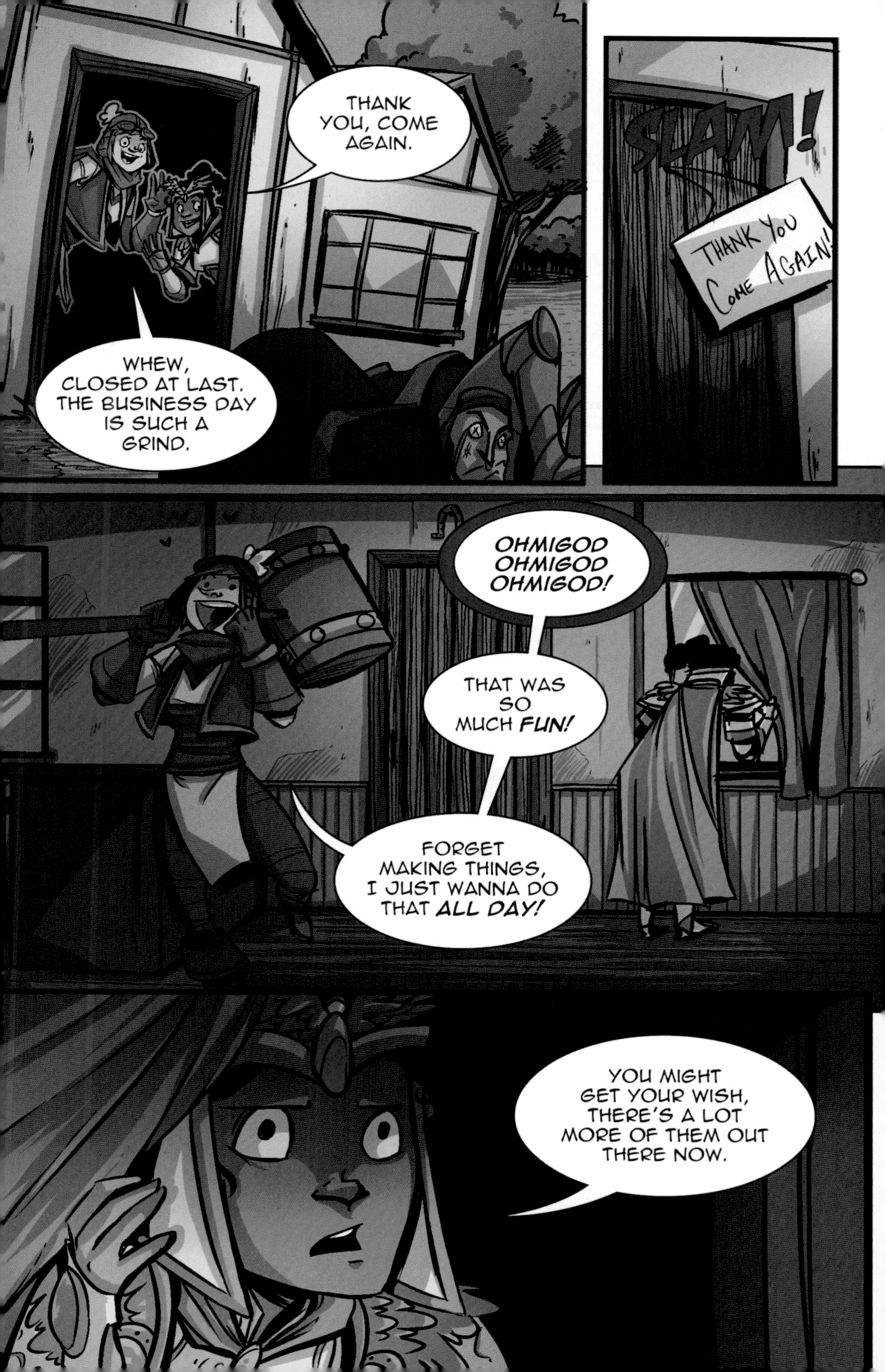
THANK YOU, COME AGAIN.
WHEW, CLOSED AT LAST. THE BUSINESS DAY IS SUCH A GRIND.
SLAM!
THANK YOU COME AGAIN!
OHMIGOD OHMIGOD OHMIGOD!
THAT WAS SO MUCH FUN!
FORGET MAKING THINGS, I JUST WANNA DO THAT ALL DAY!
YOU MIGHT GET YOUR WISH, THERE'S A LOT MORE OF THEM OUT THERE NOW.

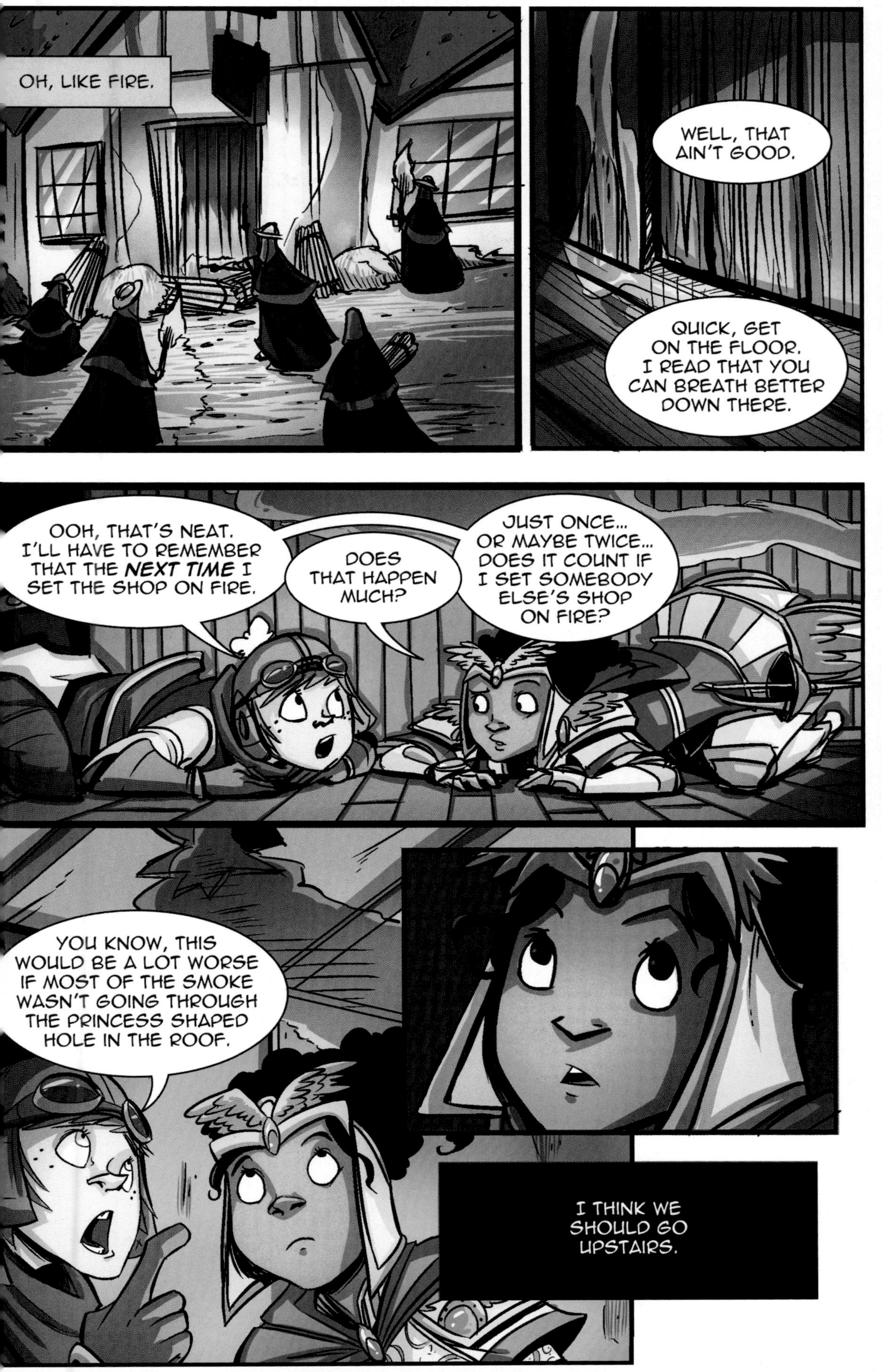
OH, LIKE FIRE.
WELL, THAT AIN'T GOOD.
QUICK, GET ON THE FLOOR. I READ THAT YOU CAN BREATH BETTER DOWN THERE.
OOH, THAT'S NEAT. I'LL HAVE TO REMEMBER THAT THE NEXT TIME I SET THE SHOP ON FIRE.
DOES THAT HAPPEN MUCH?
JUST ONCE... OR MAYBE TWICE... DOES IT COUNT IF I SET SOMEBODY ELSE'S SHOP ON FIRE?
YOU KNOW, THIS WOULD BE A LOT WORSE IF MOST OF THE SMOKE WASN'T GOING THROUGH THE PRINCESS SHAPED HOLE IN THE ROOF.
I THINK WE SHOULD GO UPSTAIRS.

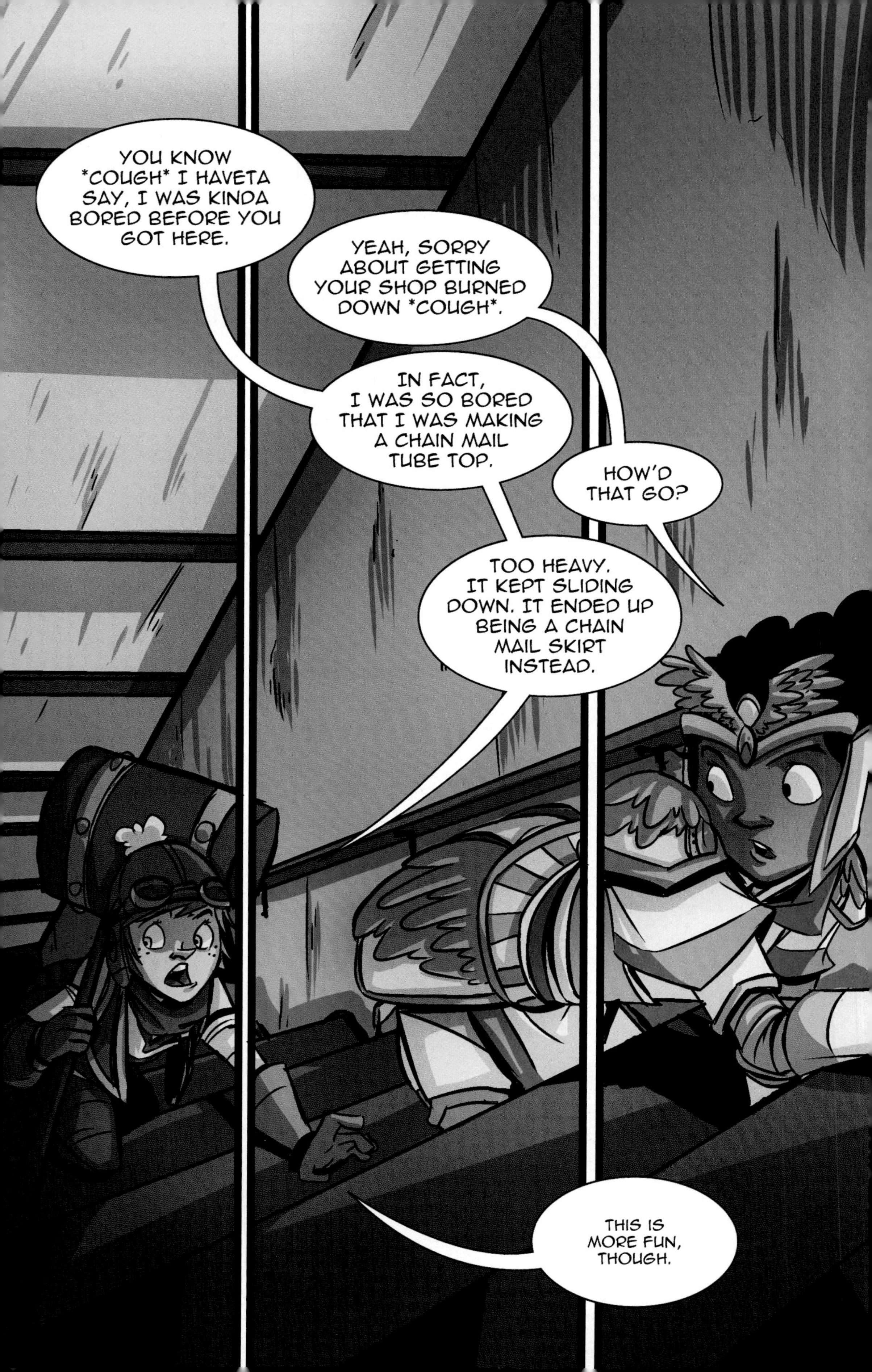
YOU KNOW *COUGH* I HAVETA SAY, I WAS KINDA BORED BEFORE YOU GOT HERE.
YEAH, SORRY ABOUT GETTING YOUR SHOP BURNED DOWN *COUGH*.
IN FACT, I WAS SO BORED THAT I WAS MAKING A CHAIN MAIL TUBE TOP.
HOW'D THAT GO?
TOO HEAVY. IT KEPT SLIDING DOWN. IT ENDED UP BEING A CHAIN MAIL SKIRT INSTEAD.
THIS IS MORE FUN, THOUGH.

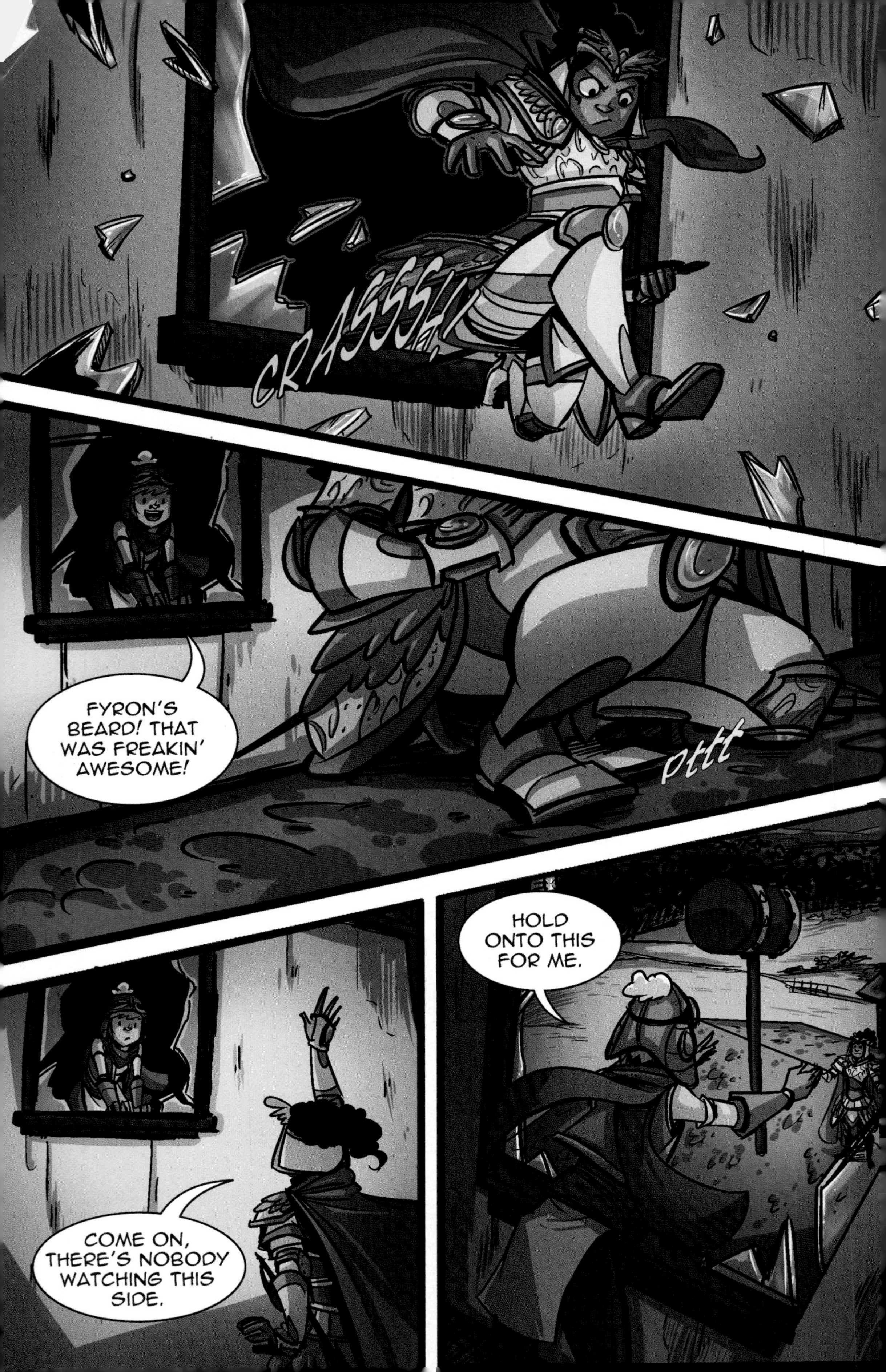
CRASSSH!
FYRON'S BEARD! THAT WAS FREAKIN' AWESOME!
pttt
COME ON, THERE'S NOBODY WATCHING THIS SIDE.
HOLD ONTO THIS FOR ME.

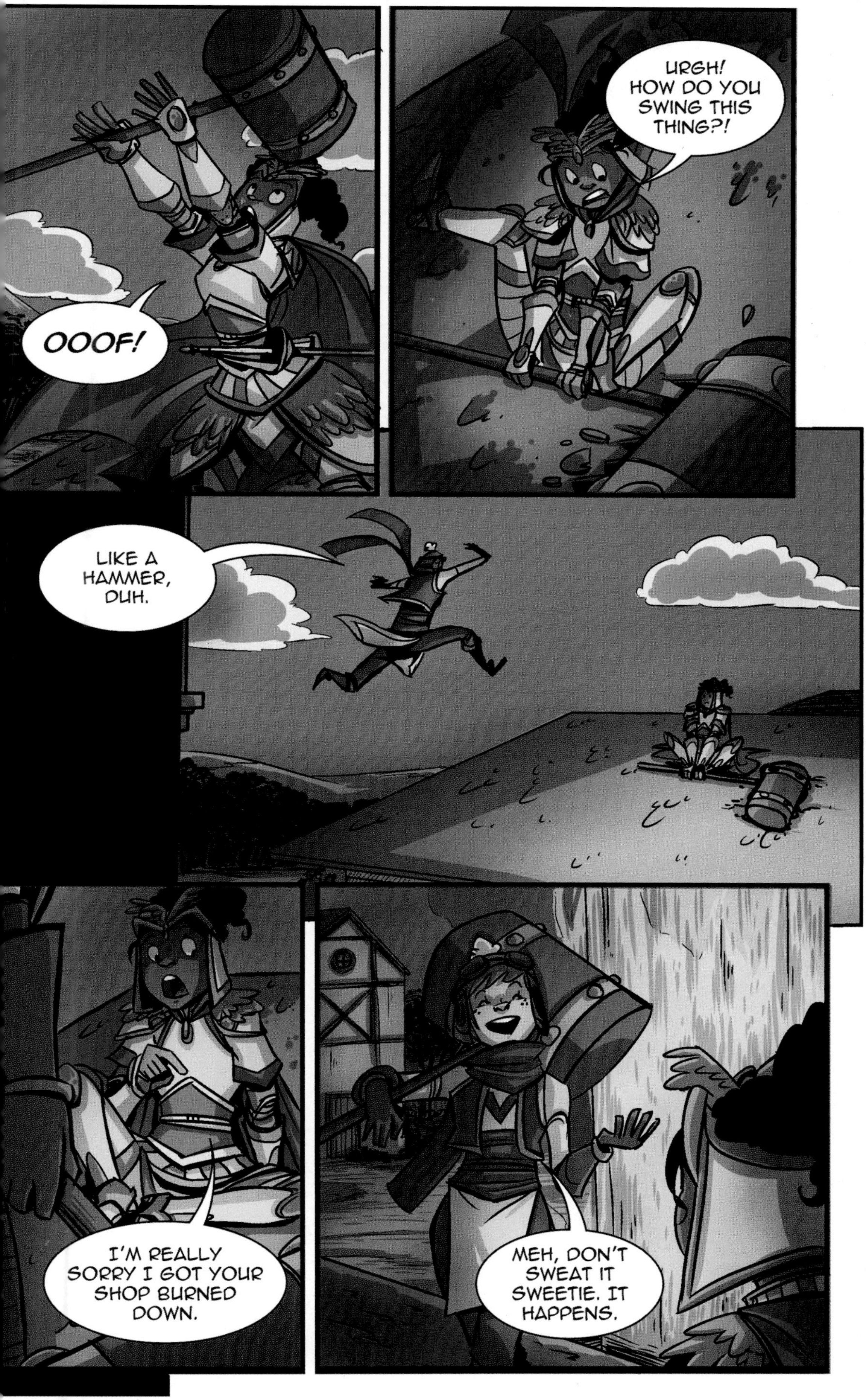
OOOF!
URGH! HOW DO YOU SWING THIS THING?!
LIKE A HAMMER, DUH.
I'M REALLY SORRY I GOT YOUR SHOP BURNED DOWN.
MEH, DON'T SWEAT IT SWEETIE. IT HAPPENS.

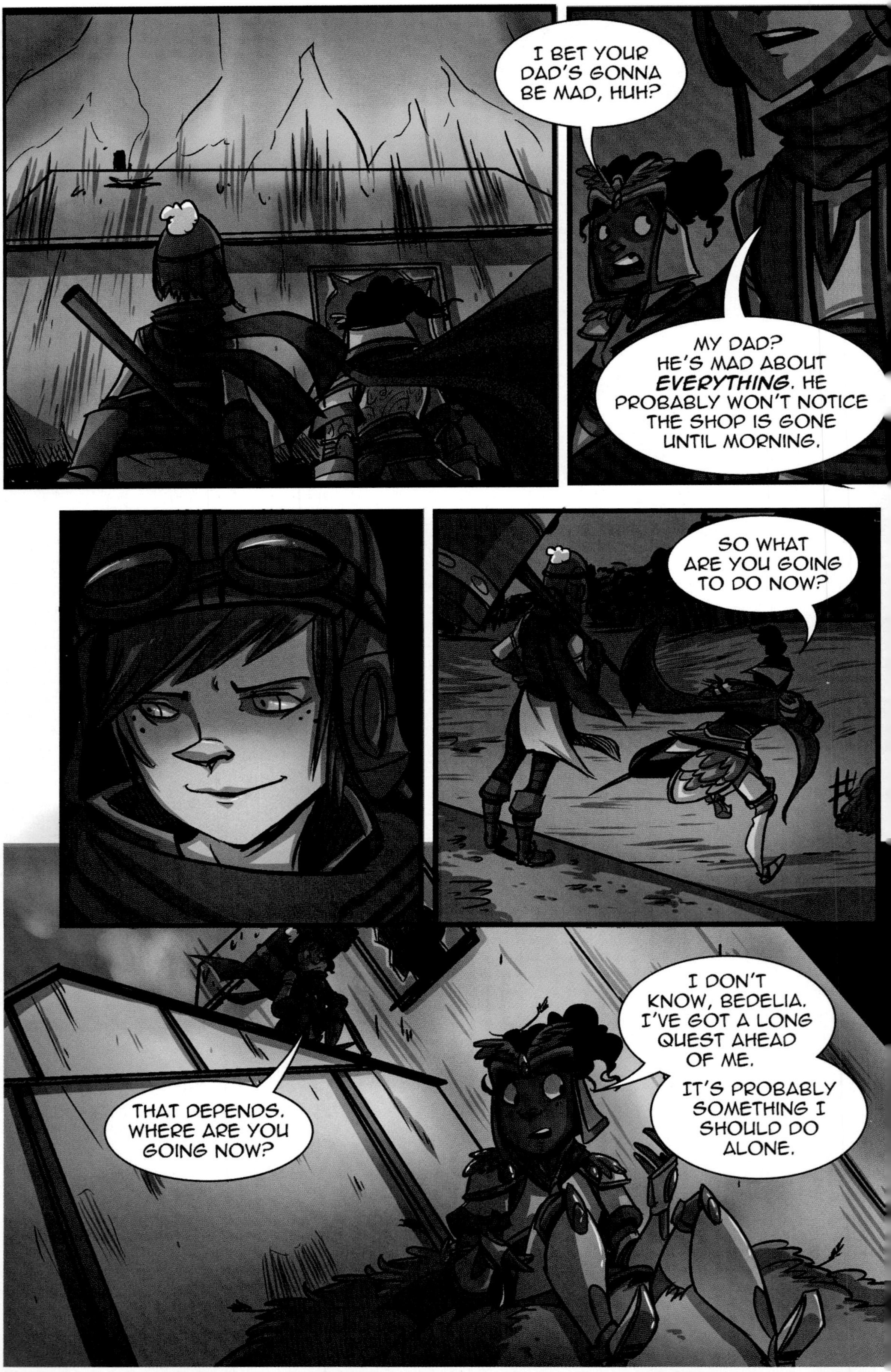
I BET YOUR DAD'S GONNA BE MAD, HUH?
MY DAD? HE'S MAD ABOUT ***EVERYTHING***. HE PROBABLY WON'T NOTICE THE SHOP IS GONE UNTIL MORNING.
SO WHAT ARE YOU GOING TO DO NOW?
I DON'T KNOW, BEDELIA. I'VE GOT A LONG QUEST AHEAD OF ME.
IT'S PROBABLY SOMETHING I SHOULD DO ALONE.
THAT DEPENDS. WHERE ARE YOU GOING NOW?

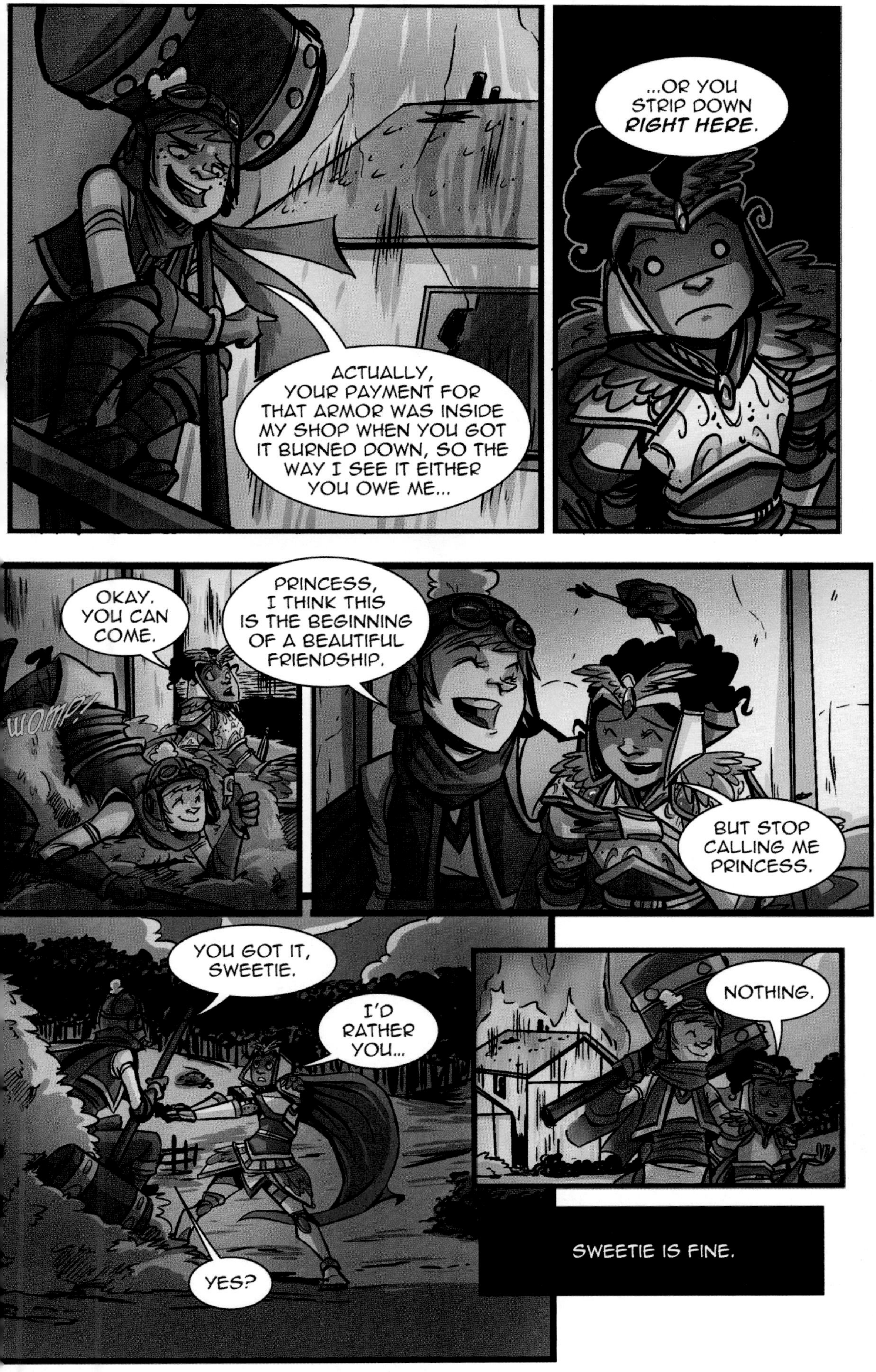
ACTUALLY, YOUR PAYMENT FOR THAT ARMOR WAS INSIDE MY SHOP WHEN YOU GOT IT BURNED DOWN, SO THE WAY I SEE IT EITHER YOU OWE ME...
...OR YOU STRIP DOWN ***RIGHT HERE***.
OKAY. YOU CAN COME.
WOMP!
PRINCESS, I THINK THIS IS THE BEGINNING OF A BEAUTIFUL FRIENDSHIP.
BUT STOP CALLING ME PRINCESS.
YOU GOT IT, SWEETIE.
I'D RATHER YOU...
YES?
NOTHING.
SWEETIE IS FINE.

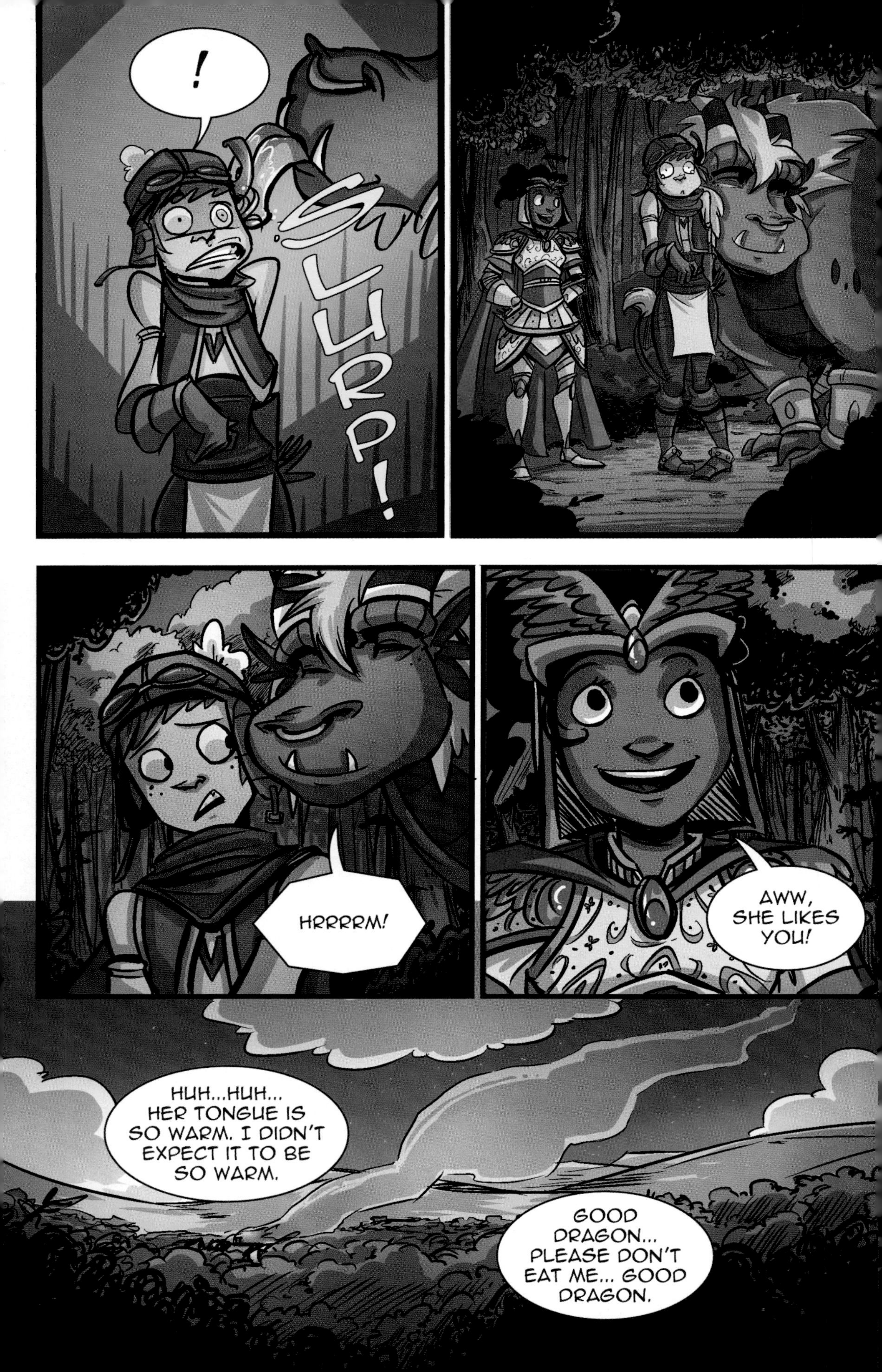
!
SLURRP!
HRRRRM!
AWW, SHE LIKES YOU!
HUH...HUH... HER TONGUE IS SO WARM. I DIDN'T EXPECT IT TO BE SO WARM.
GOOD DRAGON... PLEASE DON'T EAT ME... GOOD DRAGON.

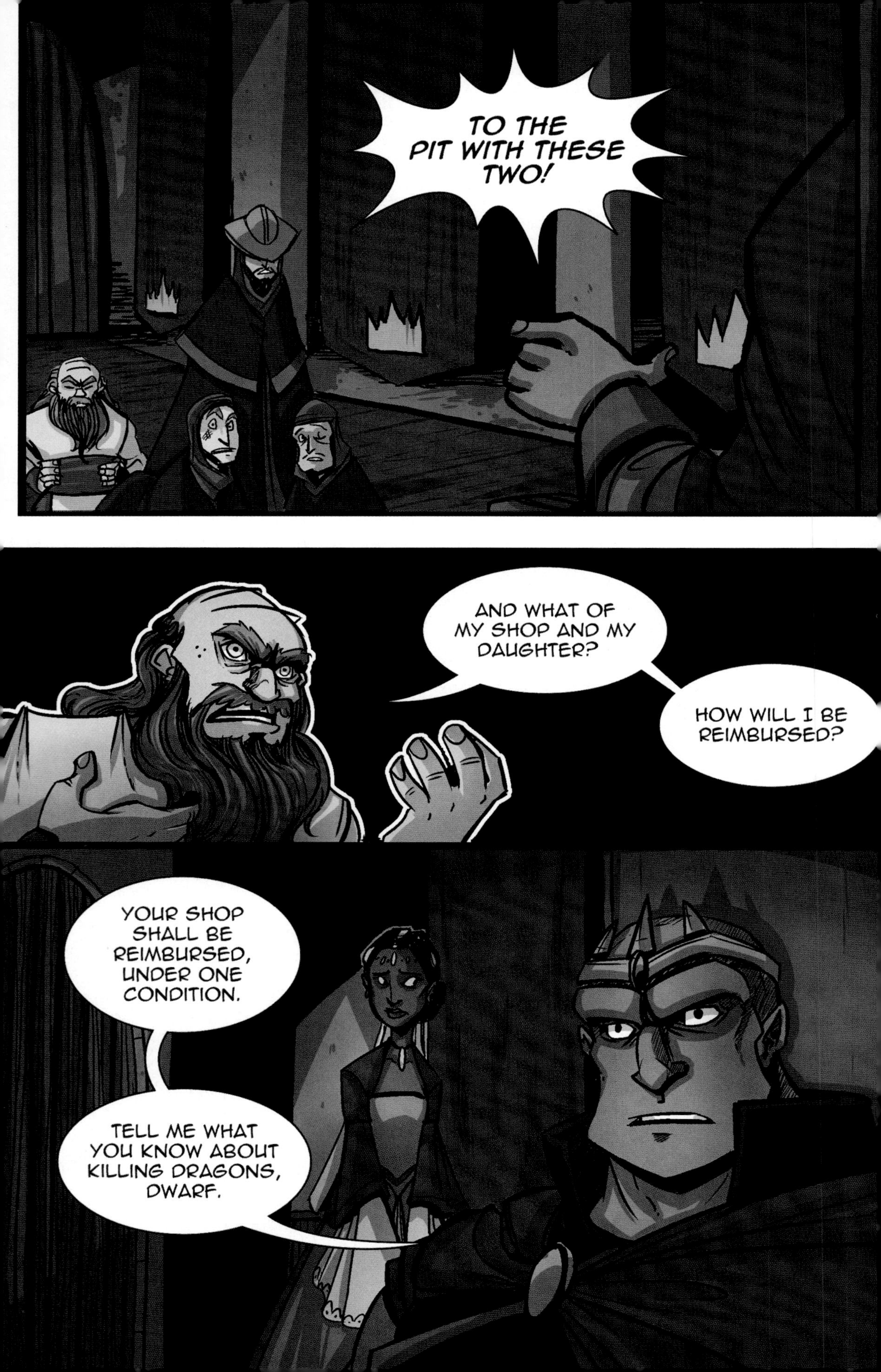
TO THE PIT WITH THESE TWO!
AND WHAT OF MY SHOP AND MY DAUGHTER?
HOW WILL I BE REIMBURSED?
YOUR SHOP SHALL BE REIMBURSED, UNDER ONE CONDITION.
TELL ME WHAT YOU KNOW ABOUT KILLING DRAGONS, DWARF.

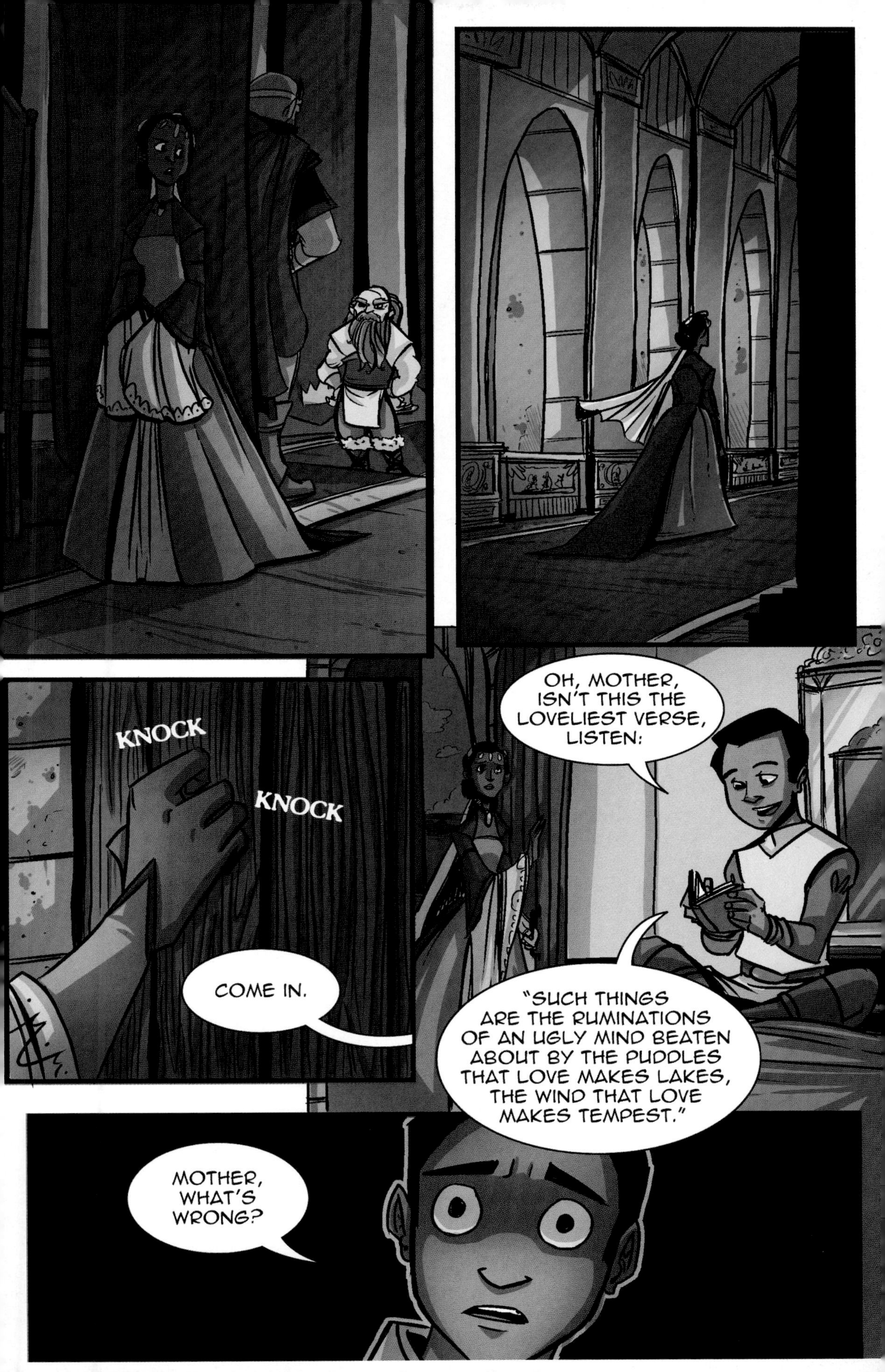
KNOCK
KNOCK
COME IN.
OH, MOTHER, ISN'T THIS THE LOVELIEST VERSE, LISTEN:
"SUCH THINGS ARE THE RUMINATIONS OF AN UGLY MIND BEATEN ABOUT BY THE PUDDLES THAT LOVE MAKES LAKES, THE WIND THAT LOVE MAKES TEMPEST."
MOTHER, WHAT'S WRONG?

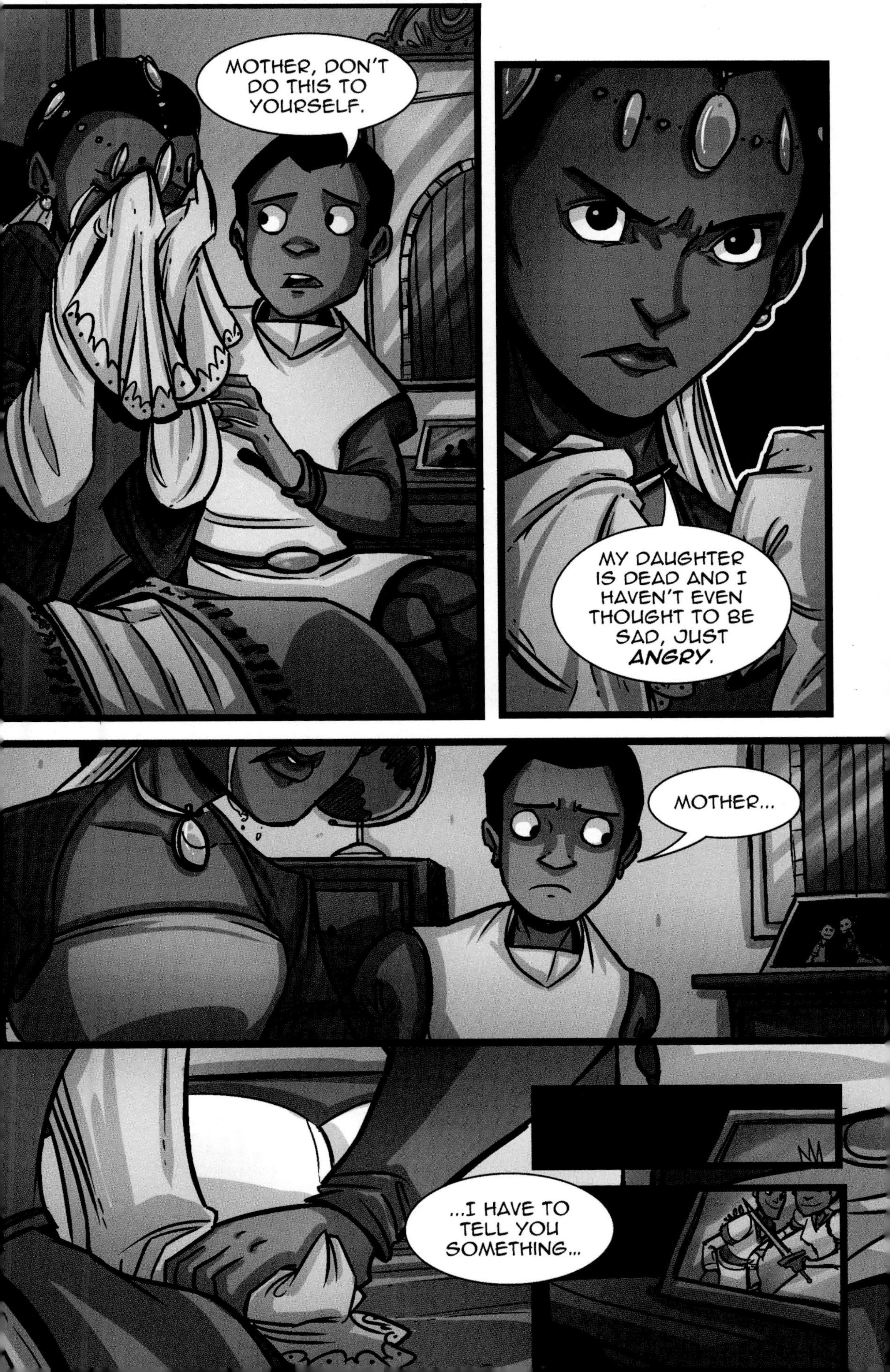
MOTHER, DON'T DO THIS TO YOURSELF.
MY DAUGHTER IS DEAD AND I HAVEN'T EVEN THOUGHT TO BE SAD, JUST *ANGRY*.
MOTHER...
...I HAVE TO TELL YOU SOMETHING...

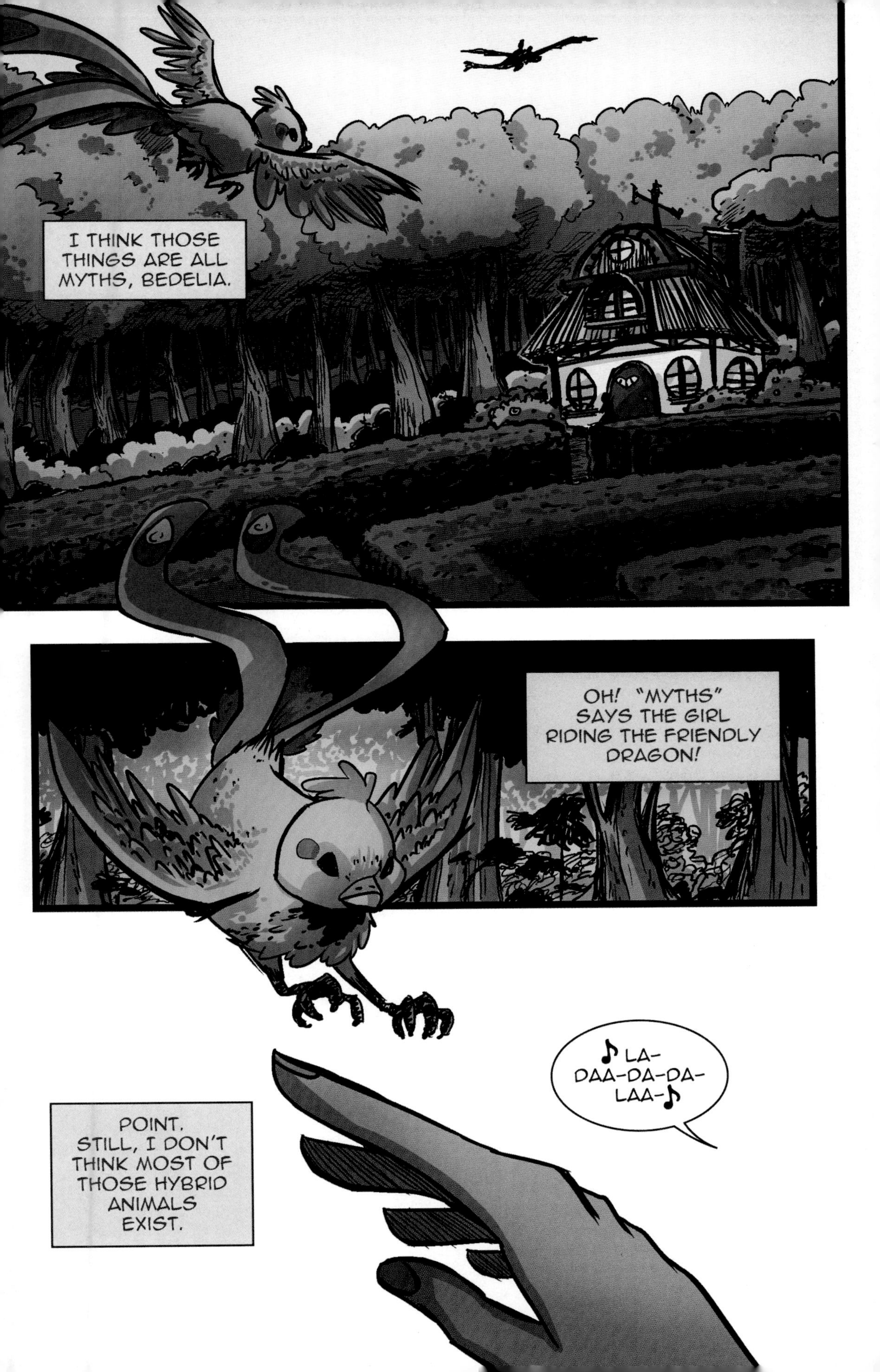
I THINK THOSE THINGS ARE ALL MYTHS, BEDELIA.
OH! "MYTHS" SAYS THE GIRL RIDING THE FRIENDLY DRAGON!
♪ LA-DAA-DA-DA-LAA-♪
POINT. STILL, I DON'T THINK MOST OF THOSE HYBRID ANIMALS EXIST.

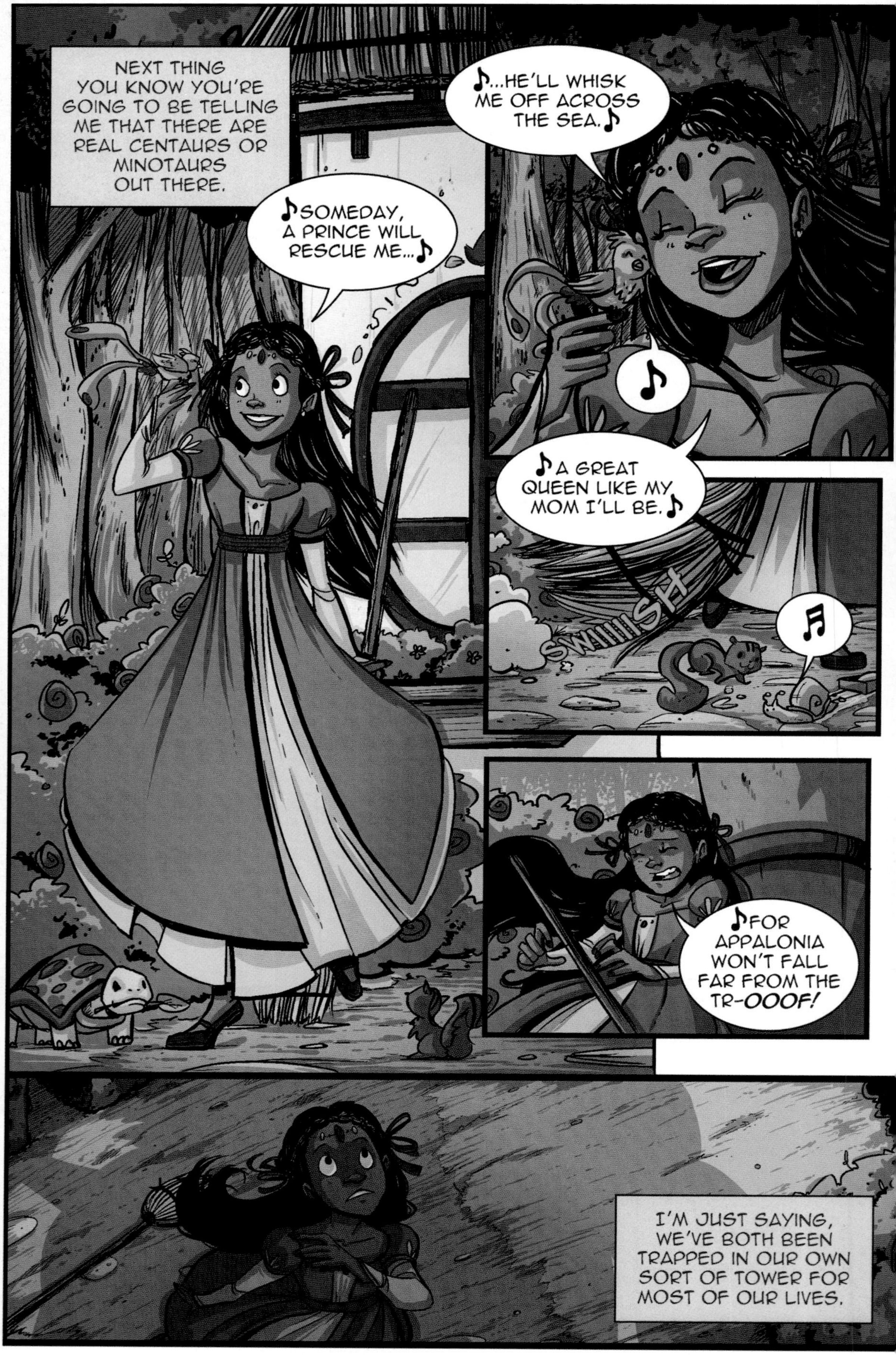
NEXT THING YOU KNOW YOU'RE GOING TO BE TELLING ME THAT THERE ARE REAL CENTAURS OR MINOTAURS OUT THERE.
♪SOMEDAY, A PRINCE WILL RESCUE ME...♪
♪...HE'LL WHISK ME OFF ACROSS THE SEA.♪
♪
♪A GREAT QUEEN LIKE MY MOM I'LL BE.♪
SWIIIISH
♬
♪FOR APPALONIA WON'T FALL FAR FROM THE TR-OOOF!
I'M JUST SAYING, WE'VE BOTH BEEN TRAPPED IN OUR OWN SORT OF TOWER FOR MOST OF OUR LIVES.

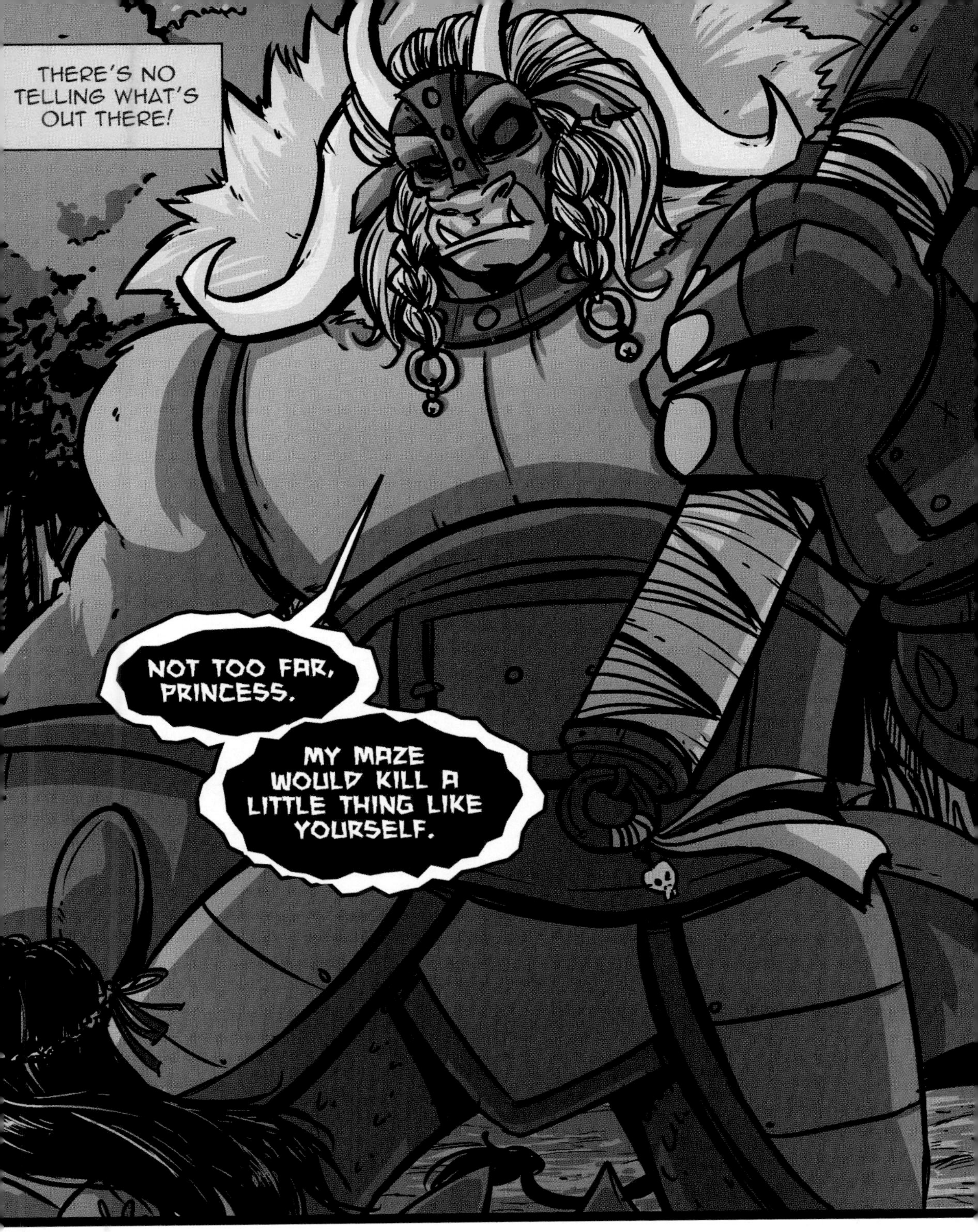
THERE'S NO TELLING WHAT'S OUT THERE!
NOT TOO FAR, PRINCESS.
MY MAZE WOULD KILL A LITTLE THING LIKE YOURSELF.
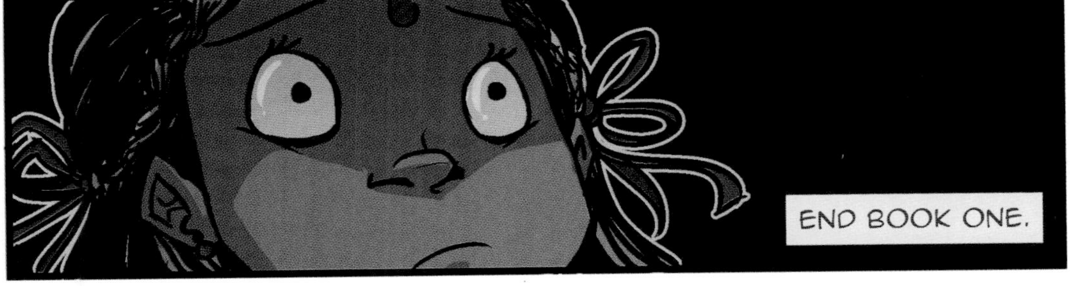
END BOOK ONE.

OUTTA DA WAY, *SHORT STUFF!*

BULLY BUMP!

ANGRY SWITCH FLIPPED!

WHO ARE YOU CALLING *"SHORT"?!*

YOU!

SEEMS WE'RE MUTUAL-OFFENDED HERE.

READY TO SHOW 'EM WHAT'S WHAT?

IF YOU SAY SO...

HEALTH ♥

PICKLES O MAN

POTIONS!

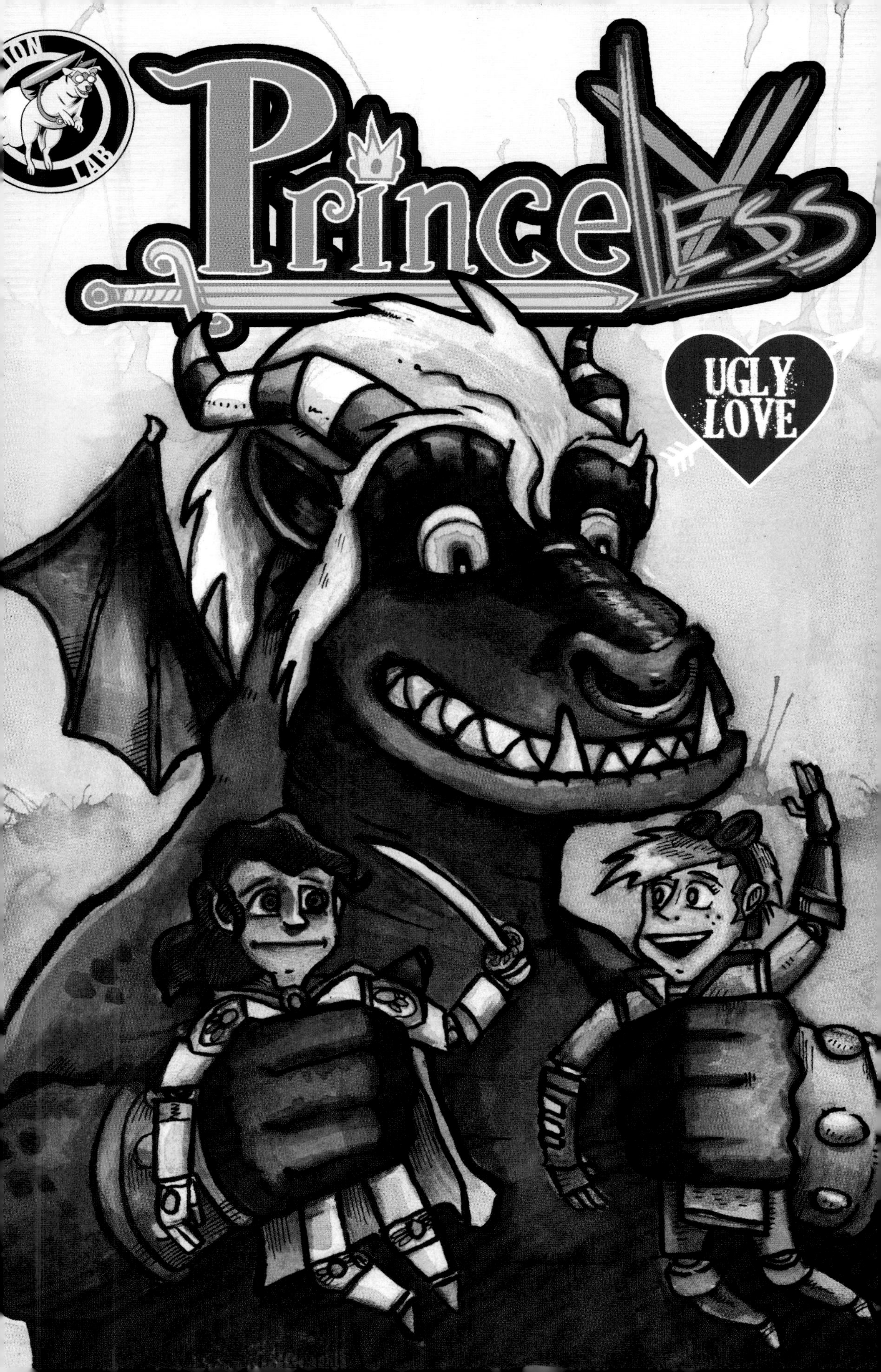
Princeless
UGLY LOVE
LAB

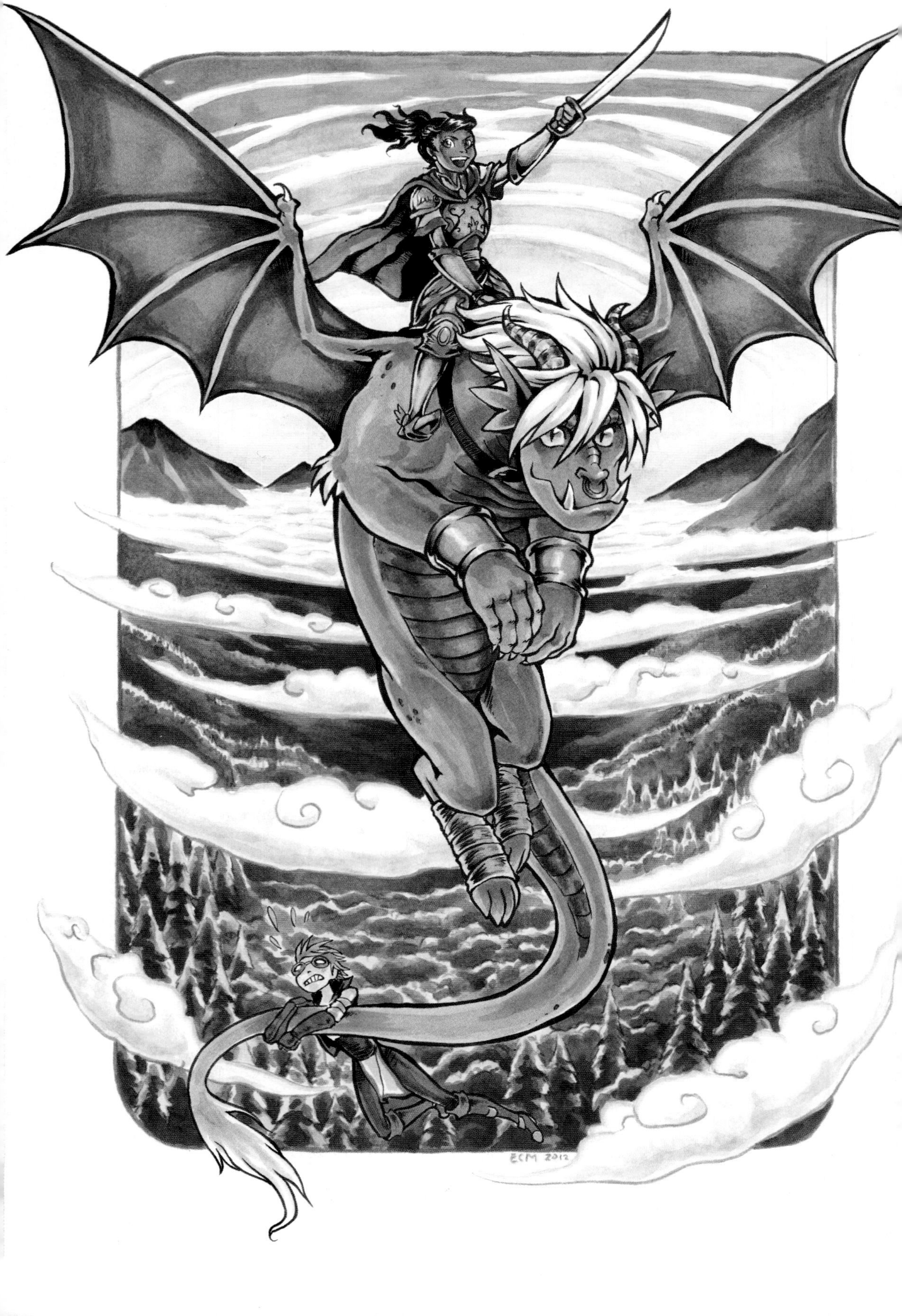
ECM 2012

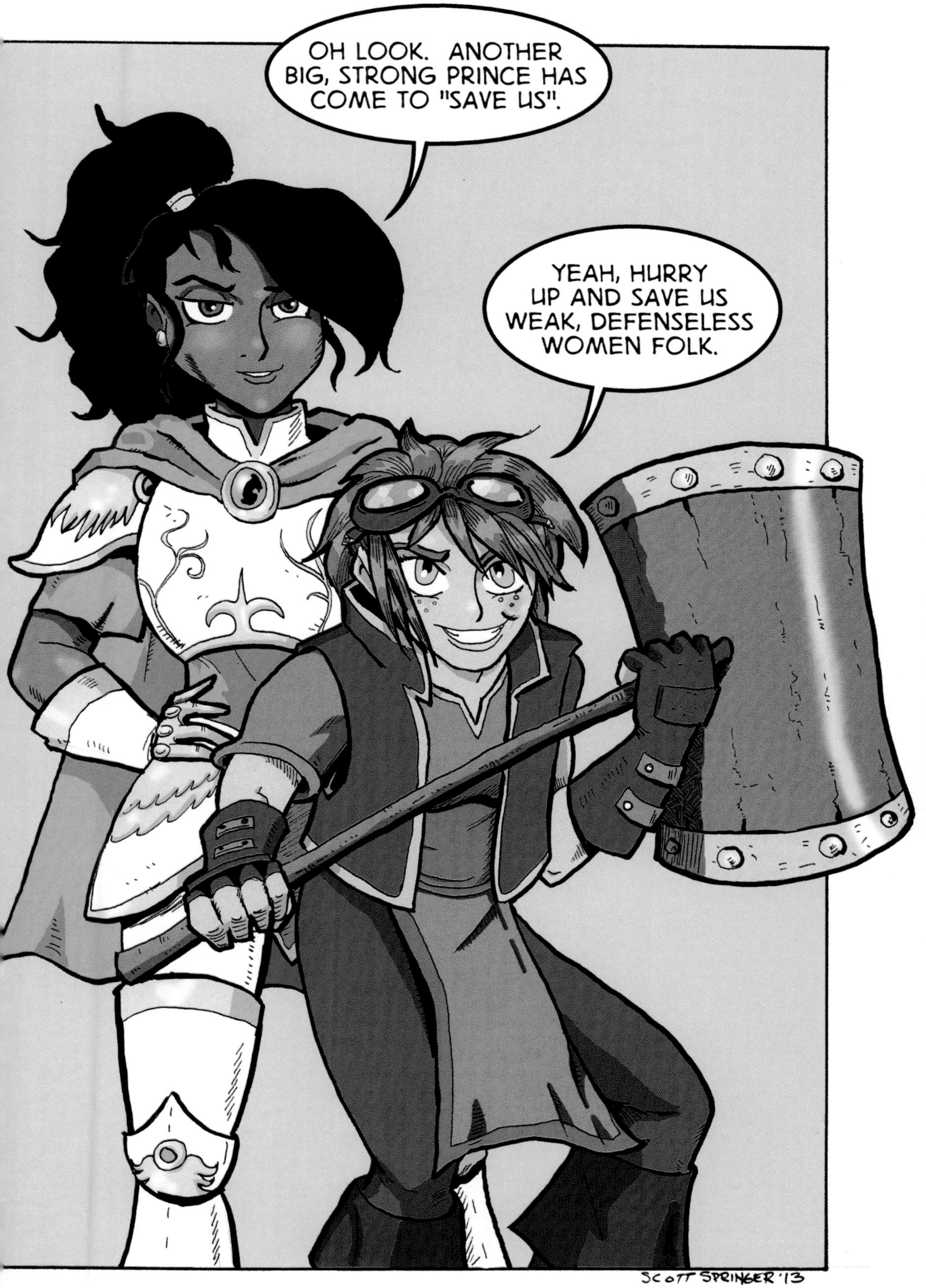
OH LOOK. ANOTHER BIG, STRONG PRINCE HAS COME TO "SAVE US".
YEAH, HURRY UP AND SAVE US WEAK, DEFENSELESS WOMEN FOLK.
SCOTT SPRINGER '13

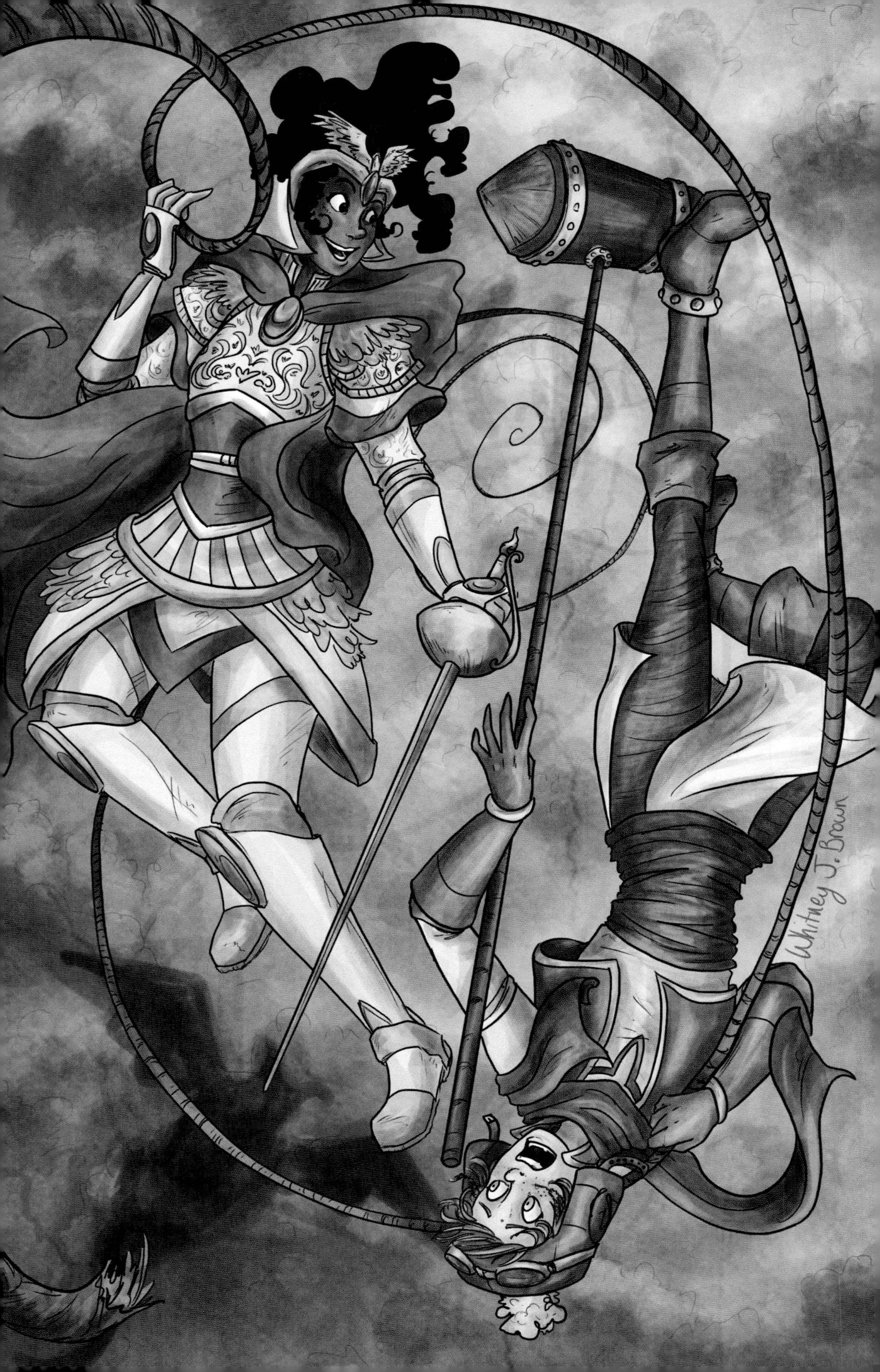
Whitney J. Brown

PIN-UP BY ELSA KROESE

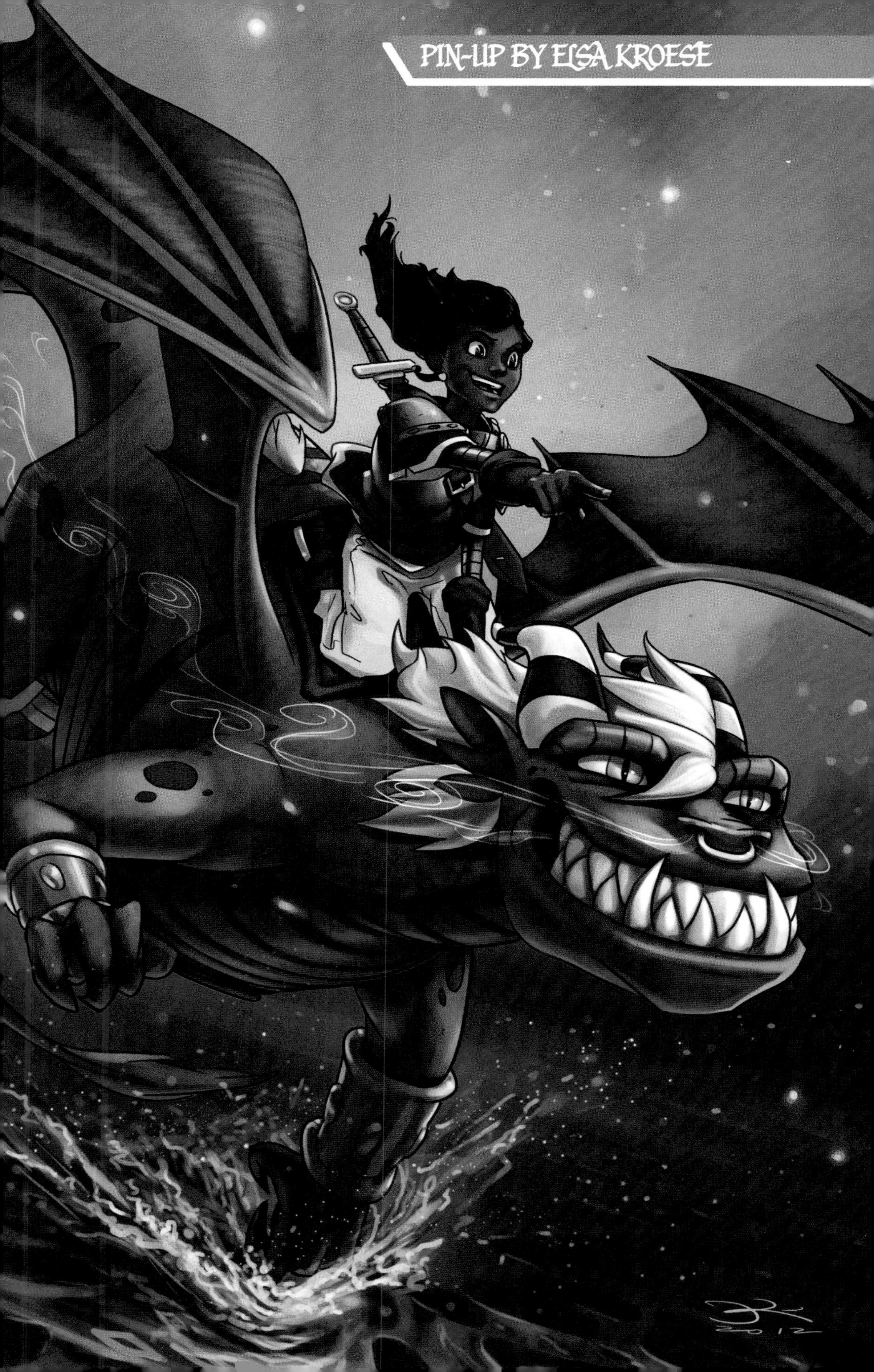

PIN-UP BY LAURA GUZZO

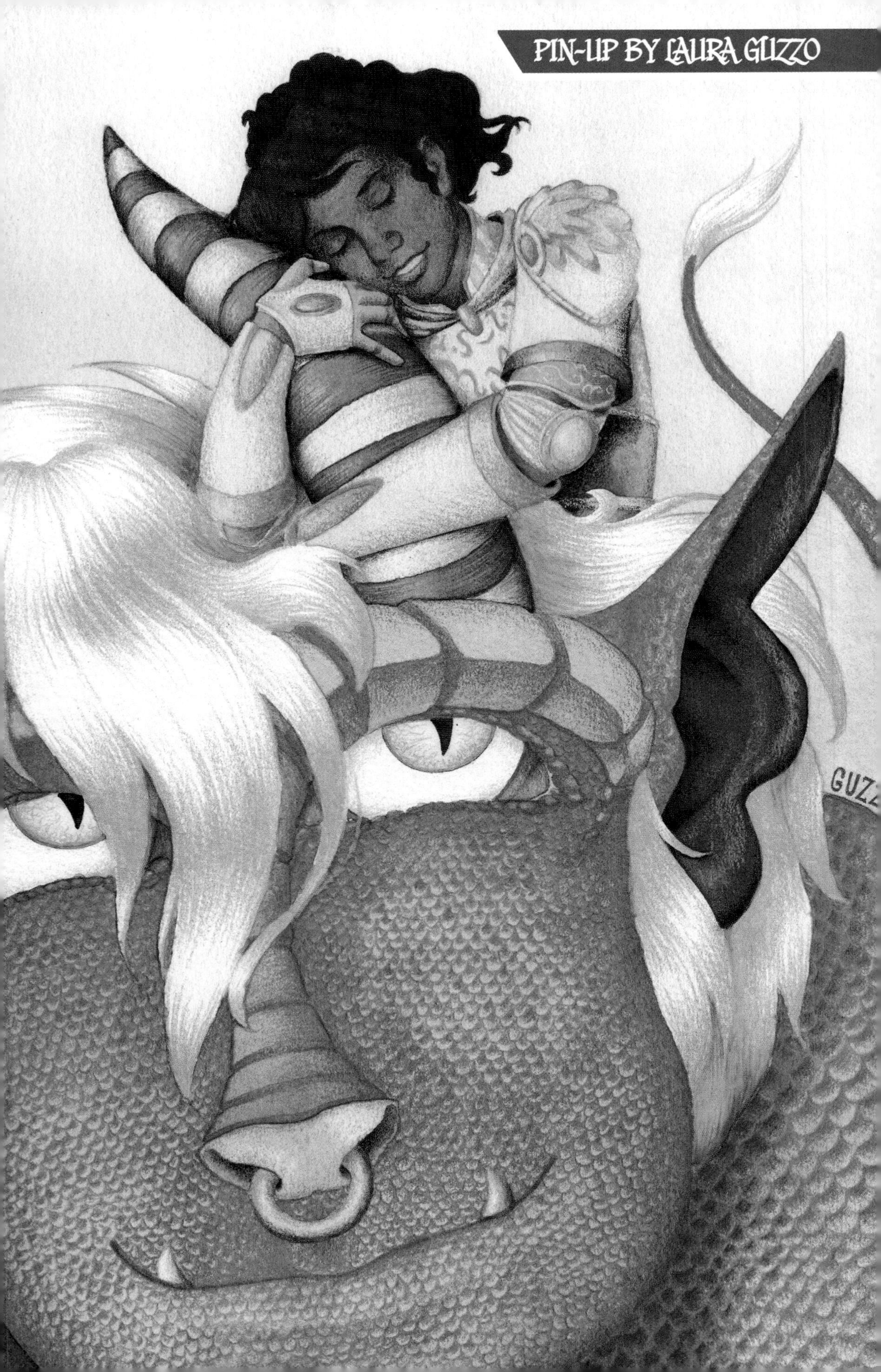

PIN-UP BY SARAH LEUVER

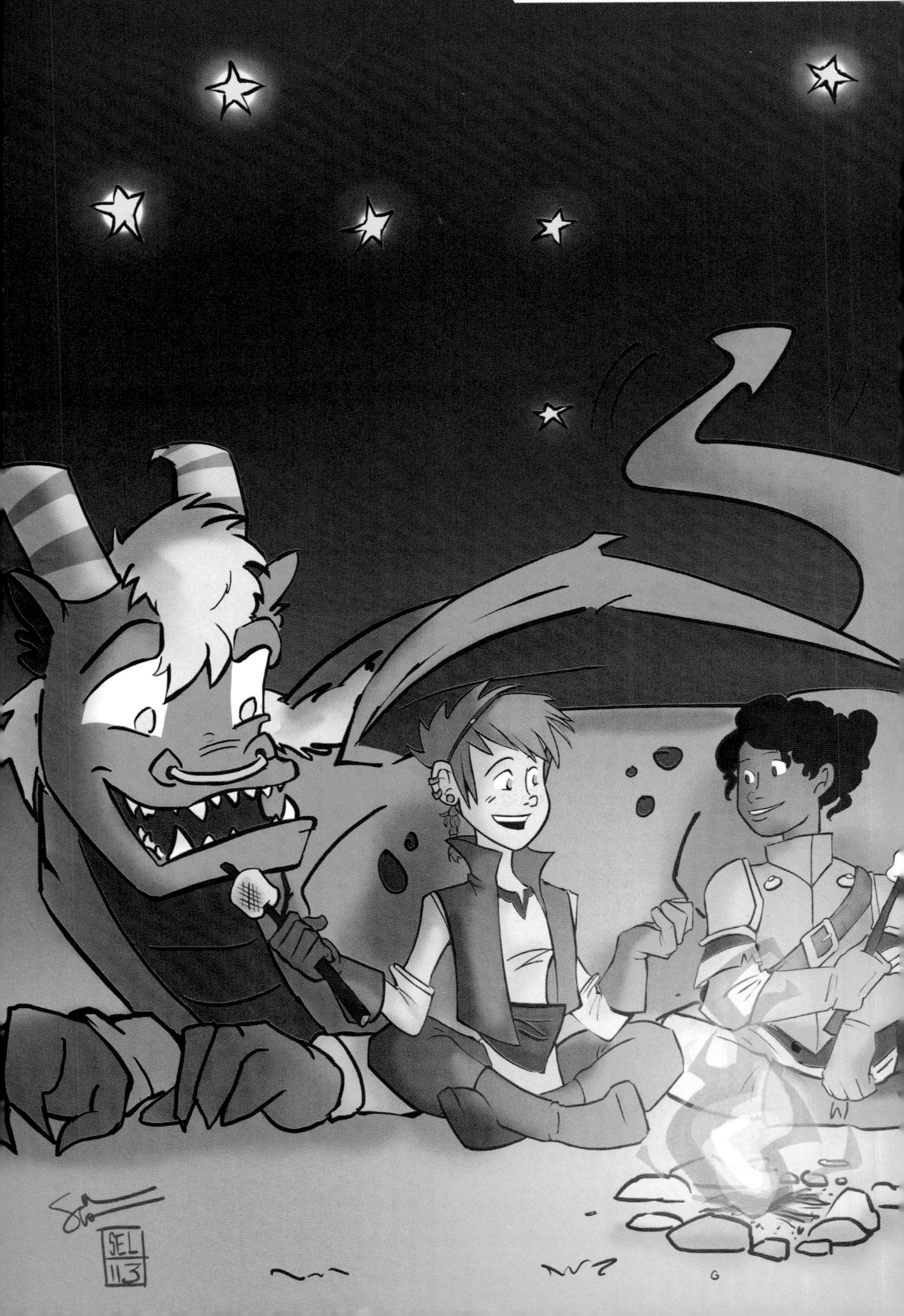
SEL
11.3

PIN-UP BY JANET WADE

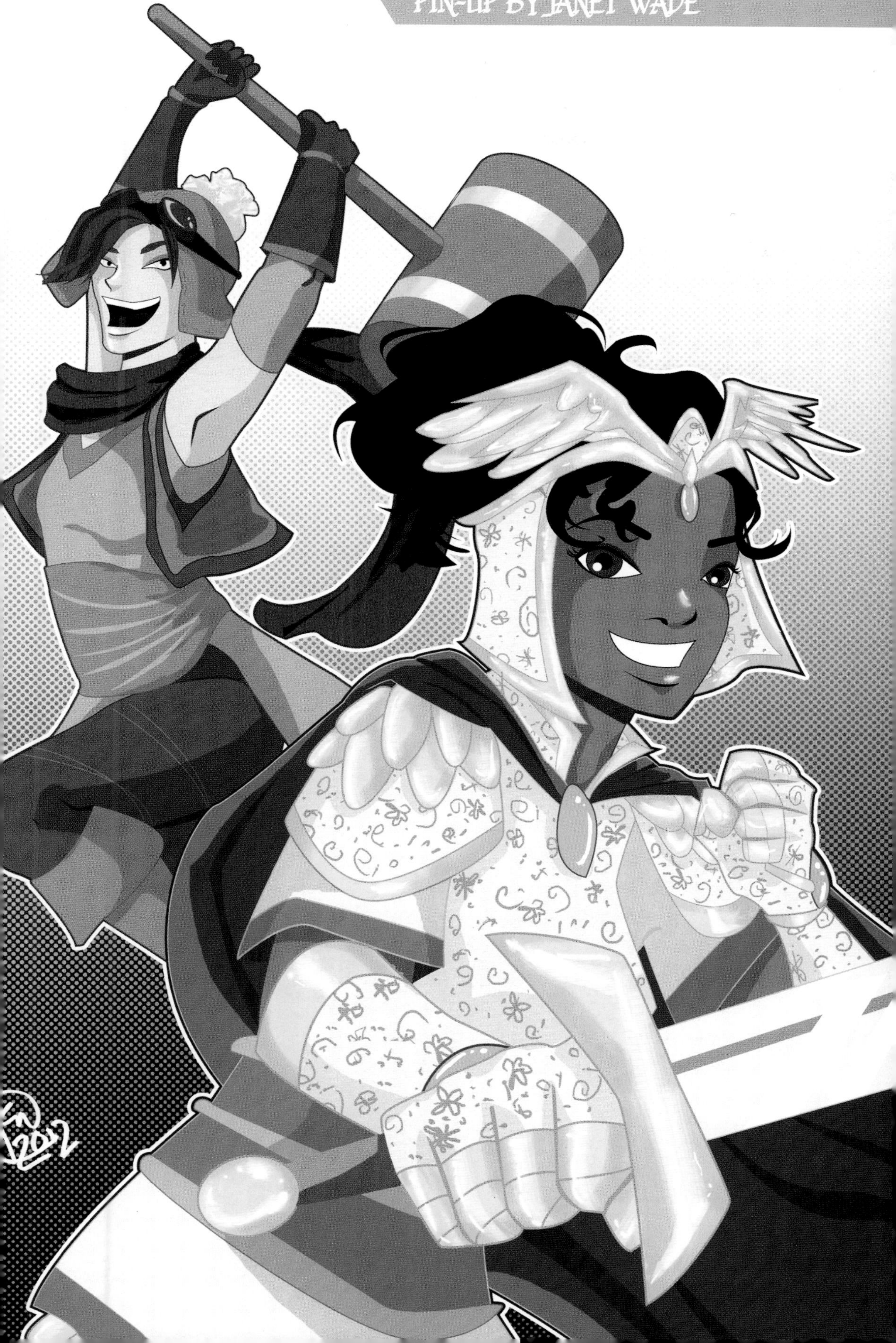
JW 2012

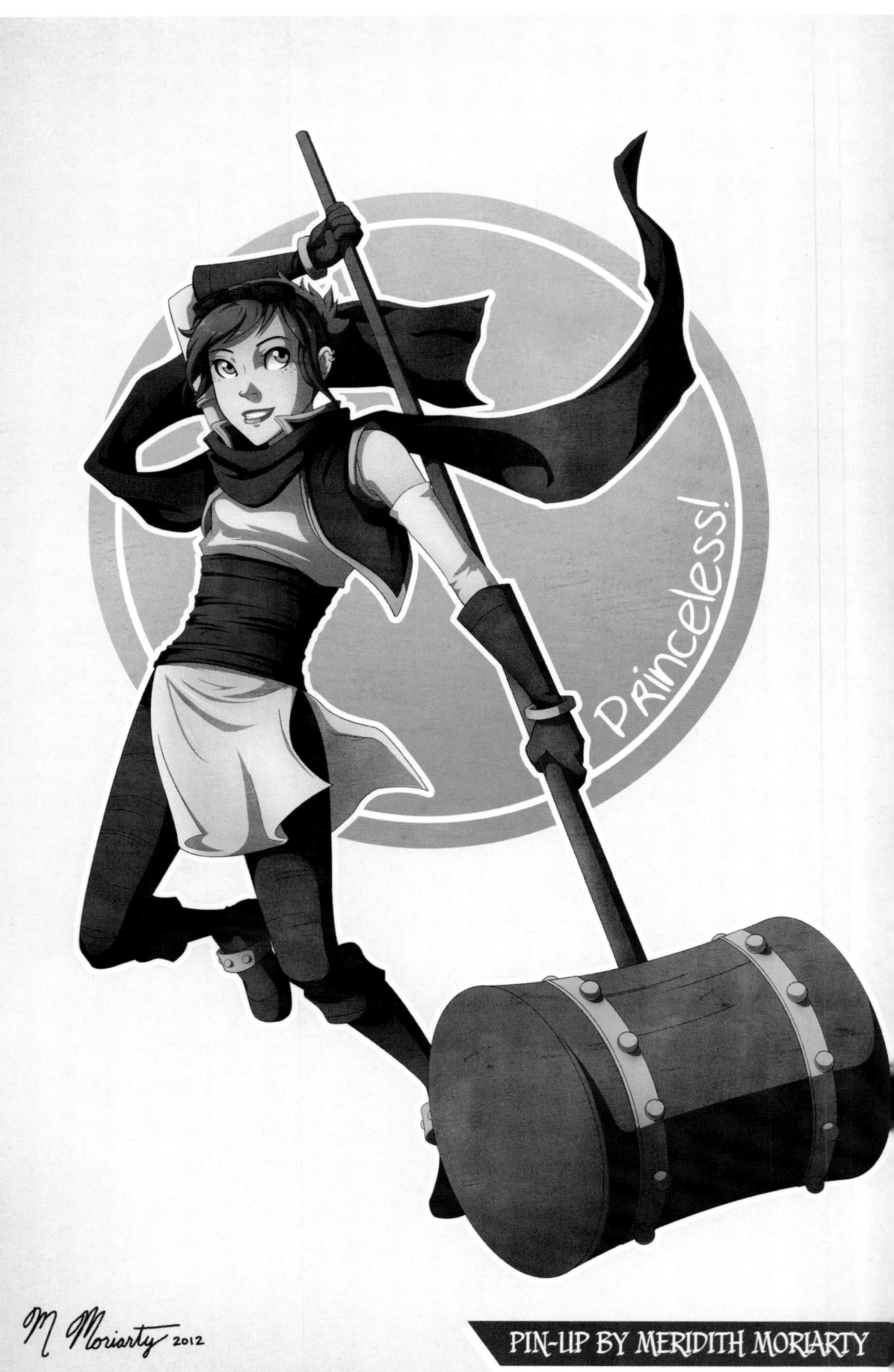
Princeless!
M. Moriarty 2012

PIN-UP BY MERIDITH MORIARTY

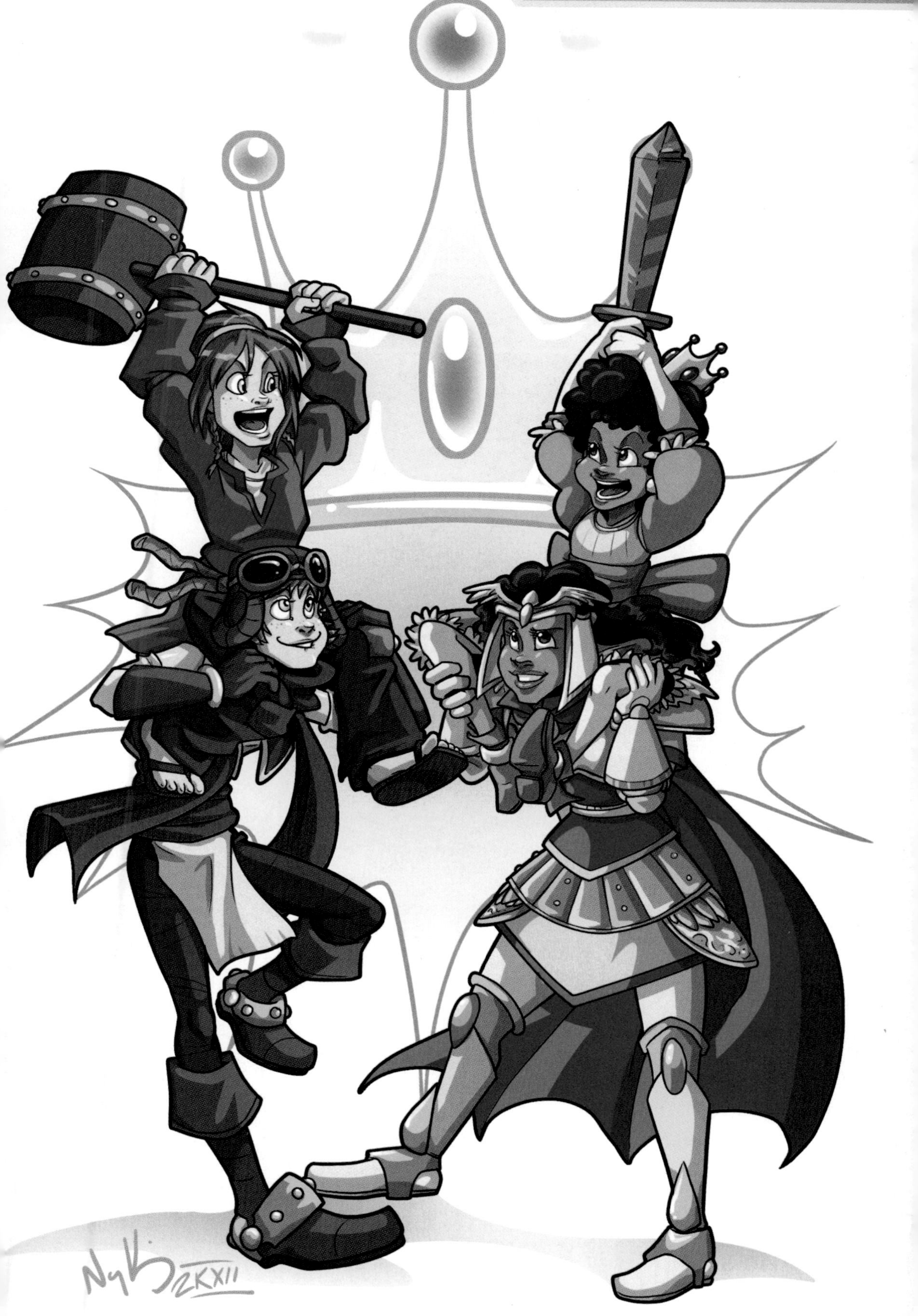